W9-CJW-540

Roosters at Midnight

*Publication of this volume was made possible
through the Katrin H. Lamon Publications Fund
at the School for Advanced Research.*

School for Advanced Research
Global Indigenous Politics Series

James F. Brooks
General Editor

With highest regards,
- Rob

Roosters at Midnight

Indigenous Signs and Stigma
in Local Bolivian Politics

Robert Albro

SAR
PRESS

School for Advanced Research Press
Santa Fe

School for Advanced Research Press
Post Office Box 2188
Santa Fe, New Mexico 87504-2188
www.sarpress.sarweb.org

Managing Editor: Lisa Pacheco
Editorial Assistant: Ellen Goldberg
Designer and Production Manager: Cynthia Dyer
Copy Editor: Sarah Soliz
Proofreader: Sheila Berg
Indexer: Catherine Fox
Printer: Cushing Malloy, Inc.

Library of Congress Cataloging-in-Publication Data
Albro, Robert.
    Roosters at midnight : indigenous signs and stigma in local Bolivian politics / Robert Albro. — 1st
ed.
        p. cm. — (Global indigenous politics series)
    Includes bibliographical references and index.
    ISBN 978-1-934691-18-2 (alk. paper)
    1. Indians of South America—Bolivia—Quillacollo—Politics and government. 2. Indians of South
America—Bolivia—Quillacollo—Government relations. 3. Indians of South America—Bolivia—
Quillacollo—Ethnic identity. 4. Local government—Bolivia—Quillacollo. 5. Stigma (Social
psychology)—Bolivia—Quillacollo. 6. Quillacollo (Bolivia)—Ethnic relations. 7. Quillacollo
(Bolivia)—Politics and government. I. Title.
    F3319.1.Q54A53 2010
    323.1198084'23—dc22
                                2009046102

 This book was printed on 10% PCR paper with soy-based inks.

Cover illustration: *Top*, blessing a truck in front of the San Ildefonso church; *bottom*, asking the Virgin
for a truck during her annual fiesta. Both photos taken by the author in Quillacollo, Bolivia.

For the artist, the bookbinder, and the analyst

Contents

Figures

Acknowledgments

As any author knows, the cliché is true: writing a book is about acquiring many debts. The present effort has been no exception. Since this ethnography has been relatively long in coming and since parts of it have been written at many different stops along the way (including years spent in Cochabamba, Chicago, Los Angeles, Boston, and Washington DC), these debts have only accumulated. I am profoundly grateful, however, for the many examples of kindness, support, and collegiality, as well as intellectual contributions, that have helped carry it along to its final completion.

These began with my original introduction to anthropology, as an undergraduate at the University of Chicago, courtesy of Ray Fogelson. While pursuing my doctoral work at Chicago, they also included a pipeline to the anthropology of Bolivia by way of the archaeologist Alan Kolata. My two most important mentors in the discipline, and the cochairs of my doctoral committee, were Jim Fernandez and Paul Friedrich. I found their humanistic and humanizing approaches to anthropology well worth the attention and their noninvasive mentoring supportive of my own preoccupations with local Bolivian politics. An abiding appreciation for the ways Jim has consistently located argument at the heart of cultural matters and Paul's efforts to sharpen the tensions between and relationships among, let's say, the biographical and the social are very much part of the present work. Chicago also provided a cohort of fellow Andeanists, the majority Bolivianists, who have generously offered insights from their own work and provided responses to mine. Over the years, this Chicago connection has included Tom Abercrombie, Stuart Rockefeller, Susan Paulson, Andy Orta, Yan Phoa, John Janusek, and Nicole Couture. Other friends and fellows in Chicago, who have been important contributors to the anthropological conversations and social environment informing my eventual fieldwork in Bolivia, include Marko Zivkovic, Tony Berkley, Mary Scoggins, Shao Jing, Tom Lyons, and Baron Pineda. From BA to PhD, the Chicago years—all twelve of them—provided a wonderful, intellectually rich, and unique atmosphere that, for better or worse, ensured my future as an endogamous Chicago product, an accusation not infrequently made but happily owned up to.

Years spent in Bolivia were also filled with support from many corners. As has been true of other anthropologists who have worked in Cochabamba, I benefited greatly from my position as a research associate with the Centro de Estudio de la Realidad Social y Económica (CERES), which supported my work and provided a forum for discussing it with others. I particularly wish to thank Rosario León, Jaqueline Gorrido, Humberto Vargas, and Roberto Laserna. Another source of intellectual support and political analysis was the Centro de Estudios Superiores Universitarios (CESU) of the University of San Simón, and especially Fernando Mayorga. In the city of Cochabamba, I also welcomed cooperation from and access to the archives of the newspaper *Los Tiempos*, the Cochabamba office of CARITAS–Bolivia, and the Federación Departamental de Clubes de Madres, as well as the regional offices of Bolivia's Instituto Nacional de Estadísticas and the Corte Departamental Electoral.

I had the great fortune to be carrying out my own research in Quillacollo during a period of renewed anthropological attention to Cochabamba, which had previously been somewhat neglected in the larger context of Bolivia. My two years of research and living in Cochabamba overlapped with those of other excellent anthropologists and friends. My relationships with many of these people began while learning Quechua from Luis Morató (a distinguished Bolivian radio personality and the first to use Quechua on the air, if I'm not mistaken). Special thanks are reserved for Dan Goldstein (and his wife, Claire), with whom I began my career as an ethnographer in Cochabamba and with whom I still enjoy talking shop; Susan Paulson, whose high energy and infectious enthusiasm brought me into a lively research community; and Aurolyn Luykx, who lived with me and my wife for many months in our two rooms on mile three of Avenida Blanco Galindo and whose accomplished ethnographic sensibilities inspired my own. In different ways and over the years, Janet Page-Reeves, Pamela Calla, Tom Kruse, Kathryn Ledebur, Ben Kohl, Krista Van Vleet, and Eduardo Gamarra have all been part of conversations while in Bolivia that have helped to give this book its final form.

Successful fieldwork in Quillacollo, particularly on something as controversial as local politics, was by no means a given. That I was able to accomplish so much is due to the willingness of so many counterparts in Quillacollo to take time out of their lives to work with me, with patience, in good faith, and often with enthusiasm for the work itself, as it took gradual shape. Quillacollo is anything but a typical provincial capital, and it has provided me with a unique chance to understand Bolivia's changing social landscape. My thanks go to the several hundred people and dozens of institutions with whom I worked in the course of fieldwork. Some people were particularly crucial. Paulino Mérida, whom I first met when he worked for Quillacollo's Department of Culture, was indispensable as a self-appointed field assistant and friend. And whatever conclusions I have reached about the relationship between cultural identity and politics in Quillacollo are largely the result of the generosity, interest, many in-depth conversations, and diverse interactions with Eduardo Herrera, Carlos Vargas, Abel Espinoza, Lorenzo Flores, Oscar Claros, Vittorio Valdéz, Narciso Lazarte, Zenon Peredo, Daniel Guerra, Nicolás Hidalgo, Guido Nájera, Ricardo Mercado, Don Rafael Peredo, and the water warrior Oscar Olivera.

Other contributors to my ethnographic work and the present book include Felix Gemio, Walter Gonzales, Waldo Rivas, Jaime Vallejos, Aurelio Flores, Adolfo Guillen, Nora Quinteros, Demetrio Terán, Mario Limache, Fernando Pereira, Walter and Gonzalo Mercado, Jorgé Beltrán, José Escalera, Max Fuentes, Juan Flores, Juan Clavijo, Carlos Becerra, Hilarión Rojas, Alfonso Prado, Doña Carmen de Caballero, Father Germán Sainz, Marcela Olivera, Gerardo Gonzales, Nicolás Orellana, Manuel and Gustavo Guerra, Luis Aliendre, Hector Cartagena, Ramiro Pinto, Raul Lopez, Salomón Peréz, Flavio Villar, René Rojas, Daniel Rojas, Carmen Peredo, Freddy Camacho, Edgar Ballón, Florentino Zelada, Fructuoso Mercado, Orlando Uriona, the editorialist Alfredo Medrano, and the author Ramón Rocha Monroy. In addition, I benefited greatly from the cooperation of many of Quillacollo's social and political institutions, most conspicuously, the mayor's office, the town council, Quillacollo's Civic Committee, the Comité Pro-Quillacollo, the Movimiento Cívico Regional, Quillacollo's Federación de Juntas Vecinales, the Federación de Comerciantes Minoristas y Artesanos, the cultural group Itapallu, the Department of Culture, the Sindicato Manaco, Quillacollo's Asociación de Fraternidades Folklóricas, and the Radio Independencia.

Over the years, before and after fieldwork, I have also received kind support from many colleagues and fellow Andeanists. Special thanks go to Mary Weismantel, Maria Lagos, and Billie Jean Isbell. At various points, each has supported my work directly and indirectly, opening their doors, writing recommendations, and reading manuscript drafts. Such collegiality is a precious commodity. Other friends and colleagues also continue to be sources of inspiration and insight, in particular, Michelle Bigenho, Andrew Canessa, Linda Seligmann, Nancy Postero, Xavier Albó, Jeff Himpele, Lesley Gill, Kevin Healy, Brooke Larson, David Nugent, Marcia Stephenson, David Guss, Guillermo Delgado-P., and Eduardo Gamarra. While living in Whittier, Mariella Bacigalupo and Jeff Himpele were great sounding boards. During several years at Wheaton College (Norton, Massachusetts), I enjoyed the support of my colleagues Donna Kerner and Bruce Owens.

After returning to my hometown, Washington DC, my work has benefited from synergies with other fellows during a year at the John W. Kluge Center of the Library of Congress. I would also like to recognize the support of Joanne Bauer, while a fellow at the Carnegie Council for Ethics in International Affairs, as well as Richard Kurin, James Early, Olivia Cadavál, Carla Borden, and Cynthia Vidaurri at the Smithsonian's Center for Folklife and Cultural Heritage, where I spent a great year as a Rockefeller Foundation Humanities Fellow. I would also like to recognize the faculty of George Washington University's Department of Anthropology, particularly the wonderful support of Barbara Miller and conversations with Alex Dent, and finally, my present academic home, the Program on International Communication in American University's School of International Service. Both fieldwork and writing have also been supported at various stages along the way with Fulbright–Institute of International Education and National Science Foundation Doctoral Dissertation Improvement grants, a faculty research grant from Wheaton College and fellowships awarded by the Carnegie Council, the Rockefeller, Mellon, and Tinker Foundations, and the American Council of Learned Societies.

My artist mother and my bookbinding father have each been creative models, if different kinds, from which I continue to draw inspiration. My children, Jonas, Maddie, and Zeke, have made these happy years of writing and frolicking, and, of course, fellow traveler, wife, and partner, Liz, has been my unfailing better angel. None of this would have been possible without her—or at least it certainly wouldn't have turned out the same!

1

Introduction
Politics in a *Ch'ajchu* City

Early-twenty-first-century Bolivia is a nation energetically confronting stubborn legacies of second-class citizenship, as part of a historic process of political transformation. Indigenous and social movement activism beginning in early 2000 and followed by years of large-scale and direct-action protests culminated in the historic election to the presidency in late 2005 of the Aymara-descended coca grower and opposition leader Evo Morales. The years of civil unrest were a spectacular expression of grassroots disenchantment and a sharp rebuke to the politics of Bolivia's neoliberal democratization, first applied with the sweeping structural adjustment measures of 1985. They also articulated a thoroughgoing indigenous, popular, and even middle-class rejection of the elitism, inequity, corruption, and occasional downright ineptitude exhibited by Bolivia's traditional "political class," which dominated national party politics since the democratic opening of the late 1970s and which had maintained a political stranglehold on the country's politics since its creation. The adoption of a new national constitution in January 2009 defining the country as "plurinational and communitarian" was an unquestionable high-water mark for indigenous enfranchisement in this majority indigenous country.

Set in the largely urban provincial capital of Quillacollo, this book is an ethnographic examination of municipal politics in the context of renewed elections of local-level officials beginning in 1987 after a hiatus of almost forty years.[1] And in the words of one counterpart in Quillacollo, "This was the moment when people of humble descent began to enter" into local politics. Understanding who these people are, how they think of themselves, and how they relate with each other politically tells us a great deal about the everyday neopopular political ground that preceded and has since been embraced by the Morales presidency, which has steadily been moving Bolivian national politics toward a greater rapprochement with its indigenous heritage. But the recent story of the undeniably historic political empowerment of Bolivia's indigenous peoples is not just the story of the Morales administration's successful constitutional referendum. It is more importantly a story about the changing significance of what it means to be indigenous in contemporary Bolivia. This story is apparent in the examination of local political relationships along the urban margin in towns such as Quillacollo, where "indigenous" has become a more capacious category of inclusion in recent decades. And this, in fact, represents a key part of the formidable grassroots support for Morales and the MAS (Movement toward Socialism).

The high profile currently enjoyed by Evo Morales, as perhaps the hemisphere's most influential indigenous figure, is often explained in the context of the increased public exposure, transnational coordination, and political effectiveness of the hemisphere's indigenous movements, from at least the successes of Mexico's Zapatistas to the present.[2] But this assessment tends to ignore more prosaic and less corporate forms of politics. Throughout this ethnography I develop the case that the present high profile of an indigenous political project in Bolivia is significantly owed to longer-developing if more under-the-radar neopopular working relationships among people often categorized as nonindigenous, diverse urban indigenous, and popular sectors, whose political activities are largely entangled with everyday and informal kinds of economic activities in the effort to make ends meet in neoliberal Bolivia.

This lower-profile process has accompanied the opening up and development of local municipal and provincial politics throughout the democratic period. The thoroughgoing interrelationship of neopopular political alternatives with indigenous projects in local politics through the 1980s to the present, particularly along the growing urban periphery, has gone largely unexamined even as it is notably transforming and expanding the terms of indigenous belonging in Bolivia. This interrelationship is apparent in the steps taken by a diverse array of urban-dwelling people with backgrounds as laborers, factory workers, agriculturalists, miners, entrepreneurs, students, shop owners, and lawyers, among others, to build and maintain political relationships in terms largely recognized by them as characteristically Andean forms of cultural practice. In the Morales era such local neopopular political experience in provincial and urban settings, as a personally relevant heritage, directly informs popular support for indigenous rights. This promises to be a continuing trend.

This book is an account of the cultural politics informing the recent neopopulist turn away from Bolivia's democratic "politics as usual"—a process that is still ongoing. Enthusiastically dubbed the "politics of the multitude" or the "democracy of the plebe" by close-up observers, academics, and social movement participants,[3] the present turn has included a surge of grassroots participation from among this nation's historically marginalized popular and indigenous sectors. In media as well as scholarly accounts, the events of the past nine years in Bolivia are often interpreted as part of the often bumpy trajectory of democratization, with the country's indigenous movements achieving greater recognition through the fits and starts of institutional reforms that have culminated with the new Constitution (Van Cott 2007; Yashar 2005), if only after a series of false beginnings, repressive state actions, and factional infighting since at least the mid-1940s. But my account takes a different starting point.

This ethnography is a product of long hours spent in the company of the several hundred or so most politically engaged men and women in Quillacollo,[4] as well as close attention to the discourses, practices, and cultural and political strategies characteristic of these most local state representatives, the mayors and town councilmen and leaders of local base organizations, who together compose the political authorities of this provincial capital.[5] None of these people are what we could call professional politicians, if many have had long careers and if politics is their abiding passion. One Bolivian political analyst has aptly called such people "politicians of circumstance more than of vocation" (Lazarte 1998:78). And circumstances require that they make a living in other ways.

During the mid- to late 1990s, "neopopulism" in Quillacollo corresponded to the UCS (Unidad Cívica Solidaridad, or Civic Solidarity Union) party, born in 1988 almost full blown from the head of its founder, beer baron Max Fernandez, who was himself born in Quillacollo.[6] For more than a decade the UCS party thoroughly dominated the town's politics. Since 2002 the UCS has been displaced by the MAS in Quillacollo. But the type of local municipal politics talked about here and the mostly urban indigenous and popular constituency to which the parties correspond are not simply a phenomenon of the UCS of the 1990s or the MAS of the 2000s. They are part of a more encompassing set of developments that emerged in close relationship with everyday struggles during neoliberal democratization, an increased informalization of the local economy, uneven provincial urbanization, the inconclusive provincial legacies of an earlier project of national identity based on *mestizaje* (cultural mixing), the effects of more recent multicultural state reforms, new incentives to embrace at least the rhetoric of indigenous politics, and greater autonomy and concentration of resources in local municipalities. Taken together, these factors have shaped local political strategies and priorities in Quillacollo.

This book, then, is about the political lives and careers of a growing urban-dwelling popular and indigenous constituency that operates primarily within the many corners of the hidden or informal economy in and around Quillacollo, a population that has experienced significant expansion throughout the neoliberal period just as Bolivia's public sector has shrunk.[7] The cultural politics informing the political and economic rivalries and relationships maintained by these people are not, I suggest, unique to Quillacollo, if they are well illustrated here precisely because of the location of Quillacollo as a social and cultural crossroads of sorts on the margin of the nearby city of Cochabamba.

The majority of people who self-identified as indigenous on Bolivia's most recent census in 2001 also happened to be urbanites.[8] This is perhaps a counterintuitive fact, given that the recognition of indigenous identity in Bolivia and in Latin America frequently has been linked to such diacritics as place (assumed to be rural), language, collective integrity, or precolonial descent. But recent events in Bolivia have invested the question "What does it mean to be indigenous?" with new relevance, since these events have highlighted the variable and situational characteristics of indigenous claims. Most notably, the high profile of Evo Morales and the MAS owes significantly to having successfully articulated a more inclusionary big tent to better frame key national issues, rights, forms of heritage, and agency in indigenous terms than previously (see Albro 2005a, 2006a; Canessa 2006).

However, once in government the MAS has also at times adopted a "with us or against us" approach. This is perhaps most apparent in the new Constitution,[9] which formally recognizes thirty-six indigenous "nations" and which defines them as collectively sharing in common a cultural identity, language, historical tradition, institutions, and cosmovision while asserting the rights of indigenous peoples to autonomy, self-governance, and territory.[10] The Constitution is a historically significant step forward for the enfranchisement of Bolivia's indigenous population. But it also begs the questions of misrecognition and of the legibility of indigenous experience vis-à-vis even a well-meaning state (see Postero 2007b), particularly for people living in marginal urban environments such as Quillacollo or El Alto, and for whom indigenous identity is at once personally relevant, a politically relevant heritage, but not necessarily recognizable in territorial or even collective terms (see Albro 2008).

Bolivia's new Constitution has not come to terms with the more variegated expressions of indigenous agency, which ironically were significantly responsible for the MAS's original rise to power. These include the more urban, overlapping, and mutually engaged interests and identities of indigenous and popular associational networks, as well as the changing boundaries of indigenous and mestizo (racially and culturally mixed) inclusion characteristic of these alliances and politics. As Andrew Canessa (2007b:208) has recently and rightly noted, the numbers of Bolivians who do not belong to a recognized indigenous community, who do not speak an indigenous language, but who nevertheless identify as indigenous in some circumstances are considerable, but "there is still virtually no research on this important segment of the Bolivian population." The present work is an effort to begin to address this.

Quillacollo's Identity Problem

Quillacollo and environs could be said to be in the grip of a protracted identity crisis, perceived in the terms of growing urban squalor, felt social anomie, and even moral decay. This is not a new problem. Quillacollo's is not a history based on tracing out successive collective locations of Andean identity, still detectable after more than five hundred years (compare to Rivera 1984). Rather it is a history told as if premised upon a cultural *absence*, upon which are enacted successive social displacements. In fact the encompassing region of Cochabamba, as a social space, has always been somewhat at odds with the sorts of explicitly Andean cultural contexts more typically made the basis of ethnographic accounts. As Xavier Albó (1987b:45–46) put it some years ago, the Cochabamba region is an "open geographic space, a point of encounter, whose identity consisted in its very *lack of an identity*" (emphasis mine).[11] The lower valley of Cochabamba is originally thought to have been populated by groups of Aymara colonists "whose nuclei were in other parts," supplanted in quick succession first by the Quechua-speaking Inca and then by the soon-to-arrive Spanish (Larson 1998:14–31; Wachtel 1982).

Founded in the late sixteenth century and first named as a Spanish parish (see Peredo Antezana 1963), Quillacollo was not a typically sleepy provincial town. Unlike all of the other towns in Cochabamba's lower valley, Quillacollo was not created as a *reducción*, or new Indian town, under the program of then-Viceroy Toledo. Its population was primarily a collection of "rootless Indians" (in colonial terms, *forasteros*), alongside a mixed-race (mestizo) artisanal class, and land owning creole townsfolk (*gente decente*). The town is described by one historian of the region even then as "notoriously mestizo" (Sánchez-Albornóz 1978:156–184). By the eighteenth century we are told that the pre-Hispanic "pattern of ethnic identification" (Larson 1998:101) had been severely undermined, and it was reported that "five hundred *cholos* [gloss: "upwardly mobile Indians"] and mestizos" (1998:179) were already hard at work in the town's incipient textile industry. A large laboring class has continued to characterize the unique demographics of the province right up to the present, most importantly in the form of the Manaco shoe factory and other smaller industrial ventures in and around the province, especially along the highway corridor on the way to the city of Cochabamba.

The emergence of a large population of petty agriculturalists, called *piqueros*, in the early twentieth century accelerated after the 1952 Revolution, feeding the growth of a thriving regional market network. This growing investment in the market on the part of rural provincials (*vallunos*) increased the traffic between rural and urban, including intimate and daily connections with the nearby city of Cochabamba. As a result of these many factors, historians of the region have consistently emphasized the social *mobility*—internal migration, displacements and superimpositions of populations, fluid shifts in ethnic identity, diversified household subsistence strategies, socioeconomic shifts—particularly characteristic of this region (see Dandler 1987a; Goldstein 2004; Lagos 1994; Peredo Antezana 1963; Rivera 1984; Rocha 1990; Rodríguez and Solares 1990; Salamanca 1931).

The academic consensus about Cochabamba's vallunos has described them as a long de-Indianized peasantry that over time has successfully manipulated vertical ties as clients to urban elites and state politicians, to solidify their own access to land, material, and capital (Dandler 1983; Lagos 1994; Larson 1998). As a regional case study, Cochabamba has thus reflected a trend within the study of peasant communities in Latin American anthropology, where "class differences and differentiation remain the basic theoretical issue" (Kearney 1996:173). This regional combination, then, of social displacement, the lack of complex indigenous cultural forms (or extended kinship ties), no long-term historical memory (or corporate organization), competitions of class, and a concomitant fluidity of ethnic categorization have all participated in producing a set of circumstances within which cultural identities are understood to be weakly defined and where questions of identity are anything but clear-cut. Take this characterization of the region by the respected historian Brooke Larson:

> However shrewd and flexible peasant families might be in their liveli-
> hood strategies, and however much they tried to balance their subsis-
> tence requirements against reciprocal obligations to kinsmen or

neighbors, they lived and worked outside the cultural and material context of Andean village society. They may have practical reciprocities, but those practices were embedded in a class context. In their daily pursuit of a livelihood or their struggle against the enduring injustices and humiliations of being Indian in colonial society, or living in the shadow of a patrón, most valley peasants faced the world alone. They did not have recourse to the material and ideological traditions of Andean communities to defend themselves against the incursion of outside claimants, the arbitrary demands of a landlord, or the ravages of a natural disaster. There was no communal tradition of group self-sufficiency, reciprocity, and distribution to buffer the peasant household against subsistence threats or to contain class forces. Valley peasants had no means of calling upon the moral economy of their ancestral kin and ethnic groups to collectively confront the outside world whenever it turned hostile. In short, the absence of a strong ethnic heritage in the valleys left most peasants without economic autonomy or symbolic integrity. [1998:303–304]

For the purposes of this discussion, it should be apparent that the complexly interrelated social facts only touched on here have routinely been used to indicate the absence of sharply defined collective cultural identities for the region as a whole. The different ways that this absence has been explained and temporarily filled over time are, in a sense, imagined to *constitute* the unique characteristics of regional history. One repercussion has been for researchers to look elsewhere for elaborated corporate or collective ethnic identities. Another repercussion has been a reduction of scale of cultural analysis, within a region characterized by a "diffuse peasantry." Hence, those who have conducted research in Cochabamba have tended to subsume questions of cultural identity to a seemingly more characteristic class analysis at the level of the household (see Lagos 1994).[12] And yet, as recently as 2000, campesino irrigators in Cochabamba's lower valley—where Quillacollo is found—mobilized collectively to defend their established "uses and customs" (that is, traditional *cultural* practices) from an attempted government sell-off of the city's waterworks (Albro 2005b).

Among the many appraisals of the current moment of Evo Morales, and the successful installation of a national indigenous project within the apparatus of the state beginning in 2005 (see Albro 2006a; Canessa 2006; Postero 2007a), the majority have been concerned primarily with the mobilization of Aymara-based social movement activism during the period 2000 to 2005, with attention focused mostly upon the city of El Alto as representative of indigenous kinds of mobilization in contemporary Bolivia

(Arbona 2007; Lazar 2008). But, beginning with the Water War of 2000, Cochabamba's lower valley has also been an important if distinct space of popular mobilization, in which Quillacollo has played a prominent role. Quillacollo, therefore, offers a fruitful comparison with the political organizing along the outskirts of other major cities like El Alto, particularly in terms of the different varieties of urban indigenous expression characterizing these places.

Brooke Larson's (1998) excellent history of Cochabamba has detailed the regionally characteristic close relationship of the rise of independent small landholders, traders, and markets at the turn of the nineteenth century alongside the emergent politics of mestizaje. The Bolivian nation-state, Bolivian organic intellectuals, as well as social scientists have all viewed Cochabamba through the twinned lenses of racial and cultural mestizaje facilitated by an "alliance of classes" (Rivera 1984; Albó 1987b, 1994). And as Florencia Mallon (1996:170) and many others have observed, being a "mestizo/a is, by definition, betwixt and between, neither Indian nor Spanish." Particularly after the 1952 Revolution, the MNR (Movimiento Nacional Revolucionario, or National Revolutionary Movement) undertook to finish the incomplete project of creating a unified citizenry with the goal of constructing a socially integrated and culturally homogeneous mestizo nation.

As a discourse of nation building, the new MNR government of 1952 understood mestizaje as the assimilation of Andean "others" through the erasure of disruptive internal differences to create a single national subject. The Bolivian critic Guillermo Mariaca Iturri (1998:190) has glibly summarized the revolutionary project of folding culture into class as a recipe for the creation of citizenship with the maxim, "Mestizo equals homogenization equals nation of equals."[13] Borrowing the words of Nestor García Canclini (2001:137), such projects represented a historical moment of the "epic affirmation of popular identity" in Bolivia. For the past quarter century, in fact, Quillacollo has taken on a starring role in advertising the supposed cultural mixture productive of Bolivian nationhood, as the site of the yearly fiesta of Urkupiña, the town's saint's day festival. Urkupiña has become a colossal yearly event of national significance, where "traditional" and "modern" Bolivia are feted as they publicly, amicably interpenetrate and coexist. In 1986 Urkupiña was officially dubbed the "fiesta of national integration."

Larson (1998:343), however, has questioned the skepticism with which researchers of Andean culture and community initially snubbed this scene, dismissively written off, in her words, as composed of "Quechua-mestizo peasantries" and "corrupt clients or penny capitalists." Quillacollo, in particular, has been understood to exemplify these trends. The province has been described as having a "weak communal tradition" (Albó 1987b:412) or, as a now-dated study by Bolivia's Ministry of Urbanism and Welfare explained, "poor social cohesion" (Rojas Rosales and Galarza Garamendi 1975:29), in large part due to its 13-kilometer proximity to the nearby city. In the late 1990s politically engaged cultural activists with whom I worked in Quillacollo regularly repeated such conclusions when complaining about challenges they faced as informal cultural workers: "Quillacollo lacks its own identity" or "Quillacollo has little in the way of tradition." Or, as one friend put it, Quillacollo is "as variable as the wind."

Dismissively described by both residents and nonlocals as a town with an expanding population of *cholos*, upwardly mobile people of indigenous descent who often also reject their own origins, the social space of Quillacollo invites comparisons with June Nash's (1979:311) path breaking description of the "cholo culture" of the miners of Siglo XX, never sharply in focus and discussed as a "culture of transition."[14] Thomas Abercrombie (1996:63) makes this point as well, noting that cholos are "defined by others as much for the identities they have not achieved as for those they have failed to leave behind." The conviction that cholos represent an ill-defined, temporary, unstable, or transitory identity—as at best a problematic weigh station— early on characterized the scant writing about the process of *cholaje* (indigenous upward mobility) among social scientists. "The cholo," as Jacob Fried (1961:25) characteristically explained while writing about mid-twentieth-century Peru, "is not really a class or a cultural entity, but a transitional, contingent, elastic category."[15]

But this book addresses how such instability of identity can be surprisingly culturally productive for the construction of political relationships in Quillacollo. As I examine throughout the chapters to follow, part of this productivity is derived from the exploitation and interplay of ongoing internal connections between the expectations of mestizaje and the undercurrents of cholaje, which such expectations potentially continue to include in the activities of provincial politics.[16] If personal association with the term *cholo* historically has been pejorative, in contemporary politics it nevertheless represents commitments to forms of cultural practice associated with popular and indigenous sources of identity that, too, enable the effective construction of political networks. Despite the assumption of the disappearance of indigenous identity, particularly as part of urbanization, in and around Quillacollo a regular discourse of alienation—which includes facts of insult and stigma and of the potential loss of identity—in fact serves to reassert shared claims to indigenous heritage among people for whom such claims help to develop informal working relationships. The figure of the cholo, now as potentially positive, has in recent decades become the surprising subject of political and cultural attention.

Contemporary Quillacollo: New Urban Periphery

As a cultural and economic crossroads, Quillacollo is a good illustration of Olivia Harris's (1995:110) apt comment about the growing complexities of Bolivian cultural identity: "Everything is mixed, but not everything is mestizo." In the words of one long time resident, Quillacollo is neither "city-city" nor "country-country," and cultural identities are not smoothly, evenly, or equitably mixed. The town is comparable to other unevenly developed, unregulated, and informal boomtowns or satellite cities that have grown up alongside Bolivia's established urbs, like El Alto next to the de facto national capital La Paz and Montero near the lowland business center of Santa Cruz. As a recent in-migrant expressed it to me, Quillacollo has "a little of everything." It is a peculiar peri-urban social space, part migrant destination, part "dormitory town" a commuter's distance from the nearby departmental capital city of Cochabamba, part provincial capital, a more urban extension of the post-peasant yet still rural goings-on of Cochabamba's lower valley, and part rustic heartland of *qhochala* (valley) cultural sensibilities, conveniently available for consumption by nearby and otherwise modern city dwellers. These characteristics are at once confounded and conjoined at this crossroads.

Though there is no precise record of Quillacollo's founding, commerce is usually offered as the primary reason. One demographic study cites Quillacollo's

> location as a key point of intersection within a vast market system where it connected, on one side, the agricultural production of the central valley with the markets of the city of Cochabamba and of the region of the altiplano; and on the other side, it forms a central part of the commercial circuit of important goods from Peru, Chile and Argentina. [Polo Nájera 1991:13]

An assessment produced for Quillacollo's municipal government in the mid-1990s concurred, emphasizing the continued regional importance of the town's weekly agricultural market:

> Fundamental factors linked to commerce and to the circulation of products in the zone of the central valley, as well as the mountainous regions of the provinces of Ayopaya, Morochata and Tapacarí, converge in the historical process of the creation of Quillacollo's urban nucleus. A consequence of its strategic placement assigns it the role of a center of interchange, commerce, as a crossroads for agricultural production, toward the centers of consumption in the interior of the

> *country and the city of Cochabamba, giving place to an incipient com-*
> *mercialization consisting of grain warehouses, deposits, and squares*
> *for regional peasant markets. [Canedo 1994:45]*

Its location has given Quillacollo a strategic importance for people looking for new opportunities and coming from points distant to settle in Cochabamba.

The son of a long-established Quillacolleño family observed to me, "Until 1960 Quillacollo was a pueblo, that is, rural, with its cows, its burros, and its horses." Since then, "it has totally changed." By 1976 the population of the provincial capital of Quillacollo had begun to skyrocket, at 19,433 doubling the previous census figure (Calzavarini, Laserna, and Valdivieso 1979:14). With the next count in 1992, Quillacollo's population had more than doubled again, climbing to 42,278 (INE 1994:3). With the most recent census in 2001, the town continued its rapid growth rate to 78,324 persons. In-migration has substantially increased with the "anarchy of the relocalized miners," to quote a local civic activist, to the point that already by 1991, 47 percent of Quillacollo's population were ex-migrants (Polo Nájera 1991:63), that is, people not born in the province. Part of a rapidly emerging urban periphery, recent estimates identify Quillacollo as the most populous provincial capital in Bolivia, with, at last measurement, an unofficial annual growth rate of 6.5 percent (Contreras Baspineiro 2001).[17]

Largely unregulated street vending has come to be synonymous with the squalor of too rapid urbanization, and in recent years it has become a major headache for the town. One economic analyst has asserted that seven of every ten new jobs created in Bolivia since the application of structural adjustment measures in 1985 have been in the "informal" sector, which now comprises up to 40 percent of the total workforce (Kruse 2001, 2003). Commenting on the local effects of the nation's persistent economic crisis, a panicked editorialist noted, "Quillacollo has been converted into a gigantic center of informal commerce, bringing together more than ten thousand venders from Cochabamba, La Paz, Oruro, and other cities" (*Los Tiempos* 2002). Today on Quillacollo's streets the signs of commerce of all sorts are everywhere, from vendor kiosks, or blaring music, to video parlors, construction shops, or cybercafes (in the past few years). A host of ambulant vendors as well as *cholas*—women with their distinctive braids *pelo al pecho* and wearing the signature gathered skirts—hawk their wares, including ingredients for a ritual table, coca leaf for chewing, and *anticucho* (grilled beef strips served with potatoes and a peanut sauce). Market women give a *yapita* (a little something extra), hoping to turn customers into *caseros* (loyal customers), who are one-half of a stable buyer-seller relationship.

Figure 1.1. Sunday market day: A Quillacollo side street crowded with the stalls of informal market vendors.

On Friday evenings in particular, vendors laying out the trappings for weekly ritual observances take over the streets. At that moment the dirt or cobblestone streets are warm, lively, and sociable. Food stalls send their smells up into the night air, if they also mingle with the occasional reek of putrefaction and garbage. But by the following Sunday, the weekly market day, the scene is much more disorderly (Figure 1.1).

> The street, Héroes del Chaco, running off the main plaza, is the town's commercial district. It runs down to the Plaza 15 de Agosto. Over the years, this street has become increasingly overrun by informal small merchants [comerciantes minoristas], and during the weekly market fair it is not passable except on foot.... A central preoccupation of the local authorities is to bring some sort of order to this growing confusion. Their stalls are everywhere. Ambulant vendors set up shop anywhere, selling anything from Hanes underwear, to tutumas [bowls for drinking chicha], to potatoes, to firewood. The stalls spill randomly down the streets.... Young chulu-wearing kh'epiris [strappers] traverse the

market with wheelbarrows of bananas.... Piercing squeals of panicked
pigs go up, as they are loaded or unloaded from trucks, or in one case
shoved terrified into the trunk of a taxi. [Author's field note, August 11,
1994]

Quillacollo's changing human landscape has generated a great deal of angst and criticism from the town's civic minded and from visitors, which is apparent in the following excerpt from a scathing open letter to the mayor's office lamenting the disorganization of the town's yearly fiesta of Urkupiña.

How profound was our disappointment, upon encountering in the
streets: chaos, anarchy, disorder, drunkenness, and filth, a filth which
particularly dismays the tourists who come to our borders, asking
themselves the same question: Does Quillacollo not have any authori-
ties? Having hardly disembarked from the vehicle that transports us
from the city...we are instantly blocked [by merchants] from our objec-
tive, the temple.... We have no interest in the doodads they hawk....
The street that leads to the sanctuary...seems a madhouse. Everyone
shouts, pushes, leaves no room to walk, since the street is full of mer-
chants.... More importance has been granted to the merchants than to
the pilgrims!... Is it that Quillacollo has no place to put its merchants,
or is it that the criteria and mentality of its communal government is
to prioritize commerce over religious faith?

This market vendor epidemic is an acute political problem for Quillacollo's authorities, and the effort to relocate this exploding vendor population has been the source of periodic friction and even violence, in the forms of protests, riots, and vandalism. As a legacy of neoliberal reform, this widespread informalization of economic life has also been extended to many other arenas of Bolivian society (see Toranzo Roca 1989), including politics.

Both a highway and a railway pass through the town. To the west, the train tracks leaving town begin to travel through fields of corn or alfalfa, with milk farmers grazing their stock on empty plots or in unoccupied neighborhood blocks (Figure 1.2). To the east, the town blurs indiscriminately into the irregular urbanscape of the outskirts of Cochabamba, connected by a road, Avenida Blanco Galindo, nicknamed the "highway of death" because of the high frequency of accidents. It composes a corridor of mostly unregulated small industry (see Dandler 1987a; Gordillo et al. 1995). This growth has added greatly to a sense of local disarray. The town's expansion has long since spilled beyond its colonial-era plan, and haphazard construction now characterizes its expanding margins.

Figure 1.2. The town's uneven urban development: A young shepherd pasturing his sheep in a barrio of Quillacollo.

Over the years, as Quillacollo's demographics have changed dramatically, Quillacolleños' perceptions of their town have changed with them. A sketch of the town circa 1950 by one of its prominent citizens described it this way: "The population of the province of Quillacollo is constituted by whites and by mestizos, with very few indigenous people, who are barely seen on market days and in some religious festivals. And these have already changed their clothing and speak Spanish" (Rejas 1950:10). And some twenty years later elite descriptions of Quillacollo continued to express a confident optimism about the town's inevitably "modern" future: "[Quillacollo's] ten kilometers of paved road, now a city avenue, are alive with feverish activity. And the lively work of the industrial establishments bordering it are notable: factories, warehouses, gas and lubricant stores, clinics, ultramodern grandiose hospitals, and multiple places for recreation. The flow of vehicles is incessant, for which the traveler arriving from Oruro or La Paz is thankful" (Cevallos Tovar 1971:12).

However accurate these glowing accounts, people of indigenous descent are much less scarce in Quillacollo now than they were in the early 1970s. And amid the town's subsequent exponential, unregulated growth, and in the aftermath of national structural adjustment—with a new generation of laid-off workers and a stiffer cost of living—this confident image of an industrious, hardworking future has given way to expressions of dismay over chaotic change for the worst, leading to "underdevelopment" and breeding disenchantment. And as with the close-by city of Cochabamba, the "purportedly deficient physical and moral hygiene" (Goldstein 2004:64) of the growing presence of indigenous ex-peasants has been understood to pose a threat to the integrity of Quillacollo, at least from the perspective of its besieged upper and middle classes.

Consider this indictment by one of Quillacollo's schoolteachers and longtime participants in its civic committee, which appeared in a local pamphlet:

> A town like Quillacollo, with such national and international honor and renown, does not merit the state of backwardness and semidevelopment to which it has been reduced: Its streets and squares abandoned and anarchic, with dirt and mud everywhere. Its public buildings: schools, offices, markets, beyond insufficient, are also ruinous, inadequate, barely camouflaged with paint and filler. Its civic, political religious, union and educational organizations barely keeping up appearances and with a desire to "shine" regardless of how. Its people: chastened and defeated, as well as indifferent, grumbling about its frustrations. Once in a while they lift up a shout of protest, or better said, of censure or rejection, of those who do not know how to defend [them]. Its culture, reduced to a minimal expression, to a slender patrimony, preserved at great cost. But it is not promoted nor permitted to grow creatively and autonomously. Its routine social life, full of prejudices, interests, and neighborly antagonisms, evokes a primitive and pharisaic form of life.

Quillacollo's promise of urban development carried along its modern avenue in 1971 had by the late 1990s become "streets full of filth and converted into public bathrooms." And this problem has not improved, with "great volumes of organic and inorganic trash strewn about the streets and piled up nearby" (*Los Tiempos* 2001b). The lack of planning and the lack of any means to regulate development are recurrent themes in Quillacolleños' own stories about their changing town (see Figure 1.3). The promise of urban planning has been replaced by "shantytowns and secret land speculation, which appear overnight without authorization." This has turned Quillacollo— "a land years ago characterized by the loveliest landscapes and places of recreation"—into a "totally disorganized expansion" (Carpio San Miguel 2001b), with unemployment, violence, lack of basic services, poverty, and suspect political authorities.[18]

Figure 1.3. An election-era mural: "*Llajtamasi*: Let's make Quillacollo a dignified, clean, and attractive city."

Nevertheless, people still seek out sociability in one of the town's many colorfully named *chicherías* (traditional watering holes)—the Electric Cat, Maria the Teacher, the Guerrilla, Chernobyl, the Miraculous Chola, the Hovel, and others. For many, chicherías correspond to a social environment reminiscent of the more pastoral years in the provinces prior to the 1952 Revolution, where people can drink, socialize, play the dice game *cacho*, cheat on their spouses, and work out political deals. Recently, though, people have also had to learn the names of new youth gangs (*pandillas*), such as the Black Bulls, the Black Sheep, the Black Panthers, Los Rodríguez, and the Vultures. One report identified at least thirty such gangs in Quillacollo dedicated to "alcoholism, drug addiction, robbery, rape, theft, and violence," the products of a "social fragmentation" increasingly associated with places like Quillacollo (*Los Tiempos* 2004).

Blamed for an alarming recent rise in crime statistics, these gangbangers are mostly "of humble origin" and come from the "sectors most punished by the crisis." In many cases, they are "orphaned of father and mother" and "display an inclination to delinquency from having been totally abandoned" (*Los Tiempos* 1992). People in Quillacollo, now considered one of the most dangerous zones in the department, recognize that their tranquil small town is now a thing of the past. Given the increasing presence of gangs and drugged-up youths—who also spend a lot of time in chicherías—people now express concern about walking the streets at night (see García 2005). Whether this is more perception than reality—I have often walked the streets at night—Quillacolleños understand themselves to be living at once amid a growing crisis and in a *ch'ajchu* (Quechua: "a little of everything") environment. This has become a crisis of citizen security that has provoked vigilante responses in the form of repeated attempted lynchings in different neighborhoods.[19] Though intimately familiar with Quillacollo, upon a return visit one of the first things a close friend felt the need to tell me was to warn me not to ride in taxis. Likely as not, he gravely explained, I might be driven out of town to the periphery, to be "robbed, shot, and left for dead." In fact the social careers described for the participants in these new gangs are surprisingly comparable to the lives of the political authorities with whom I worked.

Quillacollo's turn-of-the-century neopopulist politics, then, should be understood in the context of a local perception of chaotic urban disarray, including an expanding informal economy, and characterized by a decline of good fortune under neoliberalism, in-migration, and lack of urban planning, alongside the perception of delinquency and danger. But it also needs to be understood in the context of the town's agrarian history and the province's particular cultural traditions, which, taken altogether, have encouraged varieties of re-Indianization. The social base of relatively new popular and indigenous alternatives in national politics draws precisely from urban peripheries like Quillacollo, with their historically largely neglected but growing constituencies of people struggling in the post-peasant, urban and indigenous informal sector: artisans, market vendors, migrants, disenfranchised workers, and many others. Local political authorities of "humble origin," specifically, are in a very significant sense the partially estranged inheritors of these peri-urban circumstances. And chapters 5 and 6 in particular are concerned with the problematic public consequences of genealogy and inheritance as a cultural patrimony.

Politics and Problem-Solving Networks

An astonishingly common and readily recalled experience among the vast majority of politically active people with whom I worked in Quillacollo is that of a childhood shaped by sharp traumas and variously combining hard and even exploitative labor, acute poverty, physical abuse, father abandonment, cultural and geographic dislocation, and a hard-knocks street socialization. These are men who grew up in a wide variety of challenging circumstances, including life in isolated mining camps or as street urchins, accompanying their mothers on the itinerant trading circuit, working in the fields, or as child-aged street peddlers. Most attended school only irregularly, which was fodder for political rivals who ridiculed them with complaints that they were at best "semiliterate."

As regularly serving public functionaries, many of these men were sheepish about their lack of education, which was often little more than the equivalent of elementary or middle school. A large proportion went back to school as adults as this became possible, sometimes even up through the local public University of San Simón in the city of Cochabamba. Some of them did so to become lawyers, a profession with significant political value in Quillacollo. Others, however, were clear that they had little formal schooling but indicated that they grew up in the school of political or union life (la escuela sindical), where they became conversant with the ideologies and politics of the workers' movement and the agrarian or mining union. By their own descriptions, though, typically these are people who have over-come long—even tragic—odds, including malnourishment, illness, and vio-lence, to enjoy relatively successful adult careers as local authorities and public political figures in Quillacollo. Economic hardship is a basic social fact of Quillacollo's provincial politics at present as in the past, and when local authorities describe themselves as of "humble origins"—as they often do—they are pointedly orienting these experiences of hardship and their ongoing careers to a personal trajectory, a family history, the public recogni-tion of relevant cultural heritage, and a style of local politics, compatible with nationally emergent popular and indigenous commitments. How such family and personal careers become a basis for the negotiation of cultural inheritance as shared patrimony in the context of political expedience is the subject of chapter 6.

Over the past two decades the state's neoliberal measures have led to the proportional decline of the contract worker—locally represented by Manaco and smaller-scale industry—and an increase in an insecure and unregulated or informal economy of unemployment, temporary employment, self-employment, and small-scale commercial activities.[20] When last measured, Quillacollo's average annual income was approximately $1,448 (Bustamante, Buttorworth, and Faysse 2004:5), and it remains a relatively poor province where the use of money is not pervasive and the reciprocal or direct exchange of goods and services remains a basic economic strategy (Delgado, San Martín, and Torrico 1998:29). In the absence of more stable options, people have been moved to invest a great deal of energy in developing their own household-based diversified economic strategies. These usually include wives, children, and extended family members in different capacities, as well as involvement in trade unions and both local and regional political contacts. These diversified strategies are not at all new and in fact are well documented for the provincial context of Cochabamba.[21] But the neoliberal era has made such informal and diversified economic activities even more crucial as tactics of survival.

In addition to the resources he received directly from politics, for example, one veteran political operator—described to me by his rivals as an "urban peasant"—worked as a schoolteacher, maintained a lawyer's office on the side, and owned a taxi, as well as a hectare of land on which he cultivated corn. Economic activities prominent among the politically active men I knew well variously combined such diverse pursuits as agriculturalist, transporter, land speculator, pig or milk farmer, the illicit coca leaf industry, small business, legal work, one or another cottage industry, factory worker, chichería owner, market trader or seller, street vendor, petty functionary, local official, or staff member of a local nongovernmental organization (NGO), among other possibilities. And these are not stand-alone activities but also directly if informally connect to other political and economic benefits. Such a distribution of economic activities takes considerable energy and is a necessary compensatory strategy in a context of the scarcity and vulnerability of secure long-term contract employment.

As Carlos Toranzo Roca (1989) described early on, one of the basic experiences of neoliberalism has been an increased informalization of Bolivian society, a principle we can understand as extending beyond the expansion of the informal economy to also include the face-to-face, personalistic, familial, and network-based mobilization of political activity. The great majority of people I knew living and working in the small city of Quillacollo moved through the informal economy in various ways. This included "eating from politics," as it is said. Participation in politics was definitely a calculated part of many diversified household economies, particularly the hope that with a change of local administration one might benefit by receiving a *pega* (a political job). But no one who is politically active in Quillacollo lives by politics alone, if by that is meant making a sufficient salary as a public or party official—minuscule or nonexistent in any case. Make no mistake: people do extract resources from politics, though in more informal ways (and not excluding graft), through organized political networks that circulate economic resources, sometimes as money, basic food staples, family connections, reciprocal relations, or key information.

If the views they air are any gauge, disillusioned Quillacolleños hold their political authorities in extremely low regard. A thirty-five-household survey of political perceptions in Quillacollo administered early on in my fieldwork painted a bleak picture. The following are typical samples of people's views about Bolivia's political class: "Bolivia is ruined by those shameless men"; "They are an embarrassment for humanity"; "I don't know where corruption isn't found"; "They're corrupt. All of them look out for their personal interests"; "After they take office, they forget everyone"; "They have no interest in working for the province, but instead pocket what they can";

"There is no honorable politician"; "They are fraudulent"; "They dissimu-late"; politics is "a deception"; a *político* is "he who shouts loudest"; "For every one word I say, they say ten or fifteen." And the most often heard com-plaint is that local *políticos* "make promises they don't keep." Not coinci-dentally, politically active people in Quillacollo typically energetically deny the perceived accusation that, indeed, they are "politicians."

There was no shortage of criticism of local officials while I worked in Quillacollo, however. They were constantly publicly accused of influence peddling, accepting bribes, or the pursuit of their own material interests. The most frequent charge was that of *prebendalismo*, the exchanging of mate-rial goods for votes. This charge was particularly leveled at the UCS party throughout the 1990s, the dominant political party in Quillacollo over that period. But what is condemned as corruption in national newspaper edi-tori-als is, from another angle, a staple of the informal economy, where resources change hands to bolster ongoing and potentially productive working rela-tionships among clients.[22] Successful political operators in Quillacollo occupy indispensable positions brokering what Javier Auyero (2000:83–84) has aptly called "problem-solving networks." Auyero (2000:85) describes the problem-solving network for urban Argentines during this country's eco-nomic crisis of the late 1990s and early 2000s as "an overlapping of infor-mal networks of survival and political networks," a strategy utilized by working-class people in mostly marginal urban neighborhoods. We can understand Quillacollo's politics during the crisis of neoliberalism in com-parable terms.

For local functionaries—as people with indispensable skills and access to the municipal administrative process—making a living includes the exchange of favors in the form of influence, information, or the facilitation of paperwork up the chain of administration, in return for payment in agri-cultural goods, other perishables, or even livestock, rather than cash. Clients will often describe these as part of an informal economy of ongoing and tra-ditional reciprocal relationships typical of Quillacollo's primarily informal economy. This interpenetration of economic, political, and cultural priori-ties, through organized, personalistic, and diffuse networks that circulate both material and symbolic benefits as part of a local informal economy that includes a local politics of the purse strings, lies at the heart of the political relationships I describe for Quillacollo in these pages.

As the site of an important popular market, Quillacollo has for centuries been an axis of convergence for intensive and daily cultural interactions between smallholding peasants, itinerant traders, as well as urban-dwelling artisans, laborers, mestizo merchants, and pilgrims. As such, Brooke Larson (1998:365) has emphasized the close cultural proximity and tensions between country and city, peasant and worker, Indian and cholo, productive of a complex "interclass, interethnic mingling" of the province, which is not simply reducible to the assimilationist and nationalist account of mestizaje, and which has proved critically important in recent years in a populist expansion of the possibilities for urban indigenous political participation. Instead, the people at the center of this book are best understood as specialized political intermediaries who, often for self-interested reasons of the household economy, actively manage resources to build informal political and mercantile alliances. In the present context of the national ascendancy of an indigenous project in Bolivia, the political goings-on in Quillacollo help us to fill out an account of the evolution of the characteristically urban indigenous-popular political experience that has provided critical mass support for the current project of Evo Morales and of the MAS.

Political Careers

The people featured in this book, if mostly men, confront the challenges of representation in at least two ways. They seek to be and often are elected political representatives, if to a union post or as a member of a local party ticket. They are supposed to stand in for, and to serve, a public constituency during their term of office. At the same time, throughout their political careers they are also subject to a very public and often factional cultural politics of representation, as the subjects of arguments among allies, rivals, and the noninvested, which are most often made in the terms of ethnicity, culture, family, class, and the extent to which a person's career is or is not legible in terms of the experiences and expectations of Quillacollo's fairly diverse popular, including indigenous, sectors. This is a town, recall, itself in something like a semipermanent identity crisis: as part of the regional market circuit, a historical point of transit, popular destination of in-migration, and peri-urban zone. And these two problems of representation often coincide.

Stigma is regularly attached to the reputation of local authorities, as a "spoiled identity" (Goffman 1963), not only through a distrust of those involved in politics but also with the frequent perception that they are often cholos. As such, they are considered inappropriately mobile in a variety of ways both geographic and social, transgressing perceived unitary categories of ethnic identity while confounding civilizational models of urban progress.[23] And travel, as transgression of both place and status, is a central experience of almost all the políticos of this ethnography. The problem of the cholo and of perceived cholo sensibilities in Quillacollo's politics, as stigmatized and as historically "unintelligible" from the point of view of the nation (Soruco Sologuren 2006), is a unifying theme throughout this book.

Specifically, if in different ways, it is a central subject of chapters 4, 5, and 6. But rather than simply record the facts of infamy, disgrace, or reproach composing stigma, this book explores how stigma is also an expression of estrangement from particular kinds of indigenous and popular cultural experience, but which is often confirmed in regular references to its absence. Estrangement, then, has its political uses as a way to introduce indigenous experience and identity into Quillacollo's urban politics, if often as the factional face of local politics.

More than two-thirds of the people I knew in Quillacollo who were active in politics were born elsewhere. Some, brought up in the "historic Left," described to me their experiences in Cuba (sometimes to attend university), China, or the former Communist Eastern Europe. Others spent time as political exiles cutting sugarcane in the Bolivian lowlands or in Chile. One well-known local authority worked for many years as a salesman for Cochabamba's milk company, making regular trips to Mexico. Many other men emigrated to work illegally in such countries as Argentina, Israel, or the United States for significant periods of time. A further, and important, group of local political types has worked as long-range transporters of mostly agricultural goods, traveling throughout the nearby highlands of Ayopaya and elsewhere in Bolivia, as well as Chile, Argentina, or Peru.

María Lagos (1994:102–129) has provided a detailed account of the emergence of a regional trucker elite in Cochabamba's upper valley in and around the town of Tiraque. As she noted, however, the wealthiest trucking monopoly—reputed to have a pact with the devil—was based not in Tiraque but in Quillacollo. Mobility is as often social as geographic. For one politically active individual, this was a progression from an early life pasturing cows, to thievery, to working as a butcher's assistant, to carpentry, to small-scale transport, and, finally, to becoming a lawyer, supplemented by a municipal salary, modest land speculation, and his wife's job as a pharmacist. In another case, an individual's youth spent helping his father harvest the family plot was eventually exchanged for working on a hacienda as an assistant foreman, working for years at Manaco, a brief interlude learning to be a barber, and a later life as a successful transporter.

These checkered careers are not the exceptions. But if the men in this book are "popular leaders" (dirigentes populares, as they are sometimes called) and if Quillacollo's is in some sense a popular culture, I try to avoid uncritically invoking the popular here, since the term *popular identity* often conceals more than it reveals about political careers and the politics of self-presentation, particularly when encouraging a too easy connection to cultural studies approaches and to the well-worn grooves of the analysis of mass consumption and class (see Williams 2002), on the one hand, and of the charismatic leadership of Latin American populism (see Albro 2004; Conniff 1999), on the other. In Quillacollo, the popular includes the indigenous, which has been given short shrift in cultural studies approaches to popular identity in Latin America (see García Canclini 2001; Yúdice 2003).

The political scientist Harold Lasswell (1930:1) memorably remarked, "Political science without biography is a form of taxidermy." Focusing upon the most politically active subset of the town's population as its subject, this book is concerned with the process of publicity in Quillacollo's local politics, as it has been instrumental for the changing boundaries of popular and indigenous belonging. Concerned with some of the ways that self-expression and representation become contentious, methodologically this problem has been distilled to considerations of the intersection of collective politics with biography or life history (see Auyero 2003; Behar 1993; Friedrich 1977, 1986; Ginzburg 1980), which I discuss here in terms of "careers." I explore the public implications of political careers most thoroughly in chapter 3. Particularly given suspicions about politics, the careers of local political authorities are subject to substantial public scrutiny and competing interpretations. And the ways that careers publicly circulate, as a cultural process, is a central preoccupation of this book. This is, too, a calculated means of bringing into focus the relevance of a kind of urban indigenous experience not simply expressible as collective ethnic or territorial claims.

The career of Pancho Sánchez, a key maker and recurrent figure in this book, is illustrative.[24] He can be found every day manning his small street stall, where he makes keys. This is also his political base of operations. The disorderly modesty of the kiosk can be deceiving. The street stall offers easy public accessibility, of which Pancho takes the fullest advantage. Though a "mere key maker" (as critics point out), Pancho is a market union leader, has served several times as town councilman, has been interim mayor, and for years has been an active insider of the local UCS party. As an intermittently important member of the provincial machine of this dominant party, he is among the same group of people who took turns running things from 1985 at least up to 2002. Pancho's street stall, strategically positioned just off a major town square and along a trufi route to the nearby city, places him at the hub of the town's political commerce.[25] His stall allows him to be available and to keep current as a place where other political allies gather to discuss things, joke, plot, eat, or read the newspaper.

On any given day, Pancho can be seen industriously carrying out his main business. Though he makes a lot of keys, it is not making keys. His wife sells meat as a market vendor. Though himself not a member, Pancho represents the interests of the rank and file of her union. He spends most of his time advocating for and helping to solve problems for members of his wife's union, who stop by daily. A compadre might bring him a particular problem, which Pancho will take care of for free, abruptly jumping on his bike and disappearing for several hours. Friends can easily find him at the kiosk and cajole him to a nearby drinking establishment for a private conversation. The benefits derived from Pancho's efforts are mostly indirect. Pancho is often contemptuously identified by rivals as one or another sort of semiliterate cholo. Pancho's critics, in short, derisively insinuate his indigenous descent. And if he is often vocal in combating his critics, in other contexts the myriad often unstated connections between Pancho's critics' and his own accounts of his difficult upbringing are also potential indigenous and popular cultural capital.[26] This book explores the problematic public careers of so-called cholos of humble origins in Quillacollo, like Pancho Sánchez, as doubly representative of the new kinds of possibilities for urban indigenous politics in contemporary Bolivia.

Like most of the people in this book, Pancho Sánchez is hard to classify. After coming with his mother from Oruro to Cochabamba, Pancho spent the first ten years of his life accompanying her, a corn trader (*rescatista*), on trips along the rural back roads of the regional market circuit. He has a good command of Quechua, has known the extremes of poverty, and lived as a child "like a campesino" and "on the streets." But he would be the last person to pin himself down with any particular identity. In fact careers like his encourage us to consider limitations to the now-conventional analysis of indigenous "identity politics" (see Clifford 1988; Gilroy 1991; Hale 1994, 1997; Jackson 1991, 1995), and even the inadequacy of beginning with identity as a prevailing analytic category at all in coming to terms with politics in Quillacollo. Identity trouble is a persistent theme of this book. As I have stressed, the town's history has been told in terms of a crossroads lacking its own identity and as an increasingly unregulated urban periphery. In the words of Zygmunt Bauman (1999:22), Quillacollo provides the conditions of "identity chased but never caught."

As Charles Taylor (1994:75) noted in his widely referenced discussion, "Identity is partly shaped by recognition or its absence, often by the misrecognition of others." This ethnography dwells on the regular interplay of recognition with misrecognition, which most often exploits the perceived continuities and discontinuities between mestizaje and cholaje, as a dynamic source of cultural capital. I refer to this as the work of estrangement, and it is an important means for the movement in and out of indigenous and nonindigenous terms of local experience. If in the politics of Quillacollo identity is constantly publicly negotiated, as an ongoing and often contentious performance, this is comparable to the ways that participation in recent indigenous mobilizations has been described elsewhere in

Bolivia. Sian Lazar (2008:4) describes the tensions between collective and individual interests within the politics of El Alto's base organizations as identities built through "ritualized and embodied practices, gossip and suspicion, and the development of notions of reciprocity, authority, hierarchy, and obligation." This also effectively describes Quillacollo. And yet, if local associations figure importantly in the province, at least in recent decades Quillacollo's has not, by and large, been a primarily collective politics. It therefore offers an alternative account of the various forms that popular and indigenous political subjecthood is taking in contemporary Bolivia.

Politically active people in Quillacollo often expressed concerns to me in the terms of estrangement: stories about the displacement of cultural heritage and abandonment of the terms of community, expressed via the specter of the cholo as a public sign of the loss of cultural belonging. And if this process never precisely settles into identity, it is a constituent part of an ongoing process of identification. In Quillacollo recognition is as often as not the key to an identity politics but also its undoing. In fact, with García Canclini (2001:77–86), this book explores the impossibility of constructing contemporary collective narratives of "the popular" in Latin America. It does so in large part by tracking the political effects of estrangement—including the social, cultural, and economic incoherence of the application of a collective identitarian project—in the experience and careers of men like Pancho Sánchez.

Taylor (1994:81) has distinguished two registers of the work of recognition, those of the intimate and of the public sphere. But in Quillacollo these are problematically conjoined, where public recognition is projected through what Michael Herzfeld (1997) calls "cultural intimacy." In the following chapters this is explored as more than simply intimate knowledge of the flaws and imperfections of state institutions, as Herzfeld has emphasized. More importantly, cultural intimacy involves regular effort among political authorities to define and to claim access to interior spaces of culture in Quillacollo as claims of authenticity and as the public expression of a political career. Particularly in chapter 4, I explore the connections between intimacy and politics in Quillacollo through a discussion of publicity as the management, by local authorities, of exchanges with prototypically popular women. Men, in short, advertise relations of descent and maintain public relationships of exchange with women of indigenous descent because of the ways these women are understood to control access to the market, to the home, to agricultural practice, to chicherías, to saints, and to fiestas, all as spaces or experiences of cultural intimacy. This is one publicly important way that políticos seek to continuously reactivate the sources of authenticity of their own humble cultural backgrounds.

The work of cultural intimacy is often also connected to the activities of the informal economy under neoliberalism, which are very much a part of local political practice. Careers rather than collectivities are the form taken by the province's popular and indigenous politics, if these careers are at the same time locations and trajectories for arguments about family, community, experience, and authenticity. As Carlos de la Torre (2000:11) has suggested about the populist mystique, this requires a leader who promotes "an atmosphere of intimacy with his followers." Such political intimacy depends upon the interrelation between politics and daily life—politics as a particular way of being in the world—characterized by the overlap of the personal with the social and with the public: "This lack of differentiation between the public and the private—where not only the public is privately appropriated but also political relations are perceived as extensions of private relations—normalizes favoritism, personalism, clientelism, and paternalism, as regular political practices" (Alvarez, Dagnino, and Escobar 1998:9). Public political careers are transit points in discussions of what composes cultural intimacy. Careers act as a kind of "alchemical crucible," to use Bauman's (1999:11) lyrical term, where "private concerns and public issues meet" and where politics and personhood are mutually and locally constructed in neoliberal and democratic Bolivia.

But what Debbora Battaglia (1995:10) has called "self-prospecting" is complicated by its very publicness. I dwell throughout on political performances of cultural intimacy, as these successfully and unsuccessfully seek to bridge the gaps between public and private, past and present, or social origin and mobility, as a series of ongoing recognition dramas. But, as Herzfeld (1997:3) insists, even as recognition might promote "common sociality," it can also be a "source of external embarrassment." And it can fail, as chapter 6's analysis of the factionalism associated with one public political performance makes apparent. In this case, a series of choreographed ritual libations by the mayor designed to demonstrate his effectiveness while in office backfired, with detractors using these cultural spectacles as opportunities effectively to question and to undermine his identity as a popular leader. Quillacollo's neopopulist politics of cultural intimacy, then, rarely settles into the consensus of identity talk as it grapples with the problems of recognition and the implications of misrecognition or the essential hazards of self-representation (see Keane 1997). And this, in turn, encourages a more provisional approach to the role of indigenous heritage.

Política Criolla or Humble Politics?

The informal politics of patronage usually have been described as a matter of the ways leaders see to the loyalty of their followers by taking care of them, typically with material benefits (see Auyero 2000; Bailey 1988). But during my two years of original fieldwork in Quillacollo, people were particularly disparaging of "vertical politics," which they imagined as widely practiced varieties of patronage and clientage, virtually synonymous for many people with a personalistic, informal, self-interested, and often corrupt politics, dismissed with a flourish by at least one disgusted former mayor as "drinking, handouts, and cronies" (*"chupas, pegas, y compadres"*). During the campaign for local elections in 1993 and 1995, for which I was present, Quillacollo was regularly derided by its own candidates for office as a "nest of the corrupt." But, as F. G. Bailey (1988:5) reminds us, "leaders are often villains." One kind of villainy in Quillacollo is the practice of *política criolla*, literally "mixed politics," synonymous with the kind of self-interested conduct thought to lack an ideological or higher purpose of the public good. If most local commentators are to be believed, this would include just about everyone involved in the province's politics.

Local critics in Quillacollo in fact coincide with many social scientists, who have also pointed to problematic aspects of the practices of patronage and clientelism as at once intrinsic features of what is often described as populism—a transient and transitional kind of realpolitik—and as subject to considerable criticism (see Auyero 2000; De Vries 2002; Friedrich 1986; Gay 1998; Mayorga 2002). Indeed, patronage is often synonymous with the unequal exercise of power, with an illegitimate politics conducted in between official channels, and with a kind of face-to-face interpersonal politics understood to be an undesirable cultural remainder or holdover from traditional society. So far as it goes, such a description is true of Quillacollo's *política criolla* as well. But this is not yet a sufficient description.

People in Quillacollo complained often to me about the contraction of the state after neoliberalism, including the decrease in state services or patronage, at the same time that they indicted politicians for their mendacity—often treated as an unwanted expression of Bolivia's adopted neoliberal values. In Quillacollo patron-client relationships, then, also present cultural solutions to one version of the ongoing crisis of political representation and estrangement in the province and nationally, often articulated as a sign of the perceived failures, most recently, of neoliberalism. In ways comparable to De Vries's (2002:903) description of the Mexican cacique as "pervasive, corrupt, and violent but inevitable," *política criolla* in Bolivia is a legacy at once to be escaped but which people find they cannot easily do without.

The milieu of *política criolla* included the majority of people active in politics, whom I came to know well in Quillacollo. As participants in this milieu, all of the people figuring in this book were routinely described to me at different points as "patrons" or as "clients" of other people in this book or of people beyond present considerations. In Quillacollo there is a concomitantly rich and figurative political vocabulary of patronage and clientage. It at once describes potentially self-interested political behavior but also an exercise of building social networks that provide different avenues of connection with, and inroads to, urban indigenous worlds, as a cultural identity project and as overlapping with the local informal economy.

Sustained examination of the ways that patronage and clientage in Quillacollo are culturally productive kinds of political relationships and how these, in turn, point to an alternative kind of urban indigenous subject in Bolivia is a major unifying theme of this book. In this way, each of the chapters speaks to the others, as, collectively, they lay out the ways that patronage is an organizing cultural expectation negotiated through beliefs and practices of gender, kinship, exchange, concepts of authority, reciprocity, and other aspects of Quillacollo's moral economy. This begins with a discussion in chapter 2 of the close public relationship between patronage and stigma, as epitomized by ideas about notoriously "bad clients" and as contrasted with the normative and gendered goals of self-construction, as these organize expectations across the patron-client relationship. Chapter 3 further develops the interpretation of patronage, as articulated by the political roles of the institution of ritual or spiritual godparenthood in Quillacollo, which at once registers moral kinds of debts and obligations, changing notions of respect, and public roles of sponsorship, in contrasts drawn between the feudal *patrón* of the past, market behavior, and the apparently self-interested investments of the present. Chapter 4 dwells on the kinds of cultural analogies people draw between municipal and individual political authorities, on the one hand, and the town's patron saint, on the other, as these govern exchanges of "articles of first necessity" between politically engaged men and indigenous women, and as part of the work of political self-prospecting.

Chapter 6 complements the previous chapters, as it also considers the cultural trappings and political implications of the role of the ritual sponsor, or *padrino*, particularly ideas about intercession, as these help to determine the kinds of brokerage roles local *políticos* inhabit, if not always successfully. Finally, perhaps the central chapter of this ethnography is chapter 5, which develops an account of varieties of meaningful connection between public expectations for fatherhood and patronage (as an extension of fatherhood), as related to family histories, and conceived as a kind of cultural inheritance or patrimony. This chapter makes the case most forcefully for the different ways that patronage and clientage organize cultural practice as a kind of public knowledge that is generated through the interplay between estrangement and intimacy and that people can then claim.

Across all these chapters, arguments over expectations of patronage, and related political relationships and identities, produce what we might call an indigenous remainder, which people at once acknowledge, critique, and embrace, if in different ways. Throughout this book, then, I point to the sorts of cultural work people seek to accomplish as part of patronage relationships and as part of a local political process. The case of Quillacollo raises important questions about characterizations of Bolivia's current national indigenous project, as at least rhetorically based upon a sharp repudiation of crony capitalism and of patronage politics as legacies of the elite politics of the recent past. However, it is apparent that Quillacollo's urban popular and indigenous politics and identity are also significantly produced through the legacies and expectations of a local politics of patronage.

Complicating the political careers of most of the people in these pages is the accusation that they are, to a man, cholos (gloss: "citified Indian"), a historically pejorative racial slur and insult that is expressed in the terms of política criolla. In this environment claims to "humble" status have become a prevailing mode of self-presentation—at once a means to deflect criticism and stigma and a cultural strategy of intimacy vis-à-vis Quillacollo's popular public. In Quillacollo being "humble" is a social and cultural set of circumstances directing attention to a history and ancestry as someone "of humble origin" (de origen humilde). This book examines Quillacollo's humble politics—the everyday sorts of neopopulist and urban indigenous political practices typical of provincial municipalities and urban peripheries in Bolivia—as one solution to the problem of stigma. At the same time, it also describes the circumstances of an emergent "humble political public," a new kind of third space associated with Bolivia's urban periphery, which is not elite or simply indigenous, the implications of which I discuss in the concluding chapter. But more problematically, nor is it just mixed. And this is changing the boundaries and significance of indigenous (and nonindigenous) political projects in Bolivia.

2 *Llunk'erío*
Clientelism and the Problem of Stigma

If Evo's undeniable popularity represents new—even utopian—possibilities for an indigenous political agenda, he is not the first national indigenous leader to occupy a high-profile political post in the Bolivian government. Most recently, *katarista* Victor Hugo Cárdenas served as vice president during the first Sánchez de Lozada administration (1993–97) as junior member of a surprising partnership between the neoliberal MNR and the Indianist MRTK (Movimiento Revolucionario Tupac Katari) (Albó 1994). The decision to participate formally in the government was, however, politically costly for Cárdenas. If a media darling at the time, Cárdenas was also accused of selling out by political rivals. Once a star, he is now entirely marginal to the present currents of indigenous politics in Bolivia, accused of having exhibited a "servile and fawning attitude" (Ticona, Rojas, and Albó 1995:195) while part of the government. That is, he was repeatedly accused of being a *llunk'u* (Quechua and Aymara: "flatterer"). As another leader explained it, "When we were llunk'us we expected much and got virtually nothing!" At least in politics, the llunk'u illustrates the expectation of patronage from the point of view of the client. At the same time it is also an accusation of indigenous selling out. Cárdenas was evaluated by his peers as having displayed an unacceptably clientelistic attitude and so was perceived to have been co-opted by the Sánchez de Lozada government and its neoliberal project. As such, Cárdenas was accused of having abandoned collective indigenous responsibilities and his own identity.

The ex–vice president's downfall is a testament to the risks run when leaders of indigenous and social movements choose to participate in the process of state governance. In fact, Cárdenas was a political casualty of a recurrent problem at the heart of indigenous political projects in Bolivia and in Latin America, the predominance of an indigenous cultural politics that has informed indigenous political projects in Bolivia for decades and which continues to be highly influential and to receive substantial international support. This cultural politics assumes indigenous autonomy and a definition of indigenous belonging based upon collective cultural distinctiveness, the boundaries of which are routinely highlighted, patrolled, and defended by contemporary indigenous activists.[1]

In what follows I examine the lexicon of clientage in Quillacollo as a constituent dimension of political coalition building in this provincial capital. I am particularly concerned here with making sense of the stigma attached to accusations of llunk'us, understood to be problematic or "bad" clients. As notorious political figures llunk'us are most often defined by their transgressive qualities. And as with Cárdenas, the accusation of "llunk'u" at once indicates the expectation of patronage and its rejection. At the same time the accusation reinscribes—if in negative relief—the assumption of shared expectations for an autonomous indigenous project of identity, even in a place like Quillacollo where this makes little sense as such.

Llunk'u-like patronage-clientage relationships are an important political fact distributed across everyday and intimate indigenous and popular relationships in Quillacollo. Any effort to redraw the political landscape in Bolivia is going to need to come to terms with such problems as posed by llunk'erío: its rejection of patronage, assertion of autonomy, and reliance upon an exclusionary cultural politics that makes sharp distinctions about who is "indigenous" and under what circumstances. That is, llunk'us are stigmatized in part because they confound any clear distinction between indigenous and nonindigenous cultural locations. In this regard the term is part of the ambivalent discourse concerned with class and ethnic mobility in Quillacollo.

In the mode of condemnation, the oft-noted corrupt behavior of llunk'us represents the possible corruption of indigenous identity, almost always by self-serving cholo types. To this end, and complementing chapter 3's discussion of fictive kinship to follow, here I consider the public talk in Quillacollo generated around patron-client relations. Instead of understanding these as collisions between distinct "interests" or "social positions" represented by patrons and clients respectively assumed to be members of separable and competing social statuses or groups (compare Cohen and Comaroff 1976), I focus in particular upon the ways that supposed clients participate in the "dialogical" coproduction[2] of power-laden, everyday, collusive, and intimate indigenous-popular working relationships.

Provincial Politics from *Sindicato* to *Alcaldía*

Prior to the era of structural adjustment beginning in 1985, for many decades Quillacollo's *alcaldía* (municipal bureaucracy) had not been the center of the province's political life. At least from 1858 until right before 1952, the alcaldía formally resembled its present organization (Peredo Antezana 1963:93).[3] There was an alcalde, or mayor, and a *junta municipal*, or town council of six, as well as a subprefect. The alcalde was typically a criollo or mestizo professional (usually a doctor or a lawyer), a member of one of the region's gente decente landowning families, and a person who enjoyed the sanction of the Catholic Church and town social club called the Comité Pro-Quillacollo. Then as now there was continuous close collaboration with the nearby departmental capital, connected to the town by a trolley car from 1917 until the mid-1940s. The founding of new party options in the early 1940s did little to alter this pattern of local political life. Up until 1952, the alcalde was elected from within one of the two dominant national parties, the Liberal and Republican, in a "qualified vote."[4] Politics in these years was a matter reserved for the town's dozen or so elite families making up a small fraction of the province's population.

The formal oath of office was delivered under the gaze of the town's local *patrona*, the Virgin of Urkupiña, in the main plaza of this colonial-era parish. Local elite politics early in the century was almost wholly preoccupied with the "modernization" of the town itself and almost entirely ignored the circumstances of the much more numerous rural vallunos. As the town's self-appointed historian has commented about the institution of the alcaldía during this period: "All social and cultural activity of the developed populations revolved around the municipalities. The juntas or town councils replaced the parishes as centers of growth, where the vecinos met to exchange opinions, plan projects of urban improvement, and seek out the cooperation of the townsfolk [*vecindario*] for the benefit of the community" (Peredo Antezana 1963:94).Taking the lead in these efforts, the alcaldía restricted its jurisdiction to the urban limits of the town itself. Historically, it was left to the subprefect to resolve disputes in the nearby countryside. Despite the recent expansion of the alcalde's authority into the province's rural zones, the current law formally setting out the alcalde's duties (reformed in 1985) still emphasizes his older hat: "He has as his burden the direction, promotion, and supervision of urban development" (Ley Orgánica de Municipalidades, Tit. III, Ch. 1, Art. 39).

But the 1952 Revolution and subsequent Agrarian Reform abruptly ushered in profound changes in the regional geography of political power. In
Cochabamba's lower valley, suddenly the newly founded regional
Federación Sindical de Trabajadores Campesinos emerged as the undis-
puted force (Dandler 1971:149–158; Encinas 1989; Peredo Antezana
1963:189–196), with its headquarters in Quillacollo itself. The region's
agrarian union was controlled by the new cacique, Sinforoso Rivas.[5] His
power was based upon his role as a valuable client of the successful party of
the revolution, the MNR (including both local townsmen and national
caudillos), his authority to dispense precious land titles, and his role as
"spokesman" for the mostly illiterate valley peasantry, as well as the union's
armed militia, which was allied with the militias of nearby valley provinces.
In exchange for titles, peasants gave him "gifts" (Quechua: t'inkas) of pigs,
goats, fruit trees, and money. Amid the Agrarian Reform, he also used his
authority to annex substantial land for himself. Quillacolleños emphasized
to me that these peasant autocrats were "like the new patrons" in their sense
of entitlement, something commentators on the reform also noticed
(Simmons 1974). His status as cacique ensured that he was also a successful entrepreneur. Rivas often used his political clout to obligate peasants
(who were also rank-and-file members of the agrarian union) to sell him
their harvests at a substantially reduced rate, which he then sold at a
markup in the nearby mines. Contemporary local campesino leaders agreed,
"Overnight, he became rich."

Of popular descent, politically adept, and literate (letrado), Rivas was
not a typical peasant. Jorge Dandler has summarized concisely this eventual
cacique's early career:

> Rivas is described by friends and enemies as a sharp, cunning valluno,
> very capable as a business and political operator, literate, and equally
> fluent in Spanish and Quechua. He was the son of a colono (peasant
> sharecroppers) in the nearby hacienda of Viloma. In his early twenties,
> he worked for several years in the mines (Viloco, Catavi and Llallagua,
> during the early 1940s). There he rapidly rose through various posi-
> tions beyond what most men of campesino background achieved. He
> became an employee of the company store (pulpería), assistant in the
> payroll office and typist-accountant. He also became involved in the
> mining labor union movement and closely acquainted with its
> Trotskyite leaders and Lechín, head of the National Mining Union
> Federation at Catavi. Because of his political involvement, Rivas was
> in the company's "black list" and fired.... He returned to Suticollo and
> became...partner in the wholesale supply (rescate) of eucalyptus ties

> to the mines. This was a competitive business which involved influen-
> tial contacts in the mines and a personal network with many hacen-
> dados and campesinos in the Lower Valley. At this time (1947–48),
> Rivas also became corregidor (provincial legal agent) in Suticollo.
> [1971: 151–152]

Today Quillacolleños of both elite and popular descent have few kind words about Rivas. They described him to me as someone who "ran things however he wanted" ("*a su gusto*"). Campesinos referred to him as *tayta* (Quechua: "father"), and he was "king" of the town, "like God." At the same time he was described as an abusive "criminal," a "mafioso" who routinely extorted from and even on occasion tortured people in exchange for the promise of land titles. He was depicted as a self-serving leader of a campesino movement that at the time was "still in diapers." But, as a regional *político* of ambiguously popular descent (not, strictly speaking, a campesino), Rivas also represented for an earlier generation a local pattern of identity politics where questions of political legitimacy were posed as questions about the social origin and cultural competence of leaders.[6] This became a basic feature of local factionalism and a situation to be repeated in contemporary Quillacollo.

Rivas and the union held a tight grip on regional politics for at least ten years, until the MNR fell on hard times in 1962. The mayors of this period were puppets, directly appointed (*a dedo*) from within the town's professional population by the peasant cacique and completely under his thumb. The alcalde was virtually powerless, a bureaucrat with a rubber stamp, who could be removed at the cacique's whim. Up through the early 1960s, only one alcalde made a futile attempt to resist the hegemony of the cacique (Peredo Antezana 1963:196–197). Rivas used his official status in the alcaldía to eventually subvert the institution from within. The union occupied an office (called the Central Campesina) half a block down from the alcaldía, off of the main square. And the peasant leaders of the union during this period kept up the pretense that they were paid employees of the alcaldía, receiving their salaries from the municipality's budget.

With the succession of dictatorships, more or less without respite from 1964 until 1978, the alcalde and subprefect were again appointed directly from on high. As had been the case since the late 1940s, there were no elections during this interim. But this time, local officials were for the most part army colonels and captains, from elsewhere and appointed by the dictator himself, either Barrientos or Banzer. These military officials were not "sons of the town." They were instead rotating administrators brought in from the outside to ensure that national policies were locally applied. As interlopers, these military officials rarely benefited from the support of townspeople. At least retrospectively, they were perceived as "autocratic" and were met with the "punishment" of little local cooperation. During this period, the local political arena hardly existed as such, and the alcalde was a local representative of national political powers. Since prior to 1952, then, the position of mayor has been transformed from the elected representative of a relatively oligarchic provincial elite primarily attuned to national politics to a powerless post informally controlled by the local peasant cacique and then to the local military face of national officialdom for vertically oriented dictatorial regimes.

The years from 1982 until 1985 ushered in yet another shift. Although hyped as a "democratic opening," the new government still appointed its local officials rather than electing them. In Quillacollo, the leadership of the workers' union of the Manaco shoe factory—a major source of local employment, at the time affiliated with a key party of the coalition government and victorious in a recent power struggle with the agrarian union—effectively dictated the personnel for the alcaldía. It moved quickly to install one of its own, a former factory worker, as mayor. While widely condemned by many in town as an incompetent drunk, this *obrero* was also notable as someone who was of "humble origin." For the first time, Quillacollo's alcalde was an individual with a popular background, if not directly from within the peasantry. In the early 1980s, the mayor made a point of routinely employing popular political idioms while carrying out his official capacities.

Founded in 1940 by the Czech-Canadian Bata Corporation, the Manaco factory stands at the far end of an expanding 15-kilometer corridor of small industry, which begins with the city itself. The factory's workers' union was founded in 1944 (Peredo Antezana 1963:157) and quickly emerged as one important site for provincial and regional political organizing. The factory reached its apogee in the early 1970s, with around one thousand workers. At one time the largest factory complex in Bolivia, it was described at its zenith as a "small city." Factory workers were mostly from the immediate environs of provincial Cochabamba. The majority were described to me as "sons of peasants" who socially and culturally reflect an "original mix of Aymaras and Quechuas." As such, Manaco factory workers were typically "linked closely to farm work," both as workers and as peasants. Manaco had an active mothers' club, a dance fraternity, and a competitive soccer team and built a local high school. Beginning in 1954, the union constructed the Barrio Manaco in nearby Quillacollo, where many ex-workers continue to live. The first generation of Manaco workers felt a sense of "ownership" of Manaco as something built "with their own hands" and viewed their employer, the Bata Corporation, as "like a father." But by the end of the 1980s, as a consequence of structural adjustment, the Manaco shoe factory had reduced its workforce to around two hundred employees, or a fifth of its former strength.

Since 1985 and the application of the neoliberal democratic model, the alcaldía has largely reclaimed its preeminent provincial status, though in ways significantly different from those of the years prior to 1952. With the reemergence of local party-based electoral politics since 1987, the alcalde has become the post around which the efforts of political parties are organized (see ILDIS 1990). With decentralization, more monies now flow directly to the municipalities, and so to the alcaldes (Blanes 1992; Lazarte 1998). With local elections, larger budgets, and greater political autonomy, provincial alcaldías are no longer simply cogs in the national patronage bureaucracy, as they had been for so many years. The municipality is once again the center of gravity of local politics, eclipsing at least for now the role of peasant agrarian unions, and a larger budget is one concrete sign of the new political authority of provincial alcaldías.

The man who occupies the post is often also the hub of an influential provincial "little machine" (*maquinita*). He is someone who maintains many national and department-level connections, a variety of ties with other regional políticos, a diversified local following, and control over the local party apparatus, all of which allow him largely to control the alcaldía's resources (Albro 1999; chapters 6 and 7, this volume). From the late 1980s to 2002, this person was also the head of the UCS party in the province. Contemporary alcaldes in Quillacollo are neither local elites nor peasant strongmen nor military bureaucrats. They have, instead, consistently come from problematically popular backgrounds, and as such, they make ample use of the trappings of rural-urban popular culture for the management of their political relationships. Subsequent chapters explore the consequences of this in detail.

In 1994, while I was working in Quillacollo, Bolivia's government followed a developing regional trend in Latin America (see Hale 2002), in recognizing its own "multiethnic and pluricultural" heritage and identity, with the passage of the new Popular Participation Law (PPL). As one analysis concluded at the time, in the spirit of the emergent "*pluri-multi* discourse" of legal pluralism in the 1980s and 1990s Bolivia (for example, ILDIS 1993), the PPL legally recognized the new "national narrative of multiple nations within the Bolivian state" (Bigenho 2002:114). The state cultural politics that created the PPL, then, could be read as a public effort by Bolivia's government to resolve the "two Bolivias" problem expressed by spokespeople of the country's indigenous movements over the years, who have often referred to the social contradictions between the "Bolivian nation" and Aymara, Quechua, or Guaraní "indigenous nation(s)," or what at the time popular participation policy makers themselves called the historically "clandestine nation."

The PPL explicitly defined indigenous identity, realigned local institutional relations of state, and enlarged the power, autonomy, and responsibilities of local municipal governments while formally recognizing already existing territorially based types of traditional political organization and leadership, such as neighborhood committees, agrarian unions, or indigenous communities. At least in theory the PPL was meant to rearticulate a "popular-mestizo dynamic" (Mayorga 1994), breaking with vertical patronage politics of the past while energizing and legitimating the integrity of diverse local political cultures.[7] One of the effects of the PPL, however, was to further emphasize the importance of local cultural discourses and practice as a political resource, as a basis for claim making, and as a means of legibility vis-à-vis the state (see Albro 2005b; Laurie, Andolina, and Radcliffe 2002; Postero 2007b). This has been quite apparent in Quillacollo, where cultural claim making as part of politics is not currently in short supply. Across Bolivia, particularly since the era of "popular participation," provincial elections have also become one important doorway for the entrance of hundreds of people of indigenous descent to local political office as mayors or as town councilmen (see Albó 2002).

The Rejection of Patronage Politics?

The current Morales administration's turn away from a strictly neoliberal policy has also included a rejection of elite decision making alongside greater attention to the political needs, recognition, and participation of Bolivia's indigenous and popular majority. Since the Revolution of 1952, and particularly in the region of Cochabamba, the most characteristic political participation of primarily indigenous campesinos had been as a grassroots power base for successive regional and national leaders (see Dandler 1983; Dunkerley 1987; Gordillo 2000). They were important only when elites thought it necessary to manufacture popular voting blocs. In multiple national elections, "*runas* on trucks," as my counterparts in Quillacollo called them, were brought in from the countryside to vote en masse to maintain successive populist governments in power.

Throughout this period indigenous leaders often served as vassals and as valuable clients to national Bolivian politicians. And if not unimportant, their participation was almost entirely at the bottom of a vertical national system of political patronage. Never power brokers or policy architects, indigenous people were occasional beneficiaries of state promises and, even more rarely, of state largesse. Left-leaning local políticos of indigenous descent I knew well in Quillacollo often talked of their intention to "break with the vertical politics of the past." Such a break is in part the promise of the current Evo era on the national level, and Quillacollo is a provincial municipality currently dominated by MAS politics.

The status quo of clientelistic politics in Bolivia had been undergoing a slow but steady transformation since the onset of democratization in the early 1980s. New political options appearing in the late 1980s, like CON-DEPA (Conciencia de Patria, or Conscience of the Fatherland) and the UCS, helped to speed along the erosion of traditional party affiliation as the exclusive basis for political participation (see Archondo 1991; Himpele 2008; Mayorga 1991, 2002). And the shape of the national political arena has changed even more dramatically since 2000, with the combustive impact of a series of issue-driven, indigenous-popular social movement coalitions, which engineered largely successful direct action protests over unilateral government decision making regarding such public sector resources as water and gas.[8]

In this new context of the elevation of an indigenous project to power in Bolivia, social movement advocates have celebrated their break with the pervasive politics of patronage using a discourse that embraces a less vertical and more inclusively "horizontal" politics of participation. This has been described by the current vice president as a collective "social space of encounter among equals" (García Linera 2004:72), a form of participation understood to have taken its cue from a more indigenous-derived and face-to-face decision making through assembly (see Albro 2006a; Lazar 2008). The organization of the MAS—whose national representatives refer to themselves as "spokespeople," emphasize responsiveness to their "base," and avoid the merest suggestion of membership in Bolivia's traditional political class—is a principal illustration of these redrawn political relationships and boundaries (Albro 2005a). These efforts boil down to reversing the historical role of the indigenous masses as docile "clients" of the state. As Evo and other MAS representatives have repeatedly intoned, "We want partners, not bosses."

A national indigenous project conceived in this way, however, renders Quillacollo's urban popular and indigenous politics almost unrecognizable. In the Evo era, with its emphasis upon breaking with the vertical politics of the past, horizontally organized social movements, rejection of bosses, the goal of indigenous empowerment, and a widely prevalent Indianist identity politics of self-determination, indigenous movement leaders and local municipal authorities of significantly indigenous but also urban districts face the daunting task of finding a new political language to describe their own practice, or run the risk of being caught betwixt and between two irreconcilable commitments: participation in local and national government or indigenous collective self-determination and autonomy. They are not, in any obvious way, legible subjects of the new indigenous politics. And yet, with the everyday political activities often glossed as "clientelism," they are claiming indigenous legacies as their own.

The Cholo Client

"Quillacollo as a whole is almost completely made up of cholos," I was repeatedly informed while working there. "Now, there aren't really any true campesinos. Campesinos aren't really even campesinos." One friend playfully characterized Quillacollo's crisscrossed social landscape with the exclamation, "There's everything—*chotas*, cholas, cholos. There's pure cholos, mestizo cholos, criollo cholos..." My friend's comment framed a local dilemma of self-recognition, which one lighthearted editorialist articulated while asking the question: "What is it to be a cholo?" The answer: "The mestizo is a cholo, respond the experts in things cholo. But if it's like that, we're all cholos, I answer myself" (Pacheco Balanza 2001). As his rhetorical question suggests, *cholo* and *mestizo* might both suggest racial, cultural, or class mixture, but not in the same ways. What is the difference? And why do people in Quillacollo consider it such a cholo kind of place? Quillacolleños themselves often wonder.

In his *Nueva corónica y buen gobierno*, the late-sixteenth-century chronicler and politician Felipe Guamán Poma defended the purity of the race and recorded what would become a familiar description of cholos, which he labeled "*la mala casta*" (the debased caste):

> [They are] great idlers, gamblers, and thieves, who did nothing else but drink to excess, waste time instead of work, strum instruments, and sing. They do not remember God or King, nor any service for better or ill from them. They have no humility, charity, or doctrine, but only pride.... Traitors even to treason they go with knives and daggers, with garrotes and with stones. [1980:769]

Such a miscegenation-type mistrust or fear of mixture has persisted up until the present in Bolivia. And cholos continued to articulate, as well as cross between, schisms and fissures among Andean and Spanish worldviews, country and city, Indian and elite, rejection and assimilation of the national project, as well as male and female versions of these rents in the national fabric.

The term, then, is the inheritor of a lingering colonial suspicion and stigma associated with (racial, class, cultural) mixture. Amid the nineteenth-century fervor of a creole national movement, native-born Spaniards stood at the apex of their own new nation-state, while so-called racial mestizos were tarred as "traitors," "descendants of idolators," "violent," and "individualistic." Understood as the product of Spanish men and Andean women, mestizos were also "sterile," "illegitimate," and so, "disloyal" (Rivera 1993b: 62–69). The revolutionary legacy of 1952 has largely removed the stigma of mixture from the category of mestizaje, enshrined as the subject of a national project, but this has not been the case for the cholo. As the Bolivian sociologist Silvia Rivera (1993:67) has noted, the terms have suffered an "internal polarization," where the publicly more respectable mestizo is now associated with creole traits—whiter society—while particularly in urban contexts the cholo is now paired off with the uncouth characteristics of the indigenous world.

There is no consensus about when and how the word *cholo* found its way into the lexicons of Andean nations, or even whether the term was originally of Castilian or of indigenous (Guaraní, Quechua, Aymara) origin. Several scholars have offered apocryphal accounts. Perhaps the most common appears in the early-seventeenth-century *Vocabulario de la lengua Aymara* of Ludovico Bertonio, in which appears the word *chhulu*, meaning "mestizo" but also used as a qualifier with *anocara*, "dog." In fact, the term *perrichola* was commonly used in the colonial period as a term for the female lovers of Spanish men. In the early twentieth century in his *La vida social del Coloniaje*, Gustavo Adolfo Otero claimed that cholo was derived from the Castilian word *chulo*, a name commonly given to the lower classes of Madrid. It is interesting to observe that the origins of the term are obscure and in fact unknown—potentially indigenous or Spanish. As a cultural identity, then, the cholo does not make a particularly sound basis upon which to found a national project. If an etymology is a kind of genealogy of language, a "cholo nation" would presumably lack any clear paternity, with its very moment of birth a matter of continuous debate. And at least Bolivian elites were not keen on the idea of a bastard nation.

To be called a cholo in Quillacollo and across the Andes continues to be a demeaning and insulting slur typically referring to the pretensions of upward mobility of financially successful, uppity, or urbanized Indians (see Bouysse-Cassagne and Saignes 1992). And at least in Bolivia the term remains part of a ubiquitous vocabulary of insults and derision. People in Quillacollo—including people whom others might privately slander as cholos—often described cholos to me in unflattering terms, as more aggressive, meaner, ruder, vulgar, and "trickier" (*más pícaro*) than other people. Cholos might better themselves and then spitefully "turn on their own class." In Quillacollo I heard the insult *cholo de mierda* (shitty cholo) many times as a summary character assassination. As one authority volunteered about no one in particular, "cholos are dogs." This is the case despite the fact that people regularly participated in popular cultural practices assumed to be characteristically frequented by a cholo crowd.

The Bolivian critic Guillermo Mariaca Iturri (1998:202) has suggested that to embrace cholo sensibilities would mean to abandon traditional identity politics, since "we can no longer define his identity through traits [*por pertenencia*] because he does not have a fixed identity." In my experience in Quillacollo, when the term *cholo* popped up in daily discourse, as it often did, it always appeared alongside a qualifying adjective, which indexically shifted the conversation to a more detailed, specifically socially contextualized, level. Someone was rarely just a cholo but a *cholo refinado* (socially adept cholo), *cholo malcriado* (badly raised cholo), *cholo adinerado* (wealthy cholo), or *cholo alzado* (upwardly mobile cholo), situationally dependent upon the argument already under way. In his study of Peru's *choledad*, José Guillermo Nugent (1992:77) similarly has suggested that the term is a "taxonomic anomaly," less an identity in itself and more a "means to determine who is more and who is less" (1992:80). But more and less of what? As Nugent's comment implies, grammar might be misleading, since the term functions more like an adjective than a noun, referring to a particular way or style of being mobile that is usually thought to be decidedly disrespectful.

Most remarkable is that the felt dangers posed by cholo sensibilities are magnified with regard to politics, where this questionable figure is used to illustrate and to editorialize about the costs and excesses of political populism. Consider this stinging mid-twentieth-century condemnation by the nationalist man of letters Alcides Arguedas, which is part of his polemic cataloging the failures of Bolivian nation building, *Pueblo enfermo* (A Sick People). "The cholo político," observed Arguedas (1937:59–61), "is false and unstable in his ordinary principles, when he has them." On the broadest level, twentieth-century Bolivian writers routinely registered a moral panic at the negative social consequences of introducing cholos—that is, the popular masses—into the controlled environment of an oligarchic and urban political process. This panic was reminiscent of the literary hysteria in the mid-nineteenth century—most famously expressed by Matthew Arnold—over the perceived invasion of England's cities by the new industrial lumpen proletariat. An acquaintance in Quillacollo was blunt in response to my question: "It is a little difficult to trust a cholo. Neither is he a person of solid cultural awareness nor is he ignorant. And so, to a certain point he is dangerous."

As I was told in Quillacollo, the cholo is "with both the Moors and the Christians" or "the angels and the devils." This makes of the cholo a character particularly vulnerable to moral lapses and vice, like excessive drinking. Arguedas (1937:60) informs us, "His favorite place is the *chichería*." In chicherías, and elsewhere, cholos are supposedly the most adept practitioners of the art of the política criolla, the clever but corrupt informal politics conducted out of the public eye over invitations to drink. Arguedas (1937:58) had this to say: "The cholo never, at any moment, troubles his conscience asking himself if an act is moral or no...because he thinks only of himself." Arguedas tops off his skewering of the cholo with a list of faults: "low, egotist, false, self-interested, and disrespectful." To Arguedas's mind, the cholo was an untrustworthy and undisciplined national subject.

Arguedas (1937:58) insisted that the political danger posed by the cholo was that he is "instinctively animated by the spirit of the sheep in a flock [*ovejuno*]"—a willing member of a mob. Franz Tamayo (1910:69), an educator and another important figure of Bolivian nation building, also characterized the cholo as a blind follower of dangerous politicians and as "a clay easily molded by the crazy schemes and ambitions of our most vicious demagogues." For these writers, cholos represented the potential of disorderly mass conduct. A like-minded friend in Quillacollo, struggling to explain to me the gradual replacement of "people of the town" (*gente del pueblo*) by "people of humble origin" (*gente de origen humilde*) in positions of local political authority, shrugged and commented, "Among the blind, the one-eyed is king."

In perhaps the most sharply worded condemnation, writing after 1952 and with a very different agenda of promoting an independent Indianist movement rather than a nation-building project based upon mestizaje, Fausto Reinaga (1964:218) offered the following: if the product of the "crossing of the races," the cholo nevertheless "has a soul broken in two" and carries a "perversity deep in his blood" (1964:65). Reinaga (1964:27) vilified the cholo as nothing less than the "creator and executor of evil," in this case, the long-term repression of the Indian in Bolivia. Even if the cholo's lot is thrown in with the more indigenous characteristics of social and cultural mixture in Bolivia's polarizing ethnic discourse, he still figured as the political fall guy of Reinaga's early Indianist political project.

Criticisms of chololike attitudes and conduct help to nurture the pervasive disenchantment people throughout Bolivia express about the failures of their political establishment, particularly through the prolonged economic crisis and the more recent crisis of popular representation accompanying Bolivia's return to democracy since 1982. This was often phrased in Quillacollo as a complaint about the ubiquity of the política criolla version of politics in such economically desperate times, as conducted "through the stomach," that is, the exchange of political allegiance for jobs, chicha, foodstuffs, or household goods. Cholos, people stressed, are parasitical and have a "hunger to rob" or to "partake of the cake" (*comer de la torta*). Chicha, in fact, was perhaps the most widely offered *prebenda* at mass political rallies I attended. I remember a wry comment by a onetime councilman, ex-worker, and present transporter who described cholos in politics to me as having "long tongues but short arms." That is, they consume much but work little. Critics regularly assailed such tactics as little more than demagoguery.

As should be clear, appeals to the stomach reveal the pressing economic undercurrents in activities of política criolla as a survival strategy where the institutional state or soon-to-be state representative is depicted as a failed patron. The frequency of food- and animal-related political aphorisms and analogies in Quillacollo was a constant reminder of the hunger felt to be associated with the involvement of cholos in politics. Political power was described to me as "honey to be enjoyed." Enjoyment of the political spoils was like a "fly in a glass of milk." A political patron who did not spread the wealth might be described as a "pig that eats everything" or as a "miller's dog [*perro del hortelano*] who lets no one else eat." I heard the fall of an unpopular patron described in the following terms: "Once the dog dies, the fleas leave." Even as they naturalize the near-universality of política criolla as a practice, these analogies—and many more—epitomize the moral intransigence, absence of ideology, and cynical economic calculus attributed to the version of social mobility represented by política criolla. As these different characterizations suggest, cholo sensibilities are hierarchically located in Bolivia's political arena, not just as followers, but as problematic clients. The Bolivian political humorist Paulovich (1978:185) quips in his *Diccionario del cholo ilustrado*, "Cholo políticos always go for the bottle [*mamadera*] once finished with nursing."[9]

The quantity of animal and food metaphors associated with satisfying the stomachs of rapaciously aggressive cholo clients was sometimes connected by locals with the tradition of the "robbing of fruit," an act called the *k'ukeada*, associated in particular with adolescent high jinks. Young men who grew up in Quillacollo recalled that it was commonplace "to invade," or to make forays into, the fields and orchards of local landowners to steal quantities of still immature fruit. This was described to me as "taking the best fruit of another's garden." This activity was customarily publicly sanctioned for only a few days out of the year, during Carnival season, when groups of young people might make a festive day of it this way. During these days they might even be "invited" by the landowner himself, who would serve them chicha. The tradition of the k'ukeada was a temporary reversal

Figure 2.1. Typical anonymous graffiti: "Get out of Quillacollo political party usurers! Works yes, parasitical crooks, no."

of the usual hierarchical relationship of landowner or patron to landless clients. At least one friend reported that the verb *k'ukear* was also commonly used to refer to having a child—presumably out of wedlock—by a young cholita. Santos Rojas, the subject of chapter 5, described in detail a late childhood dominated by acts of thievery and robbery, necessitated in his words by the many "hard knocks" he suffered that included stealing corn, chickens, rabbits, and peaches, among other things. Carried out as part of a gang of largely homeless youths, such activities were perceived more as criminal than as traditional, including by the adult Rojas.

Cholos tended to be considered problematic clients based upon at least three convictions: (1) when the goods stop trickling down this purely self-serving political relationship will abruptly end; (2) in the aggregate they might transform themselves into a dangerous and unpredictable mob; and (3) as creatures of social mobility, cholo clients are primed to supplant their patrons. The bottom line was that they were simply not to be trusted. In Quillacollo's politics, people talked a lot about the likelihood of "shadowing" (*hacerse sombra*) or of "undercutting" (*seruchar*, literally "to saw off") a rival. This Bolivian idiom is also used to describe the act of stealing a person's boyfriend or girlfriend. Paradoxically reflecting the definitional intransigence associated with the cholo arena,[10] cholos at once represent the combination of the danger of the crowd and the ambitions of an equally antisocial hyper-individualist and rapacious client (Figure 2.1).

Here, I want to make clear that clientage of the *política criolla* sort was talked about as a personalistic, disrespectful, morally bankrupt, and nakedly economic relationship, with the assumption that cholos active in politics are a potentially dangerous and often corrupt Trojan horse. The figure of the cholo has been imagined as the enemy of nations, both creole and indigenous. During my time in Quillacollo cholos were most often talked about as llunk'us, that is, as culturally, ideologically, and politically unreliable clients, imagined to be fully inscribed in what Toranzo Roca (1989) has called Bolivia's political "premodernity." But this means that criticisms of cholotype behavior were also assessments of the status of political relationships.

Of the *Pinche* and the Llunk'u

If llunk'u-like behavior was thought to epitomize cholo attitudes and actions, this typically cynical, if playful, discourse about political corruption was a favorite pastime of people in Quillacollo, those both deeply involved in and largely disengaged from politics. A case in point is a tongue-in-cheek editorial that appeared in the regional newspaper *Los Tiempos*, playfully suggesting the need for a new kind of measuring device of "human servitude" called "*el llunk'ometro*" (Guzman 2000). Such a fanciful llunk'ometro would measure the enthusiasm with which Bolivian políticos suck up to powerful patrons. In the quite self-consciously Machiavellian arena of provincial politics, where, as the saying goes, things are often decided "between roosters and midnight," the llunk'u was understood to be a notorious figure, Janus-faced, treacherous, traitorous, self-serving. And as the criticism of Cárdenas suggests, it was considered to be not ultimately productive as a strategy of political clientage. This makes the llunk'u among the least redeemable of figures in public Bolivian life.

In my experience in Quillacollo, llunk'us were always someone else, always men (though women also participate in politics), and always already in a clientelistic relationship. The term *llunk'erío* most typically refers to varieties of dishonorable, usually political, shenanigans of some sort. As a political friend in Quillacollo insisted to me, the many activities of llunk'erío "damage the dignity of men." But while listening to talk of political exploits it is hard to ignore that the very same men upon whom the label of llunk'u was affixed appraised themselves as llunk'u-like in their own terms, if avoiding the word itself. In stories about such exploits, llunk'erío appeared as a *desirable* means of getting things done and of self-validation. Asked to describe the makings of a good politician, for example, Pancho Sánchez—who was often called a llunk'u—asserted, "One must be *macho*, shameless [*mañudo*] and sharp [*sagáz*]. You have to have balls [*cojones*], but character too!" In this way, *llunk'u* (and its many euphemisms) was among the key words that compose a nomenclature of public political masculinity in the cultural crosscurrents of the rapidly expanding peripheral boomtown of Quillacollo.

The term *llunk'u* regularly found its way into the code switching of people in and around Quillacollo to characterize shiftless clients. Jesús Lara's (1971:161) regional dictionary primarily defines *llunk'u* as a figurative adjectival expression for *adulador* (sycophant). In its verb form, *llunk'uy*, it is used synonymously with *rebañar* or with *arrebañar*, that is, "to glean, to gather, or to scrape together." Lara also notes a synonym for *llunk'u*, as an adjective, which is *llajwaj*, meaning *lamedor*, "licker" or "one who laps and licks." In its verb form, *llajway*, it also means "to lick, to taste, or to enjoy a mouthful" (Lara 1971:153). And as a noun, *llajwa*, it is of course the ubiquitous spicy sauce (*picante*) of ground *ají*—a staple at the table for any self-respecting Bolivian.

A more comprehensive Quechua dictionary by Angel Herbas Sandoval makes the connection between *llunk'u* and *licking* more explicit. The adjective is given to mean *lisonjero*, "parasitical flatterer, and wheedler." And a second meaning is also listed as *lamedura*, "the act and effect of licking." Sandoval (1998:242) lists a further form of the verb, *llunk'ukiyay*, defined as "to flatter, to wheedle," but also with the Spanish *halagar*, that is, "to cajole, to coax." He also lists a synonym, the verb *qhanaymay*, defined as "cajoling in obtaining some end" (1998:393). A noun form, *qhanayma*, is a "demonstration of *cariño* with gestures." This adds a slightly different emphasis. A *qhanaymachi* is a person "with some interested proposition, [who] offers praise [*alabar*] to another." Of course, *alabados* are the sacramental hymns recited by children during All Saints' Day, as they go from family altar to family altar hoping to be rewarded with sweets.

Among men, then, who counted as a llunk'u in Quillacollo? First, llunk'us were practitioners of *política criolla*. This is creole or mixed politics, one might even say mongrel politics, referring to the racial, cultural, and moral miscegenation originating with the conquest, which is at best a local brand of realpolitik and at worst loudly condemned as morally suspect or corrupt behavior. In the words of one *quillacolleño político* describing a close associate, a llunk'u "is superlatively clever [*es súmamente viváz*]! [He] is always on the lookout for people of weight [*gente de peso*], as a sycophant [*adulador*] who often acts indirectly [*soslaya*]." This makes one thing clear: a llunk'u-like stance describes the attitude of a client from the perspective of a patron. This suggests that such disrespectful and disdained conduct is also typically already inscribed within a social dyad of *patrón-pinche* (loosely, "boss-crony"). Indeed, a frequent synonym for llunk'u was *lambeculo* (gloss:

"ass licker"). One need only think of English equivalents such as *ass kisser* or *bootlicker* to get the idea. But this very disrespectfulness also makes clear the competitive possibility of role reversal, and so, the potential instability of this very dyad.

Llunk'erío, as a classifiable sort of behavior, covers a range of situations. A prototypical situation is that of political betrayal. Two erstwhile insiders in a local party opportunistically parachuted into another party. This c'est la guerre antic caused an exasperated former fellow militant, the wife of the local party leader, to call them *"llunk'ukus de doble fila"* (double-dealing llunk'us). The ultimate self-serving betrayal is that of the political informer or *alcahuete* (literally, "whoremonger"), or in Quechua *purajuya*, generally defined as someone who simultaneously "adheres to or defends two people, or contrary groups" (Xavier Albó, personal communication 2002). The alcahuete (or any llunk'u) is assumed to lack substantive moral conviction for the cause in his shameless pursuit of *egoismo* or *yoismo*. Llunk'us employ a "tactical flexibility," as the political analyst Fernando Mayorga (1991) characterized the decision making of neopopular political parties like the UCS. The llunk'u, then, lacks ideological fortitude and blows with the political winds, which in Bolivian politics is called a *pasa-pasa*. Anyone who selfishly plays a double game, presenting one face publicly while nursing secret motives, is potentially a llunk'u. If a llunk'u is structurally a client, nevertheless he is a client aggressively primed to commit political parricide.

Such self-misrepresentation points to what the anthropologist F. G. Bailey (1991) has aptly phrased the "prevalence of deceit" in politics, which can take the shape of an obvious and outright lie or a less public dissimulation. Public displays of virtue masking self-interest are another likely scenario for suspicions of llunk'erío. Such is the case with the distinctions drawn between genuine ritual compadres and *compadres de interés*, as will be discussed in the chapter to follow. This kind of behavior was understood to exhibit a lack of firm self-identity or "personality." Take this complaint by Lucho Martínez, when mayor and commenting on one of his most persistent critics: "The problem as well is that [his rival] is the fruit of a sort of manipulation. I dare say that he does not have a 'defined personality.'... His derring-do, his audacity, make him come out with certain views which aren't the fruit of knowledge." This was an indirect way of implicating his rival in unenlightened but also indigenous conduct. And here we find a similar statement from another local politician reflecting on the popular political style suspiciously associated with política criolla: "This is an example of the 'fragility of the personality.' There is no *formación*, no transparent behavior. They are devices to gain notoriety.... But they've lost their effectiveness and don't gain credibility. There is no affinity, either through tradition, or through family, or by their ideology." As they are excoriated, this fragility and lack of a well-defined personality serve as an implicit explanation of llunk'us. The "audacity" of llunk'u artists was also described as sundered from that which typically provides formación, most notably, tradition, family, or political ideology, all of which express what sociologists like to call ascribed status. The llunk'u, goes the reasoning, is defined by the absence of a basis in a well-defined identity.

Another llunk'erío was the highly elaborated, at least in Quillacollo, allegorical equation between the política criolla and adultery, best illustrated with the *aventura amorosa*. Politics, of course, was often talked about in the terms of the *aventura*. An instance of graft might be discussed as the lifting of a woman's *pollera* "to taste the dish underneath." These kinds of aventuras often figured literally in politics, as with the case of the sure-fire political tactic of getting the party higher-ups—or any potential patron—laid. But this allegory also points to deeper cultural duplicities. As will be explored in chapter 4, local men of provincial descent would commonly, publicly, and loudly proclaim the virtues of the stalwart and traditional figure of the chola. And yet many of these very same men routinely sought private liaisons with "whiter" women, whom they classified as *cambas* (lowland women) or as *rubias* (blonds), often in clandestine trips to clubs or brothels, or to round off a *viernes del soltero* (gloss: "guys' night out"). In public these women were likely to be disparaged as "*khuchi warmis*" (Quechua: "dirty women"). But while such relationships with white prostitutes might actually be consummated, talk of exploits with cholas is typically fantasy. As adultery and as political allegory, the aventura is expressive of cultural ambivalence and part of a semantic register of accusations of llunk'erío. People's political experience in fact moved regularly in this way within and between both popular and indigenous modes of cultural expression and consumption—a prevailing fact of urban politics in Quillacollo.

The Identity Problem

I recall the response of a man, himself de origen humilde, who when confronted by a ragged panhandler, offered the cold response: "Ama sua, ama llulla, ama khella, ama llunk'u!" To the famous Inca maxim of "never steal, never lie, never be lazy," he had pointedly added, "never flatter." In another moment, a local *dirigente campesino* told me of factional goings-on within the union, including his rivalry with another man he claimed was not a "true campesino" (a way of referring to indigenous identity in rural Cochabamba) but was instead llunk'u-like, trying to cash in on his leadership reputation at the expense of the rank and file. Everyone knew that the first man, his rival, did not earn a living from working in the fields but instead from running a chichería. So he was unfit for the role of campesino union leader because he was unrepresentative as a noncampesino, a point the dirigente made by issuing a public challenge with the loaded question, "How do you make a living?" A llunk'u, then, might also be anyone unlikely to reciprocate, who is perceived to want something for nothing, or who does not directly earn his daily bread with his own sweat.

The following is a field note gloss of another conversation with the same man who shot down the panhandler, a transporter by trade. The note begins, "He feels a part of the *populacho* [popular masses]. For example, in contrast to a typical politician's attitude, he described how 'when we eat with a campesino we eat the *papa wayku* ["Andean" potato], otherwise it is an insult....' Políticos, in contrast, 'live by lies.' But if you don't live by your own works, then 'one forgets his own class, his own neighbors.'" As I was told on many occasions, "work dignifies the man," or "in our culture people who don't know how to work have no value." The familiar conviction that work makes the man, often voiced in Quillacollo, not coincidentally echoes the famous slogan of the Agrarian Reform: "La tierra es para quien la trabaja [The land is for those who work it]." If llunk'us "live by lies," as I was told, "in the campo we live from what we sow." Such sentiments as these crossed both class and political allegiances in Quillacollo. In this same manner, reference to the toiling "Bolivian worker" was prominent in the several political pamphlets locally circulated by leftist parties.

In a similar spirit we have this remarkable proclamation, part of an essay published in a book compiled by Bolivian sociologists titled *El país machista*:

> Here is an aspect of modern life: the man in his shop, in the street, in the office, in the highest circles of industry, in the government, wherever he wants to be found. What does he do?
>
> He works!
>
> For who?
>
> For his woman, for his children, for his home!
>
> And the woman talks still of slavery! [Flores 1977:53]

Male value is exhibited through a transparency of the direct correspondence in kind between physical labor and the fruits of labor (like Marx's "use values"). This is what Nancy Fraser (1989:124) has called the "masculine subtext of the worker role." But for our purposes, and in marked contrast to llunk'erío, "work"—as an arena of transparent correspondences—further defined a stance of public clarity of male self-definition, as farmer, as worker, and apparently even as successful industrialist. Such clarity of self-definition publicly reinscribed traditional understandings of the relationship between patron and client, respectively, as it insisted upon visible evidence for the recognized roles of each. These male-encoded cultural assumptions of well-defined self-identity, as built into the patron-client dynamic, notably contrast with the kinds of public relationships men in politics seek to build with women—relationships of cultural intimacy.

I heard many complaints by would-be patrons about untrustworthy and shiftless clients. "Fragility of personality," as was often implied, is the moral flaw of the cholo's world and was used to support the idea that cholos more easily embrace the tactics of llunk'erío. A perceived faithlessness was often insultingly disparaged as less than masculine. In this way men of popular descent were infantilized, often dismissed as *lloqhallas* (Quechuañol: "striplings"). Lloqhallas should not be taken seriously and do not deserve respect, since they are supposed to have dishonorably discredited themselves, often through some llunk'u-like past behavior. Lloqhallas are disrespectful sons, and so, unreliable clients. As I was told, "Nowadays sons throw dirt on [*sacar la mugre*] their fathers." A subtext of the frequent laments is that erstwhile clients are more apt to disavow adherence to the official trappings of patronage relations.

As people in Quillacollo talked about it, personality seeks the authority of words. Poor public speakers "lack personality," whereas good public speakers "ask the word" (*pedir la palabra*) and make sure to "have the word" (*tener la palabra*) often. Authoritative words are treated as transparently representative. The successful possession of words, and a direct equation of words with the identity of speakers, is a part of the symbolic capital of personality. People with personality speak "*de frente*" (gloss: "face-to-face"), whereas llunk'us often speak "*detrás de las cortinas*" (behind the scenes). That this is decisively about male language use is apparent in a common complaint, "No one talks to so and so de frente. There's no one willing to wear the pants!" Similarly, a friend extolled the virtue of speaking "simply one time" in public meetings. He insisted, "It's important to define whatever. If one talks without personality, this is *chaku* talk [Quechua: "a lack of continuity"]. And so, no one believes him. In this way he loses his essence as a person." Personality, in this case, is a transparency and correspondence of meaning with words. If such a close correspondence of words and meanings is indicative, then the argot of the gender ideology of patronage celebrates the referential function of language.

Linking things to works to words as proofs of personal transparency was a primary diacritic for the dismissal of llunk'erío. While seeing is believing, since "works enter through the eyes" (*las obras entran por los ojos*), at the same time, political patrons "make promises they don't keep" (*promesan pero no cumplen*). Llunk'u politicians were often condemned for a lack of commitment to their own words, a failure felt to be epitomized by the figure of the cholo. Consider this field note recording a dirigente campesino shaking his head over the characteristic doings of a longtime cholo rival: "Campesinos speak a 'true Quechua.' Cholos talk more and say less, so to speak. They are linguistically slippery. Illustrating this point, he laughingly claims that for every one word he speaks, [his rival] would speak ten. His rival's son…is worse still, averaging fifteen words to every one of his own. 'The cholo is a braggart,' he added." Self-serving rhetoric and words not particularly bound to their objects, such as tall tales by local authorities about promised works or goods never to materialize, were considered the stock-in-trade of the llunk'erío of cholos. The llunk'u, people noted, harnesses language as its own end, "simply to shoot off his mouth" (*sólamente para pistolear* or *disparar*). Touching on the subject of speaking and politics in his memoir, Sinforoso Rivas (2000:146)—onetime political strongman in Quillacollo—approvingly repeated the saying, "Lo cortés no quita lo valiente," that is, a silver tongue is no substitute for real character. The suggestion seems to be that if ornamental or flowery language might influence appearances, it still cannot disguise the valor or value of self-worth.

These interconnected ideas also informed a pervasive attitude about cholo speech as uttering mostly *pendejadas* (loosely, "tricky stories" or "silly stories"). An example is a complaint appearing in *Los Tiempos* about the controversial Aymara leader Felipe Quispe, described by the editorialist as a "*cholo vivo*" and "*cholo pendejo*" (that is, "tricky" or "stupid cholo"). The outraged commentator begins:

> The pendejada is a meeting of deceits carried to the extreme, that is trickery [picardía]. The pendejada is an attitude contrary to that of the gentleman [caballero]. And if honor defines the gentleman, what defines the pendejo? Dishonor. Dishonor animates the pendejada. And dishonor signifies a broken promise. Not honoring the given word. And the given word is the essence of the social pact among free men. [Suárez Ávila 2002:1]

This ringing condemnation asserts the desirability of transparency between a respected public masculinity (such as "gentlemanliness") and "the given word." Speaking their pendejadas, these llunk'u-type cholos are here accused of trickiness, of cooking up corruption behind the scenes. As a feature of política criolla, the *picardía* of cholos is emphasized here as a means for local political types to distance themselves from the widely decried morally suspect underbelly of popular identity, an identity that is felt to be somehow misrepresentative. This trickiness is the source of disconnect between words and referents attributed to cholos, and it suggests an inability to exhibit a unitary identity for men from popular backgrounds engaged in politics.

The linguistic expression of this moral suspicion of cholos as llunk'us is a kind of denial of their public access to propositional signs of language. Their words are suspicious because of a felt lack of correspondence to their apparent objects or referents.[11] In this sense, cholos are accused of playing language games, where the evident linguistic object is hidden, displaced, or nonexistent. In comparable fashion, describing the language ideology of Protestant conversion, Webb Keane (2002:75) has emphasized how the "modern subject" seeks out "sincerity" in language as an expression of "public accountability." This is in conspicuous contrast to Bolivian cholos, whose tricky use of language makes them highly unreliable moderns.

These cases of public dissimulation, such as the uneasy coexistence of cultural strategies (between the stances of "respect" and "self-interest") for ritual compadres, the allegorical ambivalence of the aventura, and a penchant for language games, could be multiplied here: the scourge of illegal land speculation, accusations of embezzlement, or even the double entendre of joking (such as with the rhyming couplets sung during Todos Santos), and the like. Such cases make it clear that llunk'us adopt self-conscious and multiple stances of cultural interpretation—from respectful to disrespectful, from public to intimate, or from straight up to ironic. As critics of llunk'erío also make apparent, their transgressions of the boundaries of a unitary cultural identity are viewed with suspicion. Cholos—popular men—are not transparently self-evident. Their works, their words, and their intentions fly in the face of the glassy essence of masculine ideals in many respects. From the point of view of traditional patrons, popular men are unreliable clients.

To explore the meanings of llunk'erío, then, is also to examine the production of political subjects across relations of patronage and clientage. As a dialogical contextualization of patron-client relations, llunk'erío functions as the stigmatized underside of public male symbology, the bad client to the morally upright patron. When described from the patron's point of view, the majority of llunk'erío happens "backstage" (Goffman 1959:112)—and so outside of the patron's own purview—involving parenthetical efforts between men in political networks to manipulate each other. Patrons describe llunk'us as aggressive, tricky, and untrustworthy clients, and the semantics of llunk'erío fill out a public symbolic account of the stigmatized cholo. At the same time, the semantic theater of clientage behavior—of licking,

Figure 2.2. Ritual misas: Different kinds of prepared ritual tables available for purchase in Quillacollo's permanent market.

flattering, wheedling, cajoling, coaxing, and praising—is one of mixed messages. Clients see it differently, however. Llunk'erío is one way to move between and to manipulate multiple cultural domains.

Tales of Picardía

Lolling at his key maker's stall during a tranquil moment, Pancho Sánchez offered up unsolicited a surprising tale of his experiences with a category of person often closely associated with the indigenous world—*curanderas* (healers). He began, "You know, Robertito, here in Bolivia when we get sick we go to the doctor, the pharmacist, the curandera…to everyone." On one occasion, feeling very sick, he consulted a local curandera who told him that the owner of the house where he lived had "bewitched" (*hechizar*) him. She surmised that when Pancho was out, the owner must have carried off some personal effects, so that a *yatiri*, or specialized ritual practitioner, could then "bury them with the toad." But she promised a cure for his malady and quoted a price. She told him to buy a chicken, cigarettes, and chicha. This would "counteract the *misa negra*."[12] Armed with these ingredients, they would "go looking for the toad in the pot" (Figure 2.2).

Pancho agreed to her terms. On the appointed day, they went together to a certain place, at which point the curandera began to dig around for the buried pot. Pancho was accompanied by his wife, his mother, and several other confidants. While the curandera was poking around, Pancho's mother saw her slip a little pot out from her sleeve, which she then claimed to have found. She quickly identified it as the buried toad used to hex Pancho. Upon hearing this announcement, Pancho's mother held her tongue. In the pot was a toad, perforated with nails and thorns, a scrap of cloth (supposedly from a piece of Pancho's clothing), and a blurry photograph of someone in a soldier's uniform—supposedly Pancho himself. Pancho knew he had never owned any clothing of that sort, at which point he too became suspicious. But, like his mother, he kept quiet.

Perhaps sensing the mounting suspicions, the curandera suddenly changed her professional opinion. She began to claim that it was Pancho's wife who had in fact hexed him, wanting to punish him for his habit of maintaining several *negras* (girlfriends). Pancho then became convinced that she was simply trying to get him to give her more money. Saying nothing, he left. But later on, and behind the curandera's back, he "talked secretly" with one of her assistants, who denounced her as a "fraud" (*charlatán*). Pancho then returned to the curandera, ostensibly for the next step in the curing process. But instead he confronted her, in a heated voice accusing her of being a cheat and lambasting her for her career of trying to fool people. He threatened to take her to the police if she didn't refund his money. She did.

The problem, though, was that Pancho was still sick. A friend recommended another famed curandera living in Santa Cruz who was "definitely not a fraud." She was famous, and people came from all over to receive her treatments. People wearing "expensive suits and ties" were not even given the time of day by her. Traveling together, Pancho and his friend arrived at her "office." There they talked with a "señora" whom everyone called "*doctora*," for whom he was first asked to explain his problem. This woman expertly subjected him to a standard physical exam, "as if she were in fact a professional." After the exam she concluded that Pancho was a "good person [*buena gente*], but also a bandit, a womanizer [*mujerólogo*], and so forth." She gently chastised him, saying, "You have many girlfriends." But she agreed to try to help him. Pancho and his friend remained in Santa Cruz for ten days. During this time Pancho worked to gain the doctor's sympathy. He fixed her kitchen for free. "There was *confianza*," he concluded. Finally, she decided that the time had come to cure him, at which point she revealed that the "professional doctor" was none other than the famed curandera.

She sat down across from him, took out a deck of tarot cards, and began to blow cigarette smoke upon them. Eyeing Pancho—who must have appeared dubious—she observed, "You don't believe in these things. You must have been deceived [engañado] often." As an aside, Pancho noted to me, "She could read people." She threw her cards and the rest of her stock-in-trade into a corner and told him simply to bring a glass of water. He did this, and in the surface of the water she revealed who had been hexing him. Pancho described the water's surface as like a TV screen. In flagrante delicto in the water's surface, the guilty parties were revealed. Seeing what they were doing to him, Pancho began to tremble with both fear and anger. The procedure with the glass convinced him of the doctor's legitimacy. She is now the only curandera whom he accepts as legitimate. As further proof, once home he confronted the guilty parties, and they quickly admitted their guilt. Soon thereafter, Pancho was cured.

This is a story I would not presume to get to the bottom of. But I would like to point out some of its llunk'u-like qualities, insofar as these convey a particular cultural stance. This is, in its way, a self-consciously tricky story. It begins with Pancho's decision to seek a traditional solution to his illness. But if it is at least superficially comparable to, say, Lévi-Strauss's (1963) classic demonstration of the "effectiveness of symbols" in Kuna shamanic practice, which is concerned with the social reproduction of collective and cultural belonging, Pancho's story provides a different interpretive opportunity: a consideration of the problem of deception.

The first curandera—in fact an imposter—dissimulates to make a profit. When her poorly executed trick fails and she is threatened with being exposed, she becomes a kind of informer. The second curandera—a legitimate practitioner—presents herself as something she presumably is not, a professional medical doctor. Throughout, the story is concerned with the negotiation of social status, with Pancho working diligently in clientlike fashion to gain her trust. What she reveals to Pancho is a story of double-dealing, if in matters of the heart. Pancho, in his turn, exhibits a skeptical attitude combined with the savvy to see through the first's sham and to recognize the second's virtues. If there are particular fraudulent cases, the general category of traditional curanderas is confirmed through experience, if only as one option among a variety. The story presents a provisional relationship to traditional cultural practice as legitimate, but as often illegitimately represented, and as one among multiple options, which also requires an embrace of the deceptions at its heart. Pancho's story is less about the negotiation of changing frontiers of indigenous belonging (see Rappaport 2005) so much as it suggests that to be "inside" is far from a totalizing fact of inclusion. Llunk'u-like clientage is a problematically, and usually stigmatized, negotiation of indigenous experience as incorporated piecemeal within largely nonindigenous social contexts of interaction.

The Prison House of Culture?

From the perspective of the patron, the llunk'u is a tangle of contradictions, a social shape-shifter, and a corrupt bastard of uncertain social origin. The llunk'u is described as aggressively playing a selfish double game, rarely reciprocating or working for his daily bread. He uses language as flattery or persuasion, to achieve his ends, and his words are described as untrustworthy and not honorably bound to their objects. In these ways he is accused of misrepresenting himself and of disregarding the virtues of a well-defined self-identity. He is described as an adulterer and as a person shot through with cultural ambivalence. The llunk'u is above all *vivo*. For this reason, he is considered dangerous.

These negative associations have made it difficult to see anything else in the political activities of popular coalition building than potential corruption. This is true, however, if we accept the patron's modernist view. In a famous meditation, Octavio Paz—Mexico's patron of letters—had some unflattering words for the *pachuco*, the similarly transgressive boy child of Mexican migration to the United States. Paz saw the pachuco as caught between two cultures, two nations, and rejecting both Mexican and North American options. Paz's (1961:14) portrait of the pachuco begins, "His whole being is sheer negative impulse, a tangle of contradictions, an enigma. Even his very name is enigmatic: pachuco, a word of uncertain derivation, saying nothing and saying everything." Paz's narrative of out-migration as the erasure of cultural identity works well for the public stigmatization of highly socially mobile llunk'us in Bolivia, as one way to describe the supposedly morally corrupt popular arena in which they operate.

Paz's bird's-eye view is an account of unstable moderns defined by their *lack* of a unified self. But as I have explored for Quillacollo, within the dyadic arena of patrón-pinche relations, llunk'erío is a cultural idiom and politics that addresses Bolivia's "third republic," in the words of Rossana Barragán (1992), as a complexly urban-Andean experience. Political analysts have largely failed to identify such political experience in Latin America in terms other than temporary and ephemeral populist class coalitions (Laclau 1977). This is particularly true in nations like Bolivia where the two extremes of urban elites and rural Indians have preoccupied us more. These extremes take conceptual shape as basic antagonists in academic and policy debates. Such a polarized frame tends to locate the patrón-pinche dyad of llunk'erío exclusively or primarily within the assumed historical contrast and cultural conflict between the elite *patria* (fatherland)—and its political penetration from above in the form of patronage relations—and more localized Andean political and cultural projects.

But this makes several basic errors. First, the tacit separation of "top-down" and "bottom-up" cultural commitments overrepresents the extremes of social life at the expense of the third republic or of the typically urban middle, where indigenous-popular coalitions, and different kinds of category-transgressing peoples (see Abercrombie 1996; Paulson 2007), are the rule. Second, this is done in the familiar terms of contrasting elite to Indian, modern to Andean, and national to local, in ways allowing that these might yet be, at least conceptually, two autonomous cultural provinces of meaning and experience, which makes little sense. Third, due consideration is rarely given to the cultural role of stigmatization as an expression of the tensions between claims of unitary cultural subjects and political experience that is otherwise.

The Bolivia of Evo Morales is a country passing through a transformation that promises to create many more political opportunities for its popular and indigenous majority. At the same time, the language of the political project of Evo and the MAS derives its relevance from social and indigenous movement activism, which legitimates their projects through the maintenance of strong working relationships with grassroots constituencies. The national support of the MAS, however, is owed only in part to the support of well-defined and corporate indigenous organizations and movements. It also is owed to members of the urban and informal economy organized in terms of relations of patronage, but which also represents a popular, working-class, urban indigenous, and middle-class rejection of the neoliberal governance in Bolivia. This represents an alternative kind of indigenous subject to the one routinely celebrated by the state or by transnational indigenous advocates.

3 Fictive Feasting
The Mixing and Parsing
of Native Sentiments

Quillacollo's radio reporters, really just a handful of people, were to have their annual fiesta, and I had been cornered by the persistently apologetic fellow charged with carrying off the event. He was asking if I wouldn't throw something into the pot—in Bolivia the idiom is "to make a small cow" (*hacer una vaquita*). He must have thought my sponsorship a likelihood, since I was often lumped in with this crowd as an unconventional "reporter." Sponsors, as padrinos ("godfathers"), scared up for such events are expected to contribute the lion's share of the fiesta staples: crates of beer, barrels of chicha, food, the people obliged to cook it, the music, the amplification, and even the fiesta hall. A teetering stack of continuously replenished beer crates, a dance hall floor slick with spilled drink, or heaping plates of *panpaku* (a meat and potatoes dish) hurried to recent arrivals are the sights and smells of a sponsor's generosity. And I was used to them, having in the past been present for and been served at many similar *misachikus*, as these events are generically called.

But surprised by the unexpected request, I lamely offered to contribute a sum of money, which I then proceeded to fork over. Later, relating this to some friends, I was roundly criticized for offering money. "Who would know what you contributed?" they asked. "How do you know he won't spend it himself?" "Or drink it away?" they asked. One friend flatly informed me, "You should have offered him something of substance [*de materia*]." When another such opportunity rolled around, he and I did just that, sponsoring no small portion of the drink consumed at the yearly fiesta for a union of market sellers. During the misachiku itself he unflaggingly, and at the time I thought rather boastfully, called repeated attention to the sudsy proof of our contribution. But such strategies of sponsorship, I was eventually to realize, are a particular sort of revitalizing cultural practice in this provincial capital. And as ordinary Bolivians continue to bear the onerous burdens imposed by free market economic policies, sponsorship is one among several kinds of informal economic resources.

In unevenly urban Quillacollo, the Quechua-speaking "campesino" (and, increasingly, Aymara-speaking in-migrant) is an ever more elusive (or, as I will argue, allusive) figure in the early twenty-first century and treated as a social and cultural category that is rapidly disappearing from view, even if at present Bolivia has an indigenous president. During my fieldwork some Quillacolleños were already quite prepared to confirm the indigenous campesino's permanent demise as a part of the region's fast-changing ethnoscape. And they had their reasons. As people have said, Quillacollo's is a "ch'ajchu culture." Ch'ajchu is a regional dish, a *plato típico*, that routinely mixes strips of beef, freeze-dried potatoes, regular potatoes, cheese, cabbage, and hard-boiled egg, but also admits to regular improvisations. It has a "little of everything," and people often allowed that mixtures of things lay at the heart of a provincial experience that is typically characterized by its absence of obviously Andean traits and assumed to have rapidly given way to the more homogeneous, fast-paced, urbanized, and Spanish-speaking sensibilities. But just as ch'ajchu is a gustatory experience of what it means to live in the region, which people can still taste if they know where to go, in the same way "humble" sensibilities—those assumed to be derived from an increasingly transitory Quechua nativeness—are still indulged, if now of necessity in particular times, places, and events.

Indigenous experience is still present, if more than ever as social facts of allusion conjured as characters of history, song, story, jokes, and vanishing traditions of the so-called ancestral culture. The realities of indigenous peoples—central protagonists, if no longer always authors, of local expressive culture and subjects of a regional cultural movement—continue in a contrapuntal rhetorical tension with the urban realities of Quillacollo. These realities are currently lived by a largely disconnected collection of factory workers, self-identified professionals, piecemeal and wholesale produce buyers, small-scale agriculturalists and milk farmers, street merchants, denizens of the hidden or informal economy, transporters, new in-migrants, artisans, cholos, lowland *cambas*, townies, drug traffickers, small-time politicians, and people of the "middle class." It was apparent in my conversations with many people across the social spectrum that turn-of-the-century Quillacollo is in the throes of acute confrontation with what James Fernandez (1986:191) has aptly called the "problem of relatedness."

And yet folks still frequently, and sometimes passionately, referred to their own evanescent indigenous alter egos. Sentimental talk was perhaps the most prevalent register of choice. Typical of such talk was my friend Nestor Pavo's explanation for the turn to more popular Quechua song styles by local folkloric bands over the past two decades. In his words, these tunes "brought back the autochthonous music of the Inca." As a person whose Quechua language skills were at best imperfect, Nestor nevertheless explained such popularity in these terms: "This is so people suffer and cry more. It deepens sentimentality [*sentimiento*]. We Quechuas are very senti-mental. [This music] grabs the sentiment. Aymara is indifferent. A Quechua is more apt to shed tears [*más llorón*]." Such a sentimentalized shift to a self-identity as "Quechua" is surprising coming from an individual who regularly inveighed against perceived country bumpkins and whose self-presentation of colorful, unbuttoned, fake silk polyester shirts was more reminiscent, say, of Robert Rodriguez's Mexican gangster movie *El mariachi*, which was popular in Bolivia in the early 1990s, if also aggressively delocalized and nonindigenous.

But Nestor's claim was certainly in keeping with local politics, with its often remarked "sentiment of being a Quillacolleño." This phrase was offered up, mostly by public officials, as an expression of whatever it essentially means to be a "son of the town" and to "know our culture." This nostalgia contrasted with the pervasive popular suspicions of corruption, say, where political doings were described as baldly "improvised" and self-serving. In this expressive mode of identity politics, improvisation went right along with the perceived mixing up of things that many assumed to be the source of temptation for political corruption in the first place. This view was reflected in the frequency of discussions about political corruption in Quillacollo as the inevitable outcome of the always problematic activities of creole politics (política criolla).

But even as the popular maxim claims that "the Indian insults his own origin," congeries of sentimental associations drawn by Quillacolleños in the course of everyday conversation kept an indigenous alter ego close at hand, if just out of view, engaged in an ongoing shadow dialogue with the cultural sources of political identity and authority. If kept close at hand, indigeneity—what Nestor emphatically declared to be "the intimate fever of the race"—has for centuries been treated as a malady or a stigma meant to be cured and to disappear if at all possible in favor of assimilationist narratives of middle-class and mestizo national identity, which have historically provided the cultural content of citizenship rights (see Méndez 1996). But in

Bolivia, as cultural claim making is increasingly connected to new kinds of citizenship (see Albro 2005b; Postero 2000, 2007b), this has effectively changed the terms of recognition used in the course of political work in places like Quillacollo.

This can include the most everyday terms of self-presentation. For example, almost everyone has a nickname. Nicknames like el Negro (Darkie), Bolauma (Bighead), el Gusano (Worm), el Loco (the Crazy One), el Llorón (the Crybaby), el Topo (the Mole), el Manco (the One-Armed), el Enano (Elf), and el Yakutingas (the Prostitute) are all reminders of apparent traits of indigenous physiognomy, stature, or behavior in a Bolivian version of the irreverent irony Herzfeld (1997:4) has called "rueful self-recognition." But convivially drinking chicha with friends, one might hit a different, more synecdochic note and spontaneously "open up his heart," though this would not be the Spanish *corazón* but rather the Quechua *sonqo*. Or the iconoclast might wryly and ironically observe that a suit-and-tie rival still "gives his *indio* to his woman." Behind closed doors, it is implied, sexual passion is too uncontrollable, providing an unintended moment of truth willing out, as superficial pretensions give way to racial essences.

In short, as a legacy of the era of "popular participation," and in a national climate of the empowerment of diverse indigenous projects, as I was told with a wink, "it is suddenly fashionable to be an Indian." And one recent gathering place for native sentiments in the political arena of Quillacollo has been the responsibilities and activities associated with the practices of ritual sponsorship and fictive kinship. The quotidian politics of fictive kinship (that is, *compadrazgo*, or the responsibilities of ritual godparenthood) also appears to be a means of maintaining an ongoing shadow conversation with a rapidly disappearing—if also partly adopted, recently nationally reinforced, and politically important—indigenous heritage in Quillacollo.

My development of these ideas is indebted to Fernandez's (1998) discussion of the ways that fictive kinship can function to promote strategic essentialisms, as expressing apparently "natural" or "genealogical" identities. In Quillacollo this has translated into expressed feelings people have about their organic placement in the world, that is, a desire for the integration or right relation among parts. In my conversations with people about fictive kinship, sentiment—what Fernandez (1986:39) refers to as the "emotional subjectivity" of fictive kinship—was an idiom that self-consciously dwelled on partness, that is, ego's own manipulations of his web of given relations, and so questions of ambivalent relatedness. In this chapter my task is to trace out the ways that different parts of people's identities are figuratively and simultaneously mapped onto local arguments about fictive kinship, even as they are treated as distinct cultural strategies. This includes the ways that in the political arena fictive kinship is a public frame of solidarity and consanguinity and a point of location for an inherited indigenous legacy.

Traditional Fictions

In Quillacollo people definitely give the impression that there is, or at least until very recently was, a normative ideal of the institution of compadrazgo. Let me quickly summarize a version of this institution that at least one ethnographer of the region, for an earlier generation, identified as "genuine ritual compadres" (Simmons 1974:124). As people firmly and patiently explained when asked, this is a sacred relationship ideally forged on the basis of "respect" for another or "mutual esteem." It is also a conservative sort of relationship, as Sidney Mintz and Eric Wolf (1977[1950]:12) made clear in their benchmark study. In their words, ritual kinship is used to counter the "weakening of certain traditional obligations" in moments of rapid social change. Quillacolleños generally agreed that fictive kin ties took precedence over those of friendship, "friendships of confidence," or even first cousins. Though there are many opportunities to create relationships of fictive kinship, people rated the compadre bonds of baptism, marriage, and *quince años* (a daughter's coming-out ceremony) as the most important.

Particularly in the political theater, ritual godparenthood was largely viewed as a paternalistic institution, where men should take the lead in publicly formalizing a mutual "affection" already developed through "lifelong friendships," or long-term working associations, through what Bailey (1988:84) has called the "demotic appeal" of a familial leadership style. In ideal terms, it should be a lifelong commitment, ritually consecrated in a church, with the obligatory sanction of the priest, and, most important, "before God." As a religious bond, fictive kinship was described by people as a set of obligations and duties, but, more important as including a "spiritual sentiment."[1] Couples ideally claimed to want padrinos, or godparents, for their children whom they hoped the children would emulate in life. And with the passing years, a moral calculus holds sway over people's spiritual commitments to fictive kin. Prominent among obligations to fictive kin named by Quillacolleños were the provision of material or financial support, the lending of a hand to resolve disputes, the maintenance of relations of exchange (even if just occasional token exchanges), the doing of small unsolicited favors, and of course the favorable use of "influence" (*muñeca*) on your fictive relative's behalf. It is in the terms of this last responsibility that fictive kinship typically comes to matter for politics.

In fact shared mutual affection is almost incidental to the gravity of this filial bond. A case in point is the admonition never to *tutear* a compadre (that is, in Spanish, use the informal second-person singular *tú*) but rather to carefully maintain the more formal *usted*. Likewise, one's baptismal god-father was talked about as a "spiritual father," with all the moral authority that implies. An indication of the padrino's authority is that it is he who pays the fee and signs the baptismal registry kept in the church archive. He has the right, as was told to me, to morally castigate (*chicotear*, "to whip") a god-child gone astray with an absolutism even surpassing that expected of the biological father. The whip, incidentally, also alludes to the harsh categorical distinctions typical of the feudal hacienda (landed estate) universe prior to 1952, where owners or foremen could punish indentured servants with impunity. As María Lagos (1994:106) has noted about the management of business partnerships in provincial Cochabamba, "Ritual kinship transforms initially impersonal economic exchanges into intimate, though still unequal, relations where mutual claims are made." Particularly in politics, the relationship of fictive kinship is not typically among equals but is understood to be a cultural device for the management of patronage and clientage.

Though Quillacollo does not have a *mayordomía* system (a developed civil-religious hierarchy [compare Nutini and Bell 1980:32–36]), strictly normative talk about fictive kinship assumed it to be inextricably bound up with the sponsored fiestas of passage celebrating a person's progress through the steps of Catholic personhood. These expectations were encapsulated in the well-known aphorism, often applied to public civic and private family fiestas, that goes, "From Mass to the table" (De la misa a la mesa). As the saying makes clear, padrinos must meet expectations of largesse. Traditions from the bygone economy of the landed estate once again reinforce this skein of associations between politicians and padrinos/patrones, where the Indian workers on the estate received ritualized forms of generosity from the patrón, the white estate owner. Despite the inequality of this relationship, the patrón was expected to provide food, drink, cigarettes, and often music for the Indian field hands as part of an institution called the *saqrahora*. If no longer part of the feudal context, this expectation is still assumed as a matter of course when any major job is collectively undertaken in Quillacollo.

As an institution, the ritual complex of fictive kinship is also enshrined in yearly community-level religious and fiesta events, such as the Día de Compadres and Día de Comadres, just prior to the celebration of Carnival in February or March. On these days men and women of the marketplace publicly demonstrate their economic well-being, taking turns serving each other steaming plates piled high with regional dishes like *puchero*, another plato típico specifically associated with the Carnival season and prepared using seasonal foods such as lamb, cabbage, and peaches. Each year select individuals take on roles as *pasantes* (sponsors)—a significant financial burden—responsible for providing the fiesta finery and dressing the patron saint of the marketplace (called the Señor de Compadres for the occasion but normally referred to as either the Señor de Misterio or the Señor de Buena Esperanza). This is also a customary burden for padrinos of baptism as well as First Communion, who provide the fiesta clothes for their *ahijados* (godchildren).[2] In addition to food and the saint's clothes, sponsored festivities include a Mass in the marketplace itself, as well as fireworks, musical bands, drink, lavish flowers, and ceremonial arches (*arcos de plata*), through which the saint's image is carried. In ideal terms, people often stressed the sacred "moral debt" that should exist between ritual co-parents, godparent, and godchild, or in this case, sponsor and saint. The sanctity of the sponsor-saint relation (which is at the same time one of saint-supplicant) is rooted in one's deep "faith and devotion" toward the saint and, of course, God, as a true believer.

Local authorities also showed a commitment to present themselves in public as sponsors (generically called padrinos as well) for a wide array of public regional events, in actuality usually funded by political parties or the municipality. As I examine in more depth in both chapters 4 and 6, politicians take advantage of any opportunity to deliver food, household staples, or development projects to neighborhoods or communities in the province. An equation is drawn between political efficacy and access to material goods. Well-connected leaders, perhaps also clients to powerful national caudillos, are expected to make a show of their potency by regularly provisioning their constituencies with a variety of basic goods like cooking oil, bags of flour, or noodles, items called "articles of first necessity." As a padrino the effective politician must also be a generous patron. And political expectations such as these are allegorically reiterated by the spiritual (and often material) patronage of Quillacollo's patron saint, the Virgin of Urkupiña. Like the Virgin, political leaders are expected to follow through on their promises.

The centrality of the church and expectations of hierarchy, characteristic of normative talk about the institution of compadrazgo—most obviously in the dyadic structure of padrino-ahijado, in the expectations of a padrino as public political sponsor, and via analogies with patron saints and feudal patrones—suggest the primary pre-1952 social context for fictive kinship as a cultural practice, where Indians were a feudally subordinate agrarian underclass. It was a key idiom for dramatizing the closed corporate nature of a dominant oligarchy of mostly white (that is, criollo) provincial elites. When people insisted, as they frequently did, that in Quillacollo politics is "all about families" or that "the alcaldía is a *compadrerío*" (that is, nepotism of compadre ties), they were also obliquely referencing this oligarchic world.

These expectations are still selectively operative. Quillacolleños who understood themselves as "professionals" and who were in many cases in fact descendants of this former oligarchy still spoke in the present tense about the once-prevalent social expectations of provincial seignorial privilege.

This arena—as an oligarchy, as a set of oligarchic cultural institutions, and as relevant provincial history—is one recognized source for normative features of Quillacollo's extant moral and political imagination. The arena was largely defined by the closed triangle of the alcaldía, the Catholic Church, and the town's social club, called the Comité Pro-Quillacollo. As the three institutional legs of elite control, these relations cohered around "profound ties of friendship and family," as well as the sanctity of fictive kin bonds. By and large the membership of these three institutions overlapped. The priest and municipal authorities, of course, were also club members in good standing. And prior to 1952 the club routinely "suggested" appropriate candidates for the office of mayor. This provincial oligarchy saw itself as an island of civility set within a far-reaching and "barbarous" rural hinterland. Its basic purpose was to ensure the local presence of national symbols (which included the ancient Inca but not living, breathing campesinos). Its cultural point of reference was the *patria chica*, that is, Quillacollo as the nation writ small. Explicit and normative talk about ties of ritual godparenthood (their sanctity, clear moral obligations, and sentimentality), then, had this oligarchic vision of the patria chica as one source of inspiration.

As a "genuine" ritualized practice for extending filial ties, fictive kinship has been an effective (and affective) means to evoke and give interpersonal substance to the existence of that "complex whole," to use Fernandez's (1986:207–208) phrase, which is the basis of appeals to the "sentiment of being a Quillacolleño." As a traditional institution, it was talked about in the language of clear-cut moral rules of conduct, obligations, and prohibitions, a kind of harmonic order often aligned with the feudal and politically oligarchic social landscape prior to the Revolution of 1952. Systematic intimations of order are manifest in the familial, political, or spiritual attention paid to hierarchy (epitomized by baptismal padrinos and political padrinos, as well as patron saints), the dramatization of the stages of Catholic personhood, and also the very "sacredness" of genuine fictive ties as the proverbial social glue of a onetime oligarchic "closed triangle."

In their explanations about "genuine ritual compadres," people's relations to each other were presented to me as well defined and as determined by widely recognized religious and spiritual sanctions. I have suggested that this is an important register of sentiment in Quillacollo. One purpose accomplished by such categorical talk about ritual godparenthood is that it nicely epitomizes the "spiritual essence" (Sapir 1949[1924]:316) of the town before 1952 or thereabouts, in ways analogous to Sapir's benchmark discussion of his "genuine culture." This seignorial consensus, however, is what has rapidly unraveled in the past forty years. A sign of this for many folks has been the ubiquity of a newer, debased form of ritual kinship, now talked about in the terms of a purely strategic act. The compromising of these felt moral and cultural imperatives by strategic and self-interested alternatives of more recent vintage is a critical register often associated in Quillacollo with the negative fallout from the neoliberal era.

Convenient Friendships

Notably, friendship (*amistad*), rather than fictive kinship, was generally held to be more important for success in local politics. As was explained to me, the spiritual weight and cultural obligations of mutual compadre bonds often militated against their effectiveness in the shifting fortunes of politics, where ties of fictive kinship could come to straddle political divides, become awkward, and create trouble by limiting choices. Meaningful ties among political allies, therefore, were often described to me as between "lifelong friends" (*amigos desde la niñez*). Others emphasized daily friendships of work (*de callejón*) as the basis for shared political activities. Veterans of politics stressed that their friendships were forged through "common experiences," such as going to school together or time shared in the army. They might also be an outcome of taking part in historical political events such as the oppressive years of Banzer's dictatorship during the 1970s, when Quillacollo was designated a "red zone" by the government and it was necessary for friends to hide out for days in each others' houses to avoid the authorities.

But people also differentiated between two sorts of friendships, those of "convenience" and those of "confidence" (*amigos de confianza*). Friends of convenience were viewed as slightly more familiar than mere "acquaintances" (*conocidos*). An idiomatic way of referring to such relatively shallow familiarity is to say of another, simply, "He's given me his hand" (Me ha dado la mano). People also offered comments like the following: "While he isn't a drinking friend [*amigo de chupa*], at least we know each other." But even such political friendships of convenience carry with them recognized expectations, as the following maxims suggest: "Among friends one isn't made to wait" (Entre amigos no se hacen esperar) or "You're a better friend when under the tree" (Eres más amigo cuando en el árbol), meaning friends should make sure to keep each other happy. Friendships of this sort were considered a minimal precondition for effective political work.

I observed a marked informality among "political friends" or "friends of convenience." As I made a circuit of the town's principal plaza with Nestor Pavo, he suddenly ran over to intercept a "friend" to ask a favor. Adopting a wheedling tone of familiarity, my strolling companion began to cajole his friend, "I beg you, *hermanitay*! Do me this favor already." When the other appeared indifferent, he continued, "Don't blow me off. We're friends. Don't be that way, *papito*!" Such are the conversations among "friends of interest" (*de interés*). In such cases, the informality of friendship is a claim to intimacy, if relatively weak, as suggested by the generous use of endearments like *hermanitay* (Spanish: *hermano*, or brother, with a Quechua diminutive suffix, *-itay*, added).

The perceived moral and spiritual imperatives accompanying fictive kin ties stand in stark contrast to the off-color informalities shared with drinking buddies. As a cultural space, the chichería is legendary as the Machiavellian ambience of choice, where people draft their plans for action in relative secrecy "between roosters and midnight." One local dirigente offered the following view, "For me, it's to have friendship at the moment of having to act. If it's your compadre, you can't openly battle [*hacer la pelea*], as you can with friends." As regional historians of Cochabamba have explained it, "What politics could not accomplish, the fraternity of the chichería did" (Rodríguez and Solares 1990:142). In distinct contrast to the assumptions of hierarchy publicly structuring the social interaction of Catholic fiestas of passage, in chicherías people can more bluntly speak their minds in egalitarian terms or utter the "naked truth" (*a calzón quitado*, literally, "with dropped pants"). And, while "you have to shut up in front of a compadre," as I was told, "there's more cooperation with a friend." Like Mikhail Bakhtin's (1984:165) description of Carnival, then, political friendships in Quillacollo flourish in spaces of "simultaneous praise and abuse."

Friendships of confidence, on the other hand, often reinforce already extant relations of kinship, usually between cousins, who often form inseparable teams. If the differences between these two types of friendship are not absolute, people took care to specify "personal friends." During my time in Quillacollo, one such pair of second cousins, who also figured in the local leadership hierarchy of the MNR, took lunch together every day. When people wanted to emphasize the inseparability of friends, they would place middle finger atop index finger and use the Quechua-derived term *de nañas* (from the word *ñañasi*, "my siblings") to indicate "very close friendship." Another term for such relationships is *k'aska*, which refers to people being literally "stuck together" and which carries an almost unconditional commitment among people joined at the proverbial hip. In politics and in play, such friends do practically everything together. In my experience, drinking was perhaps the most important diacritic of close friendship, since "when people don't feel themselves to be friends, they're made uncomfortable drinking together." And this is as often as not done in relatively isolated chicherías, outside of town and "in the countryside," in order to be beyond the eyes of controlling relatives.

One "cluster" (camarilla) of four friends worked closely together as a political team for two decades. Beginning in the early 1980s, they were an instrumental group in helping to engineer the local good fortune of their political party, which by the mid-1990s had become the UCS. Self-described "intimate friends," these men have shared a tremendous amount of political adventures and often regaled me with them. They also tended to act in concert when Quillacollo's factional winds shifted. "We're a group after all," noted Pancho Sánchez, one of its members. This made the brutally critical tone often adopted by each about the others—sometimes rising to the level of character assassination—all the more surprising.

The relationship between Pancho Sánchez and Nestor Pavo—one part friendship, one part relationship of convenience, and one part saga—was illustrative. Nestor could usually be found lounging at Pancho's key-making stall, schmoozing or arguing. Each consistently borrowed things from the other. In Quechua, the doing of daily small favors is called yanapay. They tended to arrive at and depart social functions together. Quite a bit of needling and barbed punning at each other's expense went on. During the years that I knew them, their relationship was a virtual soap opera. Both would often begin statements about the other, paraphrasing, "He's my friend, but it's like this," followed by a clinical analysis of the other's errors. Generally, their friendship appeared to be a sanction for mutual criticism.

Nestor had a great many views about the opportunistic Pancho. While he named "loyalty" as the first and most important criterion for any friendship, Nestor was frank in asserting that Pancho would do whatever it took to move up the political ladder. Despite their years of comradeship, this included the betrayal of his friends. Nestor complained, too, about the ways that Pancho "exploited his friends," calling him a "manipulator" (mañudo). Perhaps melodramatically, he noted, "Ours is a hypocritical friendship. He would kill me without a thought." Nestor was routinely disparaging of Pancho, frequently referring to him in his company by his nickname, "Negro"—an insulting commentary on Pancho's swarthy complexion.

For his part, Pancho understood sincere friendship to be a political vulnerability, or in his words, "an irrational submission." He made no bones about his views of his friend Nestor: "I don't trust him." As evidence, Pancho cited the former's illegal but apocryphal career in the regional cocaine industry as a pichikhatero (a person who receives and sells bulk shipments of coca leaf for eventual processing into cocaine paste). Pancho's bottom line on

Nestor was not flattering. He was a "pig" (*chancho*), since politically speaking "he eats everything." A story they both related—Pancho gleefully and Nestor with dismay—detailed how Pancho once played a practical joke on Nestor by drilling a hole in the wall of a room where Nestor was involved with a woman and then running off to bring others to watch. For Nestor, this was a perfect example of Pancho's untrustworthiness. But despite the apparent friction, Pancho described to me their many political dealings in the terms of personal favors done simply because "he's my friend, of course." As a relationship allowing a great deal of maneuverability, friendship was explicitly contrasted with fictive kinship. And yet fictive kinship also possessed a strategic face in Quillacollo's politics.

Neoliberal Fictions

The 1980s-era structural adjustment and the local reemergence of party politics, people were quick to point out, have decisively lessened the role of fictive kinship. In an era when local elections are held every two years, current wisdom has it that the moral sanctity of ritual kinship might unforeseeably complicate things. A more important category has now become that of party *militante* (loyal party worker). Rather than the hope of strategic influence via compadres, as in the past, it has become more urgent to run a successful campaign, staffed by the frontline militants who can do all the "ant's work" of getting the word out and of popularizing their candidate. After all, exclaimed one such ant, "compadres aren't going to make your campaign." People identified new and more transitory political allegiances, which have made enduring ritual bonds less desirable as effective tools of network consolidation or expansion. People also insisted that new kinds of morally suspect compadrazgo relations have been born out of the political transitoriness of party politics. Present circumstances, they imply, mock the virtues of ritual kinship bonds.

The kinds of practices and attitudes thought to epitomize today's more unscrupulous políticos are in distinct tension with "genuine ritual compadres." At one level, the distinctions people drew represented little more than the differences between talking about this cultural institution in the abstract (the "ideal") and as put into practice. But this critical register also suggests how sentimental attachments have shifted their location. Those most active in politics in the late 1990s and early 2000s were assumed to be more indigenous, and of popular or humble descent rather than of oligarchic pretension. And not coincidentally, ritual bonds were talked of as having lost the compelling obligation of moral debt or spiritual depth, which typified them in the oligarchic context. Instead, they are spoken of as debased, as just one among a variety of strategic ploys that after 1952 and again in 1985 have been put to use in the context of a rapidly transforming regional-market political and agricultural calculus in the service of selfish efforts of upward mobility. People noted that rather than a way to close oligarchic ranks, compadre ties are now used more to close business deals.

The features of this morally suspect and more obviously strategic fictive kinship were described as if this were the all too apparent reality, in sharp contrast to the still remembered and more genuine but rapidly fading ideal. As opposed to the unquestioned sincerity of "respect," "esteem," and "moral debt," people stressed the collusive and manipulative character of compadre alliances. As one ethnographer has put it for the case of nearby provincial Tiraque, people self-servingly appeal to "culture and customs to consolidate their hold over production and exchange" (Lagos 1994:160–161) and as a way to accumulate an economic surplus.

Self-interest, as a manipulative fact of cultural expression, has received increased emphasis in the transition from the "state of 1952" to the neoliberal era of the 1980s and 1990s. Each state project successively promoted the desirability of individual economic maximization as a basis to stimulate market growth. The following lengthy explanation of compadre ties by a provincial townsperson, for example, relates how these ties began to shift in relationship to the emerging market context after 1952. And this involved a de-emphasis of horizontal in-group ties between oligarchs or between campesino ex-peones and an increased emphasis upon more vertical and intergroup alliances developed with middlemen market traders:

> The peasants who before looked for a compadre among the rural folk, be they mid-level proprietors or vendors, now look for compadres in the people who live in the city of Cochabamba: owners of shops and houses in the city. This, toward the end that these people give them guarantees when they want to buy a house, a truck, or conduct some business. Then, they make these same people bless whatever they acquire. In turn, people of the sierra or hamlets come to the provincial population looking for compadres, and always choose those who have a truck, or a shop, with the hope of collaborating with them or because they believe that with these fictive kin requests, [his compadre] will ask for less in the transport of his products or the sale of his merchandise. As well, the majority of the people who have transport sell chicha in their house, where their compadres lodge. And also, they buy from [their compadres] their entire harvest or whatever they carried from their hamlet. Many people of the sierra, when they come to sell their products, arrive at Cliza or Punata nights before and, so as not to sleep in

*the street, go to the house of their compadre to lodge, carrying the prod-
uct that they brought. Then, in the house of their comadre, they suss
things out: to his comadre he gives* chuño *[freeze-dried potatoes],
quinua, and other products that he carries to sell in the market, and in
reciprocation, she invites him to chicha and food. Then, little by little,
the comadre becomes the person who buys all the produce that the
campesino brings to sell in the market. [Barnes de Marschall and
Torrico 1971:156]*

In this account the market middleman and campesino agriculturalist are
brought together by the smell of profits. To top off a transaction with her
caserito (a market relation often routinized by ritual kinship), a seller might
throw in a little something extra, called a *yapa*—a few pieces of fruit, an egg
or two. The moral guidance of the padrino takes a backseat here, however,
to the interests of compadres as more transient business partners in the
informal economy. Fictive kinship functions more like a collusive frame
within which people might get a leg up on the unpredictabilities of the
marketplace.

This collusive interpretation was also offered with particular conviction
for the municipal political arena. In the interest of "job security," or in the
hope of "greasing the wheels" with the powerful, myrmidons typically asked
their bosses to serve as padrinos of their children. For most people, even
those actively seeking such relationships, these were rather obvious cases of
"self-interest" (de interés) and so were assumed to be virtually devoid of any
"spiritual sentiment." The Quechua term most often used to describe these
folks was *llunk'u* (flatterer)—a word to which I have already given considerable attention, but which, recall, refers in part to the unrefined bumptious
behavior of the rural peasant or Indian come to town and persistently associated with the cholo. Not surprisingly, in ways comparable to friends of
convenience, the associated sense of moral responsibility is decisively
absent, since such self-interested compadres are likely to "screw you"
(*joderte*) the instant they feel the political winds shift.

A case in point, again, was Pancho Sánchez. By way of compadres, he
has done better than his four children (three girls and one boy) should have
allowed, particularly since none are of marriageable age. By his own estimation, in the late 1990s he had approximately thirty ritual co-parents, the vast
majority of whom he had asked. A typical example is his relationship of
compadrazgo with Caesar Buendía, several times Quillacollo's mayor and
the most powerful local political figure. Pancho asked Buendía to be the
padrino de anillo (godfather of the ring) for his daughter's graduation from
beauty school in 1991. Buendía had the direct ear of the national party

head, and Pancho had hopes of moving closer to the center of local party decision making via this door. Describing the process to me, Pancho emphasized that the two had never shared a friendship and had never been drinking together. He even admitted that at the time he had doubts about whether his compadre-to-be would follow through, even despite the "moral pressure" Pancho had applied, since it was "forced." To avoid being "embarrassed," Pancho made sure to line up a willing backup.

Nevertheless, at the eleventh hour Buendía did show up, unexpectedly, to present the ring at Pancho's daughter's fiesta. He did not stay for long, however. As Pancho noted, even as this was taking place, his new compadre was actively trying to "play me dirty" (*jugarme sucio*) by removing Pancho's name from the list of possible candidates for office. This small political drama, played out in the theater of ritual kinship, was one way Pancho thought to obligate a higher-up, not to oust him. But, as both parties made clear, any expectation of enduring responsibility was never assumed to exist, either to Pancho or to the new *ahijada* (goddaughter). After the public show of respect at the fiesta itself, the deed was done. I recall an accidental meeting between the two compadres some years later, at which the still influential party leader barely registered Pancho's presence. In his turn, Pancho seemed not even to expect that much and was little surprised to be given such a pale reception.

People generally agreed that the bond of fictive kinship "now does not carry the force of influence it once had," amounting to a onetime only sort of responsibility during the fiesta event itself rather than any kind of long-term or sacred commitment. Other ethnographers of Bolivia have similarly noted a new expectation for fictive kin ties as "specifically for the fiesta" and as explicitly a "profit-making venture" (Crandon-Malamud 1993:584). Other ethnographers of the Andes have found a correlation between new access to the resources associated with participation in development projects or capital enterprises and an increase in fiesta-specific investments. Janet Page-Reeves (1999:182–185), for example, has noted a correlation between new independent sources of income generated by young women as members of a knitters' cooperative in nearby Arani and their increased investments in fiesta sponsorship. Rudi Colloredo-Mansfeld (1999:145–159) has detailed the greater frequency of "compadre fiestas" in Otavalo, Ecuador, as globetrotting artisanal vendors rely more on fictive kin ties in business while funneling more cash into fiesta-type displays of wealth. Likewise, mostly outraged by such behavior, people classified antics such as Pancho's as blatant "mercantilism." They concluded, shrugging their shoulders, "There is inflation." Fictive kinship, they argued, has "become commercialized." This critique suggests that people view changes in regional cultural relations as directly reflecting the destructive results of the application of neoliberalism in Bolivia, even when it appears clear that such changes have been longer in the making, since at least the expansion of the regional market that followed the 1953 Agrarian Reform.[3]

There is even a name in and around Quillacollo coined for this disingenuous incarnation of fictive kinship: "ritual co-parents of advancement" (*compadres de promoción*). Ties of advancement are strategically expedient, since they are "a catchall where circumstances can be fabricated," which is harder to do with more traditional and harder to jury-rig cases of baptism or marriage. Typical examples would be a fiesta for the purchase of a new taxi or a party to bless a new TV set (events entirely outside the scope of the church). In the spirit of Pancho's gambit, typical as well were the reports of enterprising opportunists who asked several people to serve unknowingly as padrino for the same child, finding pretexts to fill a child's life with "improvised" fiestas of advancement, or the naming of new categories for potential sponsors, as in one notorious fiesta that boasted of both *padrinos de video* and *padrinos de Polaroid*. For each opportunity of fictive kinship, and depending upon the relative opulence of the accompanying fiesta, there can be as many as a dozen pairs of padrinos. A typical baptism, for example, might now boast *padrinos de bautizo* (of baptism), *de aro* (of fiesta drinking), *de torta* (of the cake), *de chicha* (of chicha), *de koktel* (of sweet liqueur), *de comida* (of food), *de amplificación* (of the sound system), *de fotos* (of photos), *de colitas*, *de cotillones*, and *de recuerdo* (of different sorts of party favors), and *de sorpresa* (of the surprise). This translates into twenty-four potentially new compadres. The increasing number of compadrazgo opportunities, such as the breaking down of de foto into de video and de Polaroid, is a prime example of the inflation so many people hurry to point out. Part of the catchall quality of current fictive kin bonds these days is that, like political friendship (ideally at odds with compadre ties), they are "conveniently" and "self-interestedly" improvised to serve the needs of the moment.

The political expediencies of Bolivia's era of multicultural democratization, perhaps most important the increase of local political party activities at the municipal level, have reframed the cultural relevance of fictive kinship in Quillacollo in relation to more adaptable kinds of social relationships "of interest." Even as people highlighted the way that critical registers of friendship and of fictive kinship now took neoliberal form as strategically self-interested, mercantilist, inflated, and commercialized activities, people also interpreted fictive ties de promoción as clear instances of the notorious creole politics, or as simply expressing "the creole characteristic." This more or less corrupt political sensibility—understood to be expressed by a generic lack of morals—was particularly associated with unscrupulous market middlemen or local political authorities. Such a lack of a clear moral compass was interpreted as a sign of the outcome of miscegenation, as a part of Bolivia's colonial legacy, and as explaining the ubiquity of the culturally mixed mestizo. Such rueful self-derision marked the relish with which townspeople insisted to me, "Quillacollo is screwed!"

Native Sentiments

In his story "El padrino," the regional journalist Ramón Rocha Monroy, himself an active participant in Quillacollo's cultural movement, provides us with a contemporary updating of the familiar Andeanist genre of *indigenismo.*[4] In the story we are offered a biographical anecdote of the accumulated prosperity of a provincial merchant, Don Vito. He is a citified, jaded, and upwardly mobile figure, the notorious market trader, who appears here as an ironic archetype of Bolivia's contemporary mixed-up identity. The story's narrator begins:

> *I would say that, starting with the Agrarian Reform, the vehicle of social mobility par excellence is the truck. The campesinos who brewed this chichita—still with fat, mind you, and from pure* muco *[the tradition of women chewing ground corn to start chicha's fermentation], with the sweetness and scent of maíz, without sugar—build up in their chests, cent by cent, a desire: to come to the city and buy for themselves a truck.... You might not believe me, but Don Vito was the same. This was owed to having been born with* ojotas *[footwear worn by Indians] on his feet: Don't forget that his mother wore the pollera. But it would be false to say he was a campesino. [Rocha Monroy 1979:15]*

This story is framed as a conversation between two people, friends perhaps, drinking together in a chichería. The narrator is clear: the tale's protagonist, Don Vito, is neither indio nor criollo. And it is the story's purpose to clarify his identity. The narrator tells of Don Vito's gradual economic rise from years of working "like a slave" in the market, and at the expense of his godchildren, whom he mercilessly exploited for his own advancement. The narrator concludes his tale with a sober judgment upon Don Vito:

> *He's no indio, I've come to believe, to the point of having the soul of a patrón, or at least of a* capatáz *[estate foreman], you know. Taking a close look at him, what he has is the soul and the smell of a merchant: better put, the reek. If I were to peg him...he lives in the countryside, but this does not stop him from insulting the campesinos. How?* Indio bruto *[dumb Indian]? No, the epoch of indio bruto is past. Permit me*

a phrase: huayrapamushcas, *which today would mean that which is carried away by the wind. But the contempt has been perpetuated, the hidden violent hunger, the paternalism. Because Don Vito is padrino to his compadres, a spiritual father for generations. [Rocha Monroy 1979:19]*

Partially intended as an indictment of the mendacity of this all-too-common provincial figure, the story ends with a punch line of the García Márquez variety. The critical narrator, it turns out, is Don Vito's son-in-law. Subject and critic are members of the same family. This is thus revealed to be a story of family relations, and, perhaps, of resemblances.

Such contentious intimacy puts cynical talk of ritual kin bonds in an entirely different, and more ironic, light. Though stigmatized, these are also instances of rueful self-recognition of the transgressive movements of identity. From the critical vantage point that condemns an unholy union of sacred filial bonds and personal expedience, and which treats the moral ideal as a memory quickly receding before present and unsentimental neoliberal realities, fictive kinship sentimentally fastens upon the cultural institutions of the patrón. Verbalized as a discourse of corruption, it is nursed along by the amalgamated ills of mixture percolating in the hearts and minds of Quillacollo's thoroughly hybrid populace. But all the while, derogatorily and wistfully, the very corruption directs attention to popular and indigenous undercurrents. And this includes the "violent hunger" of the Quechua turns of phrase not yet totally "carried away by the wind." Sorted out of the mix, there is yet a cultural remainder.

Ritual kinship is not just a market strategy, but, in a provincial Bolivian arena sharply characterized by the vagaries of postcolonial experience, it is also an expressive means of conjuncture, where Andean cultural sensibilities still collect. Compadrazgo, in short, is part of what survives of "our ancestral Andean culture," as Quillacolleños put it. People made such a case to me by discriminating another strategic dimension within ritual kinship, not in itself debased. Fiesta compadres were often understood to be engaging in the primarily campesino reciprocal strategy of resource sharing called *ayni,* most often defined as an exchange of equivalents. This was part of the issue motivating people's criticism of my inappropriate use of cash described at the outset of this chapter. People felt that fictive kin practices had not precisely supplanted ayni. Nor had the latter exactly given way to less obviously indigenous practices. Rather, as a friend sought to express it while equating the role of padrino with ayni, such a practice "has carried on in this part of Cochabamba's valleys." But he hurried to clarify, "It no longer exists! But this is what has remained of all that."

A wider areal Andeanist literature has given close ethnographic attention over the years to typically ayni-like activities of Andean reciprocal practices, most often discussed as a generic expression of rural and agricultural work exchange practiced in indigenous or campesino households (Painter 1991; Skar 1995).[5] Ayni has also been interpreted as a practice of the social reproduction of collective indigenous cultural identity (see Allen 2002:72–74). Most recently, Krista Van Vleet (2008:51) has discussed "the Quechua moral order of ayni" as defining the boundaries of local and indigenous inclusion. Key features of ayni include an expectation of "strict reciprocity" in kind, where the reciprocal gesture should not be in cash but "exactly in the same type of work or good received" (Albó 1985:31). It is a basic experiential dimension of the collaborative pattern of popular work. Ayni is typically set off from other similar variants of reciprocity: *yanapa* (Quechua: "help" or "aid"), less structured, practiced among relatives, and not requiring a direct return; *t'inka*, a little gift for a favor, often treated like a bribe; *mink'a*, where payment need not be in kind and might include cash; and *faenas*, obligatory communal work parties.

But very little, if any, attention has been given to the ways so-called indigenous cultural practice such as ayni operate in more urban and what many assume to be nonindigenous contexts. In Quillacollo, even as people stressed ayni's disappearance, they identified ayni-like interests with the responsibilities of fiesta compadres. As they explained, ritual co-parental bonds are usually established "as retribution for some favor." Typical ayni-like favors are those called in to help orchestrate family-level fiestas, where ritual kin are recruited to supplement the fare, set up, cook, and serve. The orchestration of such fiestas was understood to follow the same logic as that of the defunct ayni, a point often made to me. Such circumstances, too, are collective and performative opportunities for local political authorities to build political relationships through sponsorship.

Ayni was "from person to person," people explained to me, where those engaged in ayni remembered exactly the balance of exchange. Hence, ayni-like expectations would "definitely be repaid." If "ayni no longer exists in Quillacollo," people pointed out that at misachikus it is still avidly noted who contributes and whether what goes around comes around. And so when a fiesta padrino receives deferential treatment from his host, he is likely to explain, "But it's just ayni!" ("Ayni no más es!"). Written lists are often kept by families, so that when fiesta sponsors or padrinos are sought, someone wearily responds, "OK, OK. Just sign me up. Sign me up!" ("Ya, ya. Anótame. ¡Anótame!"). This offers another way to interpret the padrino's signing of his ahijado's baptismal certificate. In the case of political rallies, as the padrino, a politician might make a "promise" of future community work. After years of broken political promises, the local representatives of neighborhood committees or unions often ask authorities to sign their official minutes (*libro de actas*). In this way, people felt that the politicians were more "obligated" to carry through on the promised favor. Ayni is in part an idiom for keeping records of who owes what to whom and when.

The identification of ritual co-parenthood as ayni-like was framed almost entirely by the food-related reciprocities specific to fiestas. Both reciprocal institutions share organic traits. Interpersonal expectations are decidedly in kind and not in cash; fiesta sponsorships and ayni reciprocate the same sorts of things (food, drink, and labor); an important motivation is personal interest (de interés) (the distribution of a financial burden); accounts are kept; both are conceived as a game of strategy, where one tries to get the better of the exchange; the exchanges are dyadic and require swift reciprocation; both almost always occur within the domestic sphere of misachikus; and finally, the exchanges are short term (characteristics that particularly mark supposed "de promoción" from more "genuine" fictive kin ties). For Quillacolleños less moved to condemn the excesses of creole politics, strategic compadre ties, insofar as they are like ayni, were described with a shrug as simply "the idiosyncrasy of the pueblo" or as "traditions of the past." As an example of the work of the informal economy and as part of the everyday course of politics, this cultural analogy and practice reconciles a deep ambivalence about neoliberal economic behavior with the reassertion of specifically Andean cultural priorities.

Bakhtin (1984:16) viewed the table talk of feasting as a moment of "carnival familiarity," and as a way for "the folk" to unofficially experience themselves as part of an organic whole—what James Fernandez (1986:200), in reference to rituals of revitalization, has called a "return to the whole." But, in a cultural climate of mixture, I've dwelled instead on a penchant for parsing, for discriminating among sentimental registers (of the patrón and the popular), types of compadre ties (the categorical and the strategic), and types of strategies (the self-interested and the ayni-like). If Quillacolleños strive to recognize the whole, it is a complex whole, often ambivalently or ruefully criticized and joked about. Along with a "sentiment of being a Quillacolleño" comes a sense that "Quillacollo is screwed," as well as constant reiterations of specifically humble cultural commitments among indigenous and popular political figures, often publicly at pains to express the pueblo's particular idiosyncrasy.

A prevailing mood in this province is one of partness, or as the idiom of fictive kinship suggests, of the potential relations between parts, whether clearcut, corrupted, or reciprocal. But each of the different registers of expressed cultural sentiment is only a partial truth of self-identity in Quillacollo (see

Clifford 1986:7), sorted out from the mixture of mestizaje. Clientelistic ties of compadrazgo are like what William James (1976:21–27) called "conjunctive relations," with the potential to bridge distinct worlds and as a way to express an indigenous remainder for political participation in the work of indigenous-popular coalitions. Fictive kinship is a cultural institution that has patrolled the borders of colonial Andean society, as an important negotiation of intimacy between the categorically different identities of patrón, peón, padrino and ahijado, or oligarch and Indian. These borders continue to be patrolled in contemporary Quillacollo, during this multicultural and indigenous moment of Bolivian politics, via the discrimination between the "spiritual sentiment" of genuine ritual godparenthood and the debased strategic ties "de promoción." As intimate and conjunctive strategies, they are also partial accounts of urban and popular practices that reproduce connections to indigenous legacies.

Misachikus, where fiesta reciprocities are orchestrated among parents, children, padrinos, and compadres, are one such synecdochic context for the emphasis of the indigenous in the popular. The ayni-like details of accounting (and a particular organization of social life implied therein) are expressed and witnessed through the etiquette of drinking and feasting: where people sit, with whom they sit, when and how much they are served, and by whom. They are also reiterated by the fiesta fare: the purplish *chicha khulli*, made specifically for fiestas with a special maize called *wilkaparu*; the burned-smelling *charki* (cooked beef); regional platos típicos such as ch'ajchu or puchero; or the waxy-tasting, freeze-dried *chuño*, which invariably accompanies everything served.[6] These palates and habits are expressions of the "humbleness" of provincial lifeways. The accounting for a place at the table, as like ayni, is one way that people continue a shadow dialogue with their indigenous alter egos within the fiesta frame.[7] A field note about the drinking order at a fiesta I attended in the mid-1990s nicely illustrates this organic orchestration of cultural parts:

> Arriving, I was served a glass of chicha, and right on its heels, a glass of beer. Both had to be drained in long droughts (called drinking "seco," or "dry"). A compadre of the couple quickly came up with a trenzito, sweet spirits served in a shot glass. This too, had to be tossed back. I was then directed to a table, along with other padrinos, and quickly served a plate of picante de pollo. Barrels of chicha were lined up against the wall. And soon I was sitting along the wall of the patio, periodically invited to gourd-fulls of chicha by compadres, going down the line of sitting people with a ladle and a bucket, handing over the gourd, saying simply, ¡Tomaykuy! ("Drink!"). These were getting tipsy

pretty fast since those inviting were also invitees. The child's parents appeared and disappeared, serving people kokteles, *another sweet liquor. The* padrino de bautizo *made a formal toast, after which folks danced the* cueca. *At the requisite point in the dance, the music was stopped and people hustled* aros *[usually glasses of beer] to each couple, which had to be downed before the dance could continue. And so it went on for hours.*

As Quillacolleños explained such legacies, on the one hand is the complex whole of the closed oligarchic triangle. On the other hand is the complex whole of the ayni-like protocols of fiesta reciprocities, expressed in the etiquette of drinking and eating. Framing a provincial past and present, misachikus conjoin sometimes antagonistic registers of the self. Such a cultural play among shifting parts is expressed in the structured orchestration of the sights, smells, and tastes of fiestas, which are revitalizing reminders of "what remains of all that." Synecdoches of this sort dwell on the continuities of provincial popular and indigenous experience even while they parse it, discriminating the genuine from the corrupt, from the popular, or the Inca from the peón, from the humble. In a cultural world complicated by intense mixtures and categorical intimacies and in a political environment of the ascendancy of indigenous identity, people continue to reimagine the right relation among parts.

4 The Chola Cult

The Political Imagination and Cultural Intimacy

Mere months after the unexpected death in March 1997 of Carlos Palenque, founder and leader of the populist CONDEPA party, Remedios Loza, the party's new de facto leader and presidential candidate, was left with the task of negotiating a coalition government with then–president elect and former dictator Hugo Banzer. Usually referred to by the press simply as the "Chola Remedios," in reference to her traditional Aymara chola garb of gathered skirts called the pollera (Figure 4.1), Remedios Loza was a powerful testament to and precursor of the assertive presence of indigenous priorities on the national political scene throughout the 2000s. The 1990s-era political parties that best accommodated popular and indigenous practices and concerns, like CONDEPA and the UCS, showed surprising staying power after bursting onto the Bolivian political landscape in the late 1980s. The UCS, as I have noted, continued to dominate politics in Quillacollo until 2002.

If the deaths of the caudillo leaders of both parties, in 1995 and 1997, respectively, sped their decline into political irrelevance by the early 2000s, these new parties paved the way for the kind of broad-based indigenous mobilizations responsible for the subsequent successes of Evo Morales and the MAS by 2005 (see Albro 2006a; Postero 2007a). This has been accompanied by an expanding role for women in national politics, most notably women from nonelite backgrounds. Throughout the 2000 Water War in Cochabamba—in which Quillacollo was an active participant—women *de pollera* were in the front ranks of the standoff with riot police and soldiers

Figure 4.1. A kiosk of polleras: A woman selling traditional gathered skirts worn by *cholas* on a street in Quillacollo.

during the height of conflict. And commentators have noted "the starring role played by women's grassroots organizations in the social mobilizations that destabilized the neoliberal order" (Monasterios 2007:33) throughout the years 2000 to 2005. In addition to their growing presence in congress, as women de pollera have been appointed to a variety of high-profile positions by President Morales. This has included former domestic worker Casimira Rodríguez, typically described as a "Quechua Indian," who until early 2007 served as Bolivia's minister of justice. It has also included Silvia Lazarte, a prominent coca grower leader, chosen by Morales to shepherd the conflict-strewn and politically charged process of Bolivia's ongoing constitutional assembly to a successful outcome.

But despite the high-profile national careers of people like Loza, Rodríguez, and Lazarte, we should not hastily assume that the political fortunes of indigenous and popular women are significantly improved at the local level. Despite a law stipulating that 30 percent of candidates for municipal posts be women, the vast majority of provincial office holders remain men, while particularly women from popular backgrounds continue to face major obstacles, including sexism, racism, and the limits imposed by family responsibilities (compare Caero 1997; Claure 2007). In national politics even high-profile women de pollera are still sometimes insulted as "ignorant cholas" by their male counterparts. However, as I develop throughout this chapter, in local and popular politics the chola (woman de pollera) has become politically indispensable for men, for whom they provide one important avenue of legitimation. In the provincial theater of Quillacollo, cholas informally mediate political access—as gatekeepers and as brokers—to the interior of the household and, as I develop here, to the intimate spaces of Andean popular culture. For this reason local authorities actively court public relationships with popular and indigenous women in a variety of ways.

Up until Palenque's death, the Chola Remedios lent her charisma to the solidification of Palenque's own populist career, constantly appearing with him publicly and on his radio show. She skillfully acted both as social mediator and as cultural broker for her political patron, bridging the gap between the mestizo politician and his largely Aymara constituency (Archondo 1991:150–154). In the era of Evo Morales, this political arrangement of the genders has continued. In an interview I conducted with the prominent coca-grower union leader Leonida Zurita in 2003, she had this to say about wearing the pollera:

> Before, I didn't wear the pollera. But the compañeros obliged me. Before, I didn't wear it. But now to change things up I put the pollera on and I bought the hat. I wear it like this [low over the eyes]. This way, government agents don't recognize me and so perhaps won't arrest me. During the Water War I would accompany Evo, and they would say, "Who is that cholita with Evo?" [laughs] They don't know Leonida when dressed in that way. I asked my mother, "Why didn't you ever dress me in the pollera?" And she said to me, "Because I don't know how to read and write. For that reason I wear the pollera. While you know how to read and write." But as a leader I always put it on.

As with Loza and Palenque, Leonida conspicuously accompanies Evo during public events like protest marches as a way to reinforce his indigenous bona fides. Leonida is clear, too, that her decision to wear the pollera is circumstantial and corresponds to expectations among union members about her responsibilities as a prominent female grassroots leader. Leonida's decision to put on the pollera was a self-conscious and strategically aware choice.

The pollera, in short, is increasingly donned as a cultural resource in Bolivia and as a way to situationally perform ethnicity, particularly in urban spaces. Susan Paulson (1996) has documented the fact that otherwise non-pollera-wearing women in rural Mizque temporarily adopt the pollera when they sell in the urban marketplace since consumers prefer to buy from cholas. We can note, as well, the controversy that followed on the heels of the coronation of Miss Cholita Paceña in 2004, when it was revealed that the winner in fact did not wear the pollera as an everyday costume, or at work, but only during periodic fiestas (see Forero 2004). On the one hand, the adoption of traditional gathered skirts and hats is a sign of indigenous empowerment. On the other hand, a newer generation of young women, at once indigenous, urban, and professionally ascendant, embrace so-called modern Bolivia while seeking to honor the customs of the past. If a means of performing Andean ethnicity, the stance of the chola is also, to borrow Mary Weismantel's (2001:69) words, a "vantage point from which to critique, to reject and even to transform" this identity. Donned strategically and periodically in association with explicitly traditional political and festive activities, the pollera has become a resource of display and a vital link to Bolivia's indigenous Andean heritage, especially in cities.

During my period of fieldwork, political leaders in Quillacollo actively pursued public relationships of exchange with women de pollera in part because their mediatory role between the indigenous and mestizo worlds includes the potential reconversion of culture as an urban indigenous identity. As Elinor Burkett (1978:106) emphasized, during the early colonial period urban Andean women were already special intermediaries, given their "intimate daily contact" with the society of the conquerors (typified by sexual relations between Spanish men and Andean women) and the exclusiveness of their "direct relationship to both sides" of colonial society. Interpreters of contemporary circumstances have also made much of the status of women de pollera as mixed-race "hybrid females" (Seligmann 2004:145). As such, they can be uniquely effective as intermediaries—bringing together in often uneasy relationship the intimate and the public, rural and urban, or indio and mestizo—and also frequently as a buffer by defending largely powerless indigenous people from the abuses of the criollo patrón (compare Stephenson 1999:16), even while challenging prevailing ethnic and sexual codes of conduct.

Across the many descriptions of cholas as intermediaries, they have been most often characterized as informal market brokers, articulating so-called traditional nonmonetized "peasant" economies with "capitalist" modes of production and markets (Seligmann 2004:45) or, alternatively, production and consumption across spheres of exchange (Rivera 1996). They have been identified specifically as linking the informal and formal economies and as a mechanism by which "surplus value is transferred" (Babb 1985:289) within the capitalist system, thereby connecting the production and distribution of goods by an "extension of women's household roles" (Babb 1989:3) into the marketplace. And within this domestic environment, cholas have been viewed as the "dynamic nexus" of a diversified household economy dispersed across space and types of social relations (Paulson 1996). Perhaps more than any other social category, the chola has been thought to connect up the different parts of mixed Andean economies, in the process extending the household economy into the more public spaces of the official economy.

Cholas have also been associated with less obviously economic varieties of cultural mediation, such as the destabilizing and ridiculing of reified national ethnic categories (Seligmann 1993), the projection of a critical margin of Andean alterity as against Western modernity (Stephenson 1999), the "managing of contrasting gender ideologies" (Miles 1992:125), and the inversion of the public and the private (Weismantel 2001:70–79), as well as presiding over locations for the temporary erasure of class distinctions and the creation of social *communitas* (Rodríguez and Solares 1990), but also for the accumulation of power (Lagos 1994:110), such as the chichería. The chola has shown a considerable capacity to put up particular resistance to imposed social classifications while demonstrating deft skill in navigating among them and even transforming them.

But in the provincial political context of Quillacollo, it is her richly documented history as an intermediary that has also transformed the chola into an omnipresent but static caricature of electoral propaganda. One contemporary challenge in urban Andean political contexts like Quillacollo's is how to define and to claim membership in a category—the urban Andean—the boundaries of which are notoriously ill defined. In the words of one folklorist living in Quillacollo, "Men themselves have gone about creating the chola." The flamboyant mediatory potential represented by the chola includes what in another context Lauren Berlant (1998:285) has called an "aesthetic of attachment," which political leaders work to put to good use. The chola's image has now become widespread, recruited into local politics as an engendered instrument of cultural mediation, to the end of negotiating cultural intimacy as itself a source of an otherwise largely invisible indigenous identity.[1]

Politics and Cholas

Given the often difficult economic straits that accompany living in neoliberal Bolivia for most people from among the popular sectors, the most compelling political issue is relief from economic uncertainty. And state decentralization has placed a proportionally greater part of this burden upon local provincial economies. In Quillacollo these circumstances have renewed political recognition of and investment in the importance of household economies in the effort to make ends meet. In Cochabamba's lower valley the neoliberal era has promoted a reemphasis upon the historical primacy of the diversified household as the region's basic economic unit (compare Dandler 1987a; Lagos 1994; Larson 1998; Paulson 1992, 1996).

Given the perceived failure and demagoguery of established political parties, more recent political options, including the UCS and the MAS, have responded to popular disenchantment with politics by distancing themselves from the established platforms of both the political Left and Right. Rather than one or another retreaded ideological option, these parties have opted instead for a more direct appeal to the immediate needs of this demographically dominant and culturally traditional Andean popular sector. To effectively establish themselves as representative of this world, local political authorities seek symbolic access to the intimate household economy via specific regional cultural traditions associated with this productive domain. Authorities in Quillacollo further advertise their effective engagement with this intimate arena by establishing municipal programs of support for and collaboration with the family economy and the household.

In Quillacollo the chola's image is put to this end. In the words of provincial politicians and folklorists, the chola is a "basic symbol," a "symbol of the valley," and the "engine of man." Many say that out of pride the true chola never changes her costume; she never switches to modern dress over the pollera. She thus literally embodies the living intransigence of tradition itself.[2] At the same time, the chola provides unique access as the critical link to key locations of the regional economy in her incarnations as market woman, agriculturalist, *chichera*, and bulwark of the household economy. These multiple roles of the chola define the parameters of engagement with a regional political economy that functions on the basis of a diverse array of reciprocal exchanges. Local politicians make constant public reference to the "valiant efforts" of the woman de pollera as a way to remind anyone present that they themselves are also from humble origins and that their mothers (or grandmothers or great-grandmothers) are or were de pollera as well.

Trucking between mestizo and indigenous arenas, the mediatory potential of the chola is comparable to what linguists call a *shifter*, a cultural figure whose identity cannot be determined without reference to an immediate context of reference. In much of the contemporary Andes, the woman de pollera typically has been described as an upwardly mobile former Indian woman, who has made a successful transition to the city from her rural community of origin. But in Quillacollo cholas are more regularly viewed as indigenous, if urbanized, women and as embodying the regional qhochala or *valluna*. During the colonial period the chola's traditional outfit (its many variations notwithstanding) was traditionally worn not by upwardly mobile Indian women but by *criolla* or *mestiza* women who were part of the rural town elite, as an easy means of distinguishing themselves from other social statuses.[3] Libbet Crandon-Malamud (1991), for example, recorded the coexistence of generations of upwardly and downwardly mobile women in Kachitu, both wearing the pollera, although some are former *vecinas* (members of an erstwhile rural agrarian elite, which dominated the town prior to 1952), and some are Aymara Indians. Similarly, in Quillacollo there are signs that the women of the town's elite were still regularly wearing the pollera prior to the 1952 Revolution. As one current leader of the local Federation of Mothers' Clubs explained it, herself a Quechua-speaking and self-described *campesina* from a small community in the lower valley, "I believe that in the past, the ancestors, the señoras [provincial women of elite status], were de pollera.... That's to say that Cochabamba, more or less, is de pollera, the majority is from the pollera." This is an important point when considering from what sorts of families provincial authorities might be descended. But in the current era of the ascendancy of neopopulist and indigenous political projects in Bolivia, when men claim an ancestry of the pollera they are also claiming a "humble" and indigenous background, as if in fact descending from either a *vecino* or a campesino family.

The emphasis upon a female ancestor de pollera was critically marked in the daily sentiments voiced by male political authorities in Quillacollo about their mothers and motherhood, and in contrast to their fathers. The earnestness of the celebration of Mother's Day suggests that even as adults these men express a strong attachment to their mothers. By way of contrast, as we will see in chapter 5, in the majority of cases they hardly knew their fathers. Many fathers either passed away, left for good, migrated for work, or maintained professions that kept them on the road. Meanwhile, I knew adult men with families of their own who routinely ate meals at the nearby houses of their mothers instead of with their wives and children. In Quillacollo, it was common for políticos to insist that their mothers still wore the pollera "with pride," as does this local leader while relating his life history: "I have campesino roots.... I'm inclined to women de pollera.... I feel very proud that my mother is de pollera. I walk with a strut [*me pavoneo*] when out with her." Finally, if with hostile, comical, or supportive intent, political rivals and allies often used short descriptions of one anothers' mothers as a way to identify class or ethnic standing. Casual conversations often produce such observations as "Sure so and so's a teacher, but he's of campesino origin. I saw his mother once...a fat, swarthy woman with the pollera [*gordita, morena y de pollera*]." And local cultural activists used just such synecdochic logic when referring to popular culture in the abstract: "We think about the cholitas"; or simply, "So and so is from the pollera."

If men readily publicly credited the dogged persistence of mothers to provide for their children in the face of significant adversity, this does not mean their relationships with their mothers have been trouble free. Pancho Sánchez offered me vivid testimony of his earliest travails at the hands of his mother. He was driven to escape from her desire "to control me" and from a life "like that now lived by campesinos." About his mother, he was blunt:

> Since my mother was uneducated, she always saw me as something to exploit.... And many times I slept in the street, or with some friend, because my mother had a very special character. She gave me terrible beatings! So I saw my mother as an aggressive, violent person. She had a very rigid character. Irrational. And, well, whatever fury she nursed she passed on to me. She gave me terrible beatings. Terrible! Ferocious, no! She beat me that way. She lashed me! I had terror, fear, about my mother. So I had to flee. At times I slept in the chacras [corn plots], or in the fields, in order to escape her ire.

If Pancho's mother was admittedly abusive, Pancho held no grudge, maintained a relationship with her, and said that it was life's difficult conditions, or even simple ignorance, that explained her behavior. What is important to note is that, regardless of the status of particular relationships, publicly and in politics men were moved to idealize the role of the woman de pollera in their lives as a cultural resource. They were more concerned with the symbolic efficacy of the highly visible and recognizable figure of the chola.

Speaking of the Bolivian case, Silvia Rivera (1996:24) has noted that it is not enough simply to account for the gender of native women in political discourse. Women, furthermore, must be able to realize their own historical agency as active subjects and not simply as rhetorical objects of state action. In Quillacollo since the late 1980s, and in response to the greater importance of municipal politics in post-reform Bolivia, a regional cultural movement has sought just that: to revalorize a stigmatized popular cultural milieu.[4] The members of this movement have promoted the chola as an active agent and as a positive basis upon which a regional Quillacolleño identity might rest. In the rhetoric and activities of this cultural movement, the regional chola has been viewed as a local protagonist making cultural history rather than as simply a passive object and victim. The cultural proselytizing of this movement has had its influence upon the local political arena. Local cultural activism has emphasized the traditional mediatory role of the woman de pollera between such venues as the household, the fields, the market, and the chichería as a validation of the region's unique patrimony.

We can also point to continuities between the recent positive revaluation of the popular and indigenous in Quillacollo (including the promotion of the chola's image) and a preexistent corpus of regionalist and indigenist writing and thinking upon which the present cultural movement expressly relies. As will become apparent, even given the positive revaluation of the woman de pollera by cultural activists and political types who are themselves of humble origins, her role in the mediation of the popular at once combines the chola's evident fit with the priorities and technologies of the self characteristic of neoliberalism and her evident role as protagonist in a folkloric discourse characteristic of a bygone era of agrarian feudalism. In this essentialist midcentury idiom, the popular sector and indigenous women in particular lacked significant access to a political voice. But now the combination of post-neoliberal municipal politics and resurgent regionalist folklore has provided a new shape to the current possibilities for the circulation of the chola's image.

Gender and the *Prebenda*

The active promotion of indigenous heritage has become a prevalent strategy for local political success. In Quillacollo this has been encouraged by a national process of neoliberal and multicultural government reforms that have indirectly reinforced a new public investment in the cultural and economic venues associated with the chola. Here I explore the male political imagination in Quillacollo, as focused upon the cultural features attributed to the regional woman de pollera. In their public dealings with cholas, politically ambitious men hope to take advantage of these women's brokerage of popular economic and cultural spaces of intimacy as a strategy of legitimation. And the intersection of economic and popular cultural strategies is most apparent in the development context, where políticos regularly stage token exchanges with these representatives of the popular sector. Such tokens most typically take the form of political party and municipal programs dedicated to delivering development aid and domestic goods to cholas, who, as the traditional representatives of the household, receive these goods. I examine the various ways that a new neoliberal political economy of development, with the accompanying incentive to promote the "*usos y costumbres*" of popular participation,[5] has emphasized the culturally mediatory and political role of the chola.

Just before local elections in the town of Quillacollo, renewed only in 1987, it was hard to ignore the profusion of colorful electoral propaganda amid the dirt and cobblestone streets of the colonial center. Such propaganda was usually painted or posted by groups of young party "members" (militantes) under cover of darkness, often on ancient adobe walls. Posters were hurriedly slapped over storefronts and private residences, even against the owners' wishes. The propaganda featured both regionalist and popular images. Common images included the church of San Ildefonso, which houses the internationally renowned image of the Virgin of Urkupiña; ceramic *puños*, used in the elaboration and storing of chicha, a traditional brew of fermented corn; the regionally symbolic *molle* tree, expressing ecological concerns; and, most common of all, a *cholita*, with her typical stovepipe hat, earrings, braids, tassels, and pollera and a provocatively seductive expression. With this ubiquitous and idealized semblance of the cholita, parties hoped to overcome a native distrust of politicians among voters. Such images were also meant to be statements of self-identity about the presence of immediate female ancestors—ideally one's mother—themselves de pollera.

The image of the cholita would seem to court the vote of a demographically dominant but historically disenfranchised population—the popular sector, more specifically the popular woman, even more specifically the woman de pollera, with her conspicuously autochthonous dress style. And yet conversations with politically active women de pollera suggested that they were not taken in by such election's-eve notoriety. When interviewed, leaders of the regional Federation of Mothers' Clubs claimed the image of the cholita was pure "political propaganda," a superficial device to imply a phantom political following. In their words, such images were a "manipulation" (*manipuleo*), "humiliating," and designed to "confuse people." Political parties, they noted, want to refer to their "ancestors" in order to project an image as an "authentic creole party" that is "native to this place." These de pollera leaders in fact assumed that *políticos* merely wish to project a popular image. They were acutely aware of the ways that their image was used for self-serving electoral ends.

Both men and women have also recognized that the ubiquitous image of the *chola cochabambina* (the regionally specific variant of the woman de pollera, the qhochala or valluna) is doubly problematic, since an ever larger portion of the cholas living and working in the town and environs are from elsewhere and sport a slightly different costume featuring a bowler rather than a stovepipe hat. The desired electoral effect—to convince certain voters that the chola is being taken into account in the new and more grassroots-oriented political landscape—might backfire in this case. It might create a perception of regionalist chauvinism alienating to the many highland and Aymara-speaking migrants.

But as one leader of a mothers' club (*club de madres*) jokingly put it, once the elections are over, "They forget us. It's like [a married man] seeking out his sweetheart [*novia*]!" This comment, humorously tossed off by a female leader as a paraphrase of taken-for-granted political realities of exploitation, is telling for several reasons. In politics, goes the implication, men come to women only in the short term and for immediate gratification. Politics was equated allegorically with the love affair (aventura amorosa). From the point of view of politically active women and wives, the electoral courting of women was like a man's adultery. The relation of the sweetheart to the husband is illicit, covert, risky, notorious, unreliable, based on self-interest, and temporary. In recognized contrast to the long-term commitment of marriage, with its accompanying and public landscape of social relations, the love affair is an ephemeral and socially quite invisible relationship. In fact, from the male point of view, the skills of intrigue and deception used in "womanizing" (variously referred to as negrear, cholear, or k'alinchear), vis-à-vis concealment from gossip and from the wife, were quite similar to the strategic duplicity often prized in politics.[6] This comment pointedly draws attention to the corrupt political conduct that Bolivians typically refer to as creole politics (la política criolla).

We can compare this local allegory of politics as an illicit love affair with the early colonial situation in the Andes, where the mestizo de sangre (person of mixed race) appeared as the offspring of the often unwilling "sexual service" provided to the colonizing Spaniards by Andean women (Rivera 1993b:62; see also Burkett 1978; Silverblatt 1987). At the start of the colonial era in the sixteenth and early seventeenth century, such unions violated a social hierarchy that elevated the Hispanic and subordinated the Indian races. But in contemporary Quillacollo they have become a popular basis for the political affirmation of indigenous identity. Although, and sometimes problematically, mothers are often referred to as de pollera, wives are almost invariably de vestido and often considered to be chotas. (Chota is disrespectful slang used to refer to a mestiza de vestido, or a woman who has taken to wearing Western skirts.)

Despite their cynicism, women still have dealings with political parties. The acute need felt by regional políticos to carry the women's vote is expressed in another more concrete and time-honored tradition of regional political parties, the giving of gifts, which are often laundered through local NGOs. These are usually food staples, or so-called articles of first necessity, meant for use in the home. Typically, these are quantities of flour, rice, or cooking oil, or combinations of these, given as a basket of foodstuffs (alimentos) or, on occasion, clothes and kitchen appliances. Parties establish a provincial foothold through a local male leader, who uses personal contacts—often his wife or female relatives—to organize local women's groups. Such gifts are then given to these women, members of a specific barrio or mothers' club, during programmed political rallies (k'arakus). These rallies also usually involve the distribution and consumption of chicha, amid much political rhetoric, while local authorities extol the "principal role of the woman as the family base."

This sort of rhetoric, commonplace in political and development contexts, echoes one of the typical rationalizations for sexual discrimination within indigenous societies, as spelled out by Aurolyn Luykx (2000:157): the notion that "gender relations are located within the private sphere of the home", and so should play no part in any public political forum. In terms of the possibilities for women's political mobilization in Bolivia, there are signs that this rationalization is also an axiom accepted by women for the possible extent of their activities. Lagos (1997), for example, quotes female coca growers as expressing the need for "our own methods of struggle." However, in her account of Bartolina Sisa, Rosario León (1990:135) stresses the ways that peasant women have "bridged the apparent gap between the private sphere of the family and the public sphere of politics." As León explains, "Their socio-political activity is based on their social condition as women, which is defined by their role as consumers, administrators of peasant production, as the principal traders in rural markets, as mothers, wives and daughters of peasants." Nevertheless, alongside the comments of Quillacollo's politicians, these statements seem to equate women's political possibilities with their domestic roles. If this is at all representative, municipal and NGO programs are appealing to women's own views about their political participation. And yet the politically active women de pollera with whom I spoke condemned such activities as hypocritical.

In the context of widespread domestic economic hardship, exacerbated by the MNR's structural adjustment policies beginning in 1985, such basic foodstuffs do offer much-needed and welcome, if occasional, relief. Indeed, as people strive to earn their daily bread (el pan de cada día), such biannual political gifts have come to form a calculated part of many increasingly diversified household economies in Cochabamba's lower valley. Savvy family providers might even be able to take advantage of the largesse of multiple parties at once during the several months that the regional campaign lasts. In a sense, then, political parties and popular women, as representatives of the domestic economy, use each other.

Local leaders of women's clubs with whom I spoke were not particularly seduced by such largesse. As leaders explained to me, "The parties only give...when the elections are near. Once the elections have passed, they give nothing of the offer made." Or, if the parties actually do deliver the goods, they are in "minimum quantities." In fact, "never have they given in large quantities, or at the level of the federation." In order to show support for a local authority, parties often hold k'arakus, which people are encouraged to attend "with threats or with the offering of foodstuffs." In such cases, "the people go without knowing why they are going." As these regional leaders de pollera emphasized, such political gift giving is self-serving and short term and makes one-time-only offers, with scarce tangible benefit for families. Describing the moral economy of Sullk'ata in rural Bolivia, Krista Van Vleet (2008:55) has recently argued that the everyday and ongoing work of reciprocity, exchange, and balance keeping among an "intimate network of relationships" is what produces and maintains social relatedness. Onetime gifts, with their apparent neoliberal logic, can potentially backfire. Perceived instead as one sided or nonreciprocal and as anonymous intrusions by extralocal figures, they might create the opposite effect from intimacy.

Grassroots and opposition leaders, men and women alike, often contemptuously labeled such gifts *prebendas*, a word virtually synonymous with public political bribe. At least since an earlier populist moment—the entrenchment of the MNR political party in power after the 1952 Revolution —this practice of electoral gift giving (*prebendalismo*) to the popular masses has been the standard modus operandi. And it is a practice rooted in long-established cultural expectations in the region between patrón and peón, where, for example, food and cigarettes were usually supplied by a hacendado and then prepared by the wives of field hands for the traditional saqrahora during planting or harvest. Yet this practice is still routinely cited in editorials in the regional newspaper as an important indication of the thorough corruption of the Bolivian political system. One disillusioned former participant in local political activities aptly described the prebendalismo of distributing noodles, cooking oil, sugar, rice, and so forth as a case of políticos "hiding beneath the gathers of women's skirts." Nevertheless, there is substantial ambivalence about the prebenda in part because, as a cultural activity, it closely resembles much more acceptable and established practices. I mention only two here.

On the one hand, the prebenda could be and has been viewed as a recognized sort of all-purpose exchange relation expressing the well-known "Andean system of reciprocity and redistribution" (Medina 1992:184), along with comparable forms of community or family self-help practices such as ayni—a principle of exchange recognized by locals as previously typical in Quillacollo. In a more general sense, such practices of exchange are typical of how social relations are managed in many other arenas. The local cult of the Virgin of Urkupiña is a case in point. Devotees make a "promise" to the Virgin with a yearly *ch'alla* (libation) accompanied by food and drink. In exchange, devotees hope the Virgin will grant them mostly material well-being, such as a new truck or house or, perhaps, an academic degree. In this case, local authorities provide basic foodstuffs in exchange for at least a verbal guarantee of the vote from their popular constituency.

They hope to influence the popular sector in a way not dissimilar to devotees' propitiations of the Virgin with food and drink, designed to appease her often capricious behavior. Once again, however, an important difference between the prebenda and people's exchanges with the Virgin is the discrete transactional nature of the former (where parties deliver specific goods for support in a given election), as compared to the ongoing and productive commitment with the latter, which usually requires commitments of from one to three years.

Though the prebenda is a successful political strategy typically directed toward female domesticity, many politically active women felt strongly that it was in fact directly contrary to their best interests as a bloc. The case of one former political activist is instructive here. This young woman de vestido was enticed into politics through her efforts teaching the Catholic catechism to women from nearby rural zones. As a woman and a young community leader who was well known, she was asked by a political party to work directly in this same zone to help facilitate the "participation of the women" in the party. Taking this as a sincere request, she earnestly began her labor among the wives of "active party militants of humble origin from peripheral barrios." She focused upon obtaining sanitary posts, sex education, and general consciousness-raising about key provincial issues. Witnessing her success in galvanizing the interest of the women, the party leaders themselves soon began to pay attention. In their turn, they immediately promised that the party would "provide clothes, appliances, articles of first necessity, and at times, cash," in exchange for loyalty to the party. For the activist, this proved a great disappointment. She saw the immediate positive reaction on the part of the local women she had been working with and soon understood that "they in fact expected such material gifts from the party." She saw that "there was no clear conception on the part of women." And when she strove to formalize a secretary of women's issues within the local party structure, she encountered grave difficulties and recalls the many fruitless "clashes against the machismo of the *compañeros*." Frustrated and disillusioned, she eventually gave up and now no longer participates in the party. She summarized the participation of the party leaders as "very strategic, astute, and jealous of their influence."

Relations between popular women and local government or development NGOs have for some time functioned on the basis of similar forms of exchange.[7] And, in fact, through their gift giving, political parties take on the attributes of NGOs. NGOs are, not surprisingly, also often small fiefdoms of political parties. They are, at the same time, used as one of the ways that indigenous identity is actively promoted in Bolivia (see Healy 2001). A case in point was the local program started during the era of the UDP (Unidad

Democrática y Popular) in the severe economic crisis of 1984–85 to deliver scarce basic foodstuffs in bulk to local community groups, such as the regional federation of "neighborhood clubs" (juntas vecinales), which were then distributed by an anointed provisions committee. More contemporary is the case of the "food for work" program (alimento por trabajo) run by CARITAS. This Catholic charities program was inaugurated in 1986 on the heels of the MNR's new economic policy. Its stated goal is to provide a "palliative" to the "family basket" (canasta familiar) by mobilizing the available "unutilized" and "unskilled" workforce—primarily women—to work on public projects. Rather than cash, these women work in exchange for quantities of wheat flour, bulgur wheat, corn cooking oil, rice, sugar, and salt.

Since approximately 1985 the local municipality has become the primary institutional vehicle of regional development, replacing the now-defunct regional development corporation. The CARITAS program has also been described as part of Bolivia's "gender technocracy," where women are understood to be "beneficiaries" of NGO projects. NGOs like CARITAS also maintain a strategic alliance with the neoliberal state, as one expression of the privatizing logic of neoliberalism and as an important mechanism whereby, in cooperation with local municipalities, local NGOs are supposed to pick up the slack for a downsizing public sector (see Monasterios 2007). CARITAS in fact worked directly with Quillacollo's mayor's office, which in turn actually distributed the foodstuffs to the mostly de pollera workforce.

In Quillacollo, such food distribution programs were an integral part of the alcaldía's own program of "self-help" (auto-ayuda), in which community organizations contributed both financial and labor support for development projects (obras) in their barrios. Women's groups themselves usually did the work, in ways comparable to traditional practices of communal labor (faena), such as the yearly cleaning of irrigation ditches or the agricultural harvest. CARITAS officials tended to view such projects in apolitical terms as promoting the "welfare of the family" and these women's communal identity. One CARITAS representative described to me the typical practice of the "communal cooking pot" (olla comunal), where women provide shared food and child care for each other during such work projects. Municipal authorities, in their turn, viewed these economic and cultural goals as coinciding with traditional Andean practice. A member of the mayor's staff equated their self-help program with an "Inca socialism" of the popular imagination, rooted in the ayllu (a traditional ethnic federation based on kinship) and reflecting the Andean institution of ayni, the strict exchange of equivalents. In practice, this relation can easily become one of patronage, a political carrot, between the party or parties in control of the alcaldía and women's groups.

This conception of the popular woman in the context of development exchanges, with the implicit emphasis upon her lack of professional skills and primary role in the family, was reproduced in local, including female, representations of the chola or cholita. At the same time, as Nancy Postero (2007b:179–180) makes the point for Guaranís working with NGOs in suburban Santa Cruz, the self-help programs of the alcaldía and programs like CARITAS also seek to inculcate, in Michel Foucault's (1988) terms, neoliberal "technologies of the self," encouraging self-reliance, individual responsibility, and efficient money management. These, however, work hand in hand with the widely reputed, traditional self-reliance and resourcefulness attributed to the chola. Women de pollera were willing to be defined in such terms under some circumstances, for short-term economic gain. Rather than simply interpret these development exchanges in typical top-down clientelistic terms, we should recognize that they are also strategic decisions by women employing the diversified logic of the household economy.

Chola Incarnations: Fields, Fiestas, and Folklore

As a representatively regional native woman, the woman de pollera has been a point of convergence for local discourses of traditional cultural identity, neopopulist and indigenous politics, and neoliberal economic development in Quillacollo. For this reason, as a critical mediating agent, the chola has been the subject of extensive cultural elaboration. For Quillacolleños, the chola is emblematic of the peculiarities of women's power and, more importantly, of the uniquely local political culture. As men expressed it to me, she "represents the human being in this place," "the nucleus of the family and of society," and "the process of consolidating our cultural roots." Here I describe the cultural relevance of the chola across an array of political and folkloric expressions, including political propaganda, direct dialogue with políticos, journalistic polemics, participation in fiesta and festive events, public municipal exhibits, traditional wordplay, and regional indigenist writing. The sum total of this cultural production represents a corpus of mostly male writing, talking, reminiscing about, romancing, working with, and otherwise interacting with cholas.

People discuss the pollera as a conscious act of choice, and even as a cultural stance against modernity. And yet an older woman de vestido once instructed me on this fact about the chola. As she explained, "The chola is very moral. She is never moved in arguments between husband and wife. She loves and marries among her own kind." This truism was distilled in the saying, "La raza se abraza" (that is, "Each race embraces itself"). In contrast, she added, the cholo, the chola's male counterpart, is not nearly as intransigent.

He was dismissed in our discussion with an impatient wave of the hand, "The cholo has no loyalty." Typically socially mobile political leaders enlisted the stability of the chola's image in the popular imagination as a means to publicize their engagement with the increasingly invisible and intimate features of the popular cultural landscape, including people's livelihoods, the home, the body, and sex. In what follows, I highlight several incarnations of cholas in fiestas, the home, romance, and the fields. These are complementary cultural and folkloric attributes, in the role of the controlling matriarch, aggressive market woman, tireless agriculturalist, and potentially subversive object of men's amorous attentions. Taken together these incarnations—frequently overlapping and mutually supporting—compose the symbolic efficacy of the woman of popular descent,[8] and they provided political leaders with transit between the agriculture and the neoliberal economies, between the country and the city, and between the traditional and the modern.

The Chola as Mother and Matriarch

In an essay originally appearing in a monograph authoritatively titled *Bolivian Cultural Anthropology*, published by the Bolivian anthropologist Mario Montaño Aragón (himself familiar with Quillacollo), the "matriarchal chola" is described as

> generally dedicated to lucrative commercial or business activities: seller of food, and agricultural produce, butcher, called "mañasa" in the Cochabamba valley, and chichera; in a modern version one finds the seller of illegal contraband who, upon the lack of sources of income for her husband, works to maintain the home.
>
> This situation of supplementary work in order to attend to the family's needs, done by the woman, gradually moves her to become the person who decides what is best in the house and for her children. Along with this she controls the house finances completely. And the logical outcome is that the husband is relegated to the role of assistant or inferior.
>
> The commitment of the matriarch to her own family is enormous; the members of the husband's family are treated very diplomatically, if not with cold courtesy or even rejection.
>
> Her role as a dominant woman obligates her because her children must receive "the best" of society, principally hispano-criollo society. And she spares no effort or expense in order to obtain it. If she has daughters, they will not have to wear the pollera, and she will aspire to give them an education in the best schools. This is carried to such

extremes that she might sacrifice her social personality, disappearing from the panorama of relations of her children so as not to threaten their possibilities for ascent, embarrassing them with her presence. [1977:195–196]

In contrast to the evident visibility of the pollera, here is an account of the chola as a transitional figure but also an indefatigable backstage facilitator of the next generation's escape from her own predicament—indigenous and socially invisible. This is at her personal expense and begins with her own family. If the chola is traditionally assumed to broker a generational transition from indigenous to nonindigenous society, contemporary políticos have moved in the other direction by offering public reminders of the ostensibly invisible role of women de pollera in their own lives as a way of asserting that they have come from within one or another popular sector. In so doing, they can extend a relationship with the chola from the intimate politics of the home to more public settings.

The local conception of the chola as firmly in control of the household economy is particularly illustrated through her use of language, rather than a more direct authority, as suggested in Silvia Rivera's account of the chola cochabambina:

In contemporary talk among male and female friends of the rural or urban middle classes, the informal reference to a Cochabamba "matriarchy" is unanimous. This is expressed in the mode that women of the popular and middle class strata control their men through exuberant endearments, which include Quechua diminutives, and an abundant and varied regional cuisine. [1996:30]

Peredo Beltrán's (1992:150) analysis of chola market women in La Paz makes a similar point: "In terms of men, or their husbands, the women interviewed develop self-images as independent and maternal, with the power of decision, a certain sense of emancipation and capacity to cut off their husband" (see also Paulson 1996:104–107). In this kind of account, the matriarchal chola is of more account than her male counterpart precisely because she controls—as an essential economic and linguistic broker— productive networks of social relations. She does so through her skills as an independent and individual operator, often working against the interests or counterproductive behaviors of her evidently less enterprising husband.

As one de pollera coca-grower leader commented to me, "The earth [*la tierra*] is a mother and we are also mothers." Not surprisingly, in regional folklore a close association is drawn between the roles of the chola as mother and in agricultural productivity. Her productivity is both economic and fertile in nature. Mother's Day, for example, is an occasion for a public commemoration organized by the municipality. During this event, poems are read aloud by schoolchildren. The following representative sample, "Así es mi madre" (Such Is My Mother), was volunteered by one young local cultural activist and extensively develops the transformational theme between polleras and fertile agricultural fields:

> She wears the pollera,
> A shawl and *sap'anas* [braids],
> With a face the color of wheat,
> And teeth white as the corn.
>
> She's from the campo,
> She comes from the wildflowers,
> From the smell of garlic,
> From the bittersweet taste of the quince tree.
>
> Her pollera,
> made from green onion.
> Her blouse, from peach flowers.
> Her strength: of corn and wheat.
>
> Her sandals, of leather,
> her feet, dirty from working the earth,
> her hands, callused…
> But firm as the poplar trees!
>
> She has a gift, my mother,
> which multiplies with the potatoes, the bread,
> with nourishment,
> to satisfy my hunger.
>
> She's affectionate one moment,
> and severe the next.
> She speaks to me in the exquisite idiom
> of her ancestors,
> but also in the sour idiom
> of vulgar men.
>
> Such is my mother!
> Tender as the rose,
> strong as a rock,
> soft as the breeze,
> but also with the ire of the gusty wind.

Such is my mother!
With pollera and sap'anas,
face the color of wheat.
But as beautiful as the flowers of the cottonwood.

Whether good poetry or not, this is a good example of the pastoral as incorporated into the identity of the multiply gendered chola, now focused upon the pollera and equated with the visible agricultural landscape. In similar fashion, patron saints can be both male and female. Many attributes of the Pachamama, including Quillacollo's Virgin of Urkupiña (particularly her penchant for "punishments" if crossed) are also culturally male.[9] These include her market aggressiveness, her capacity for work, and, as this poem implies, her linguistic mastery of a largely culturally male Quechuañol idiom. The matriarchal chola can be said to incorporate into her person a gender complementarity, at once as mother and as masculine, a combination that is essential to her productive success and mediatory skills.[10]

Perhaps nowhere do the various features of what I am calling the matriarchal chola better coincide than in an extended description of provincial Carnival, celebrating the impending bountiful harvest, which appears in Medinaceli's national folkloric classic *La chaskañawi* (Quechua: "starry or velvet-eyed cholita"), parts of which were first published in 1929, and from which I will quote at length:

> For days the youth of San Javier worriedly fretted over [curcuteaba, from the Quechua kurkuy "to worry, to harass"] the preparations for Carnaval. This was the occasion where excess [borrachera, "drunken revelry"] was indulged, the world and its rules forgotten, celebrating to the glorious god Momo, which there should have been called the god Mona, given the excess to which the men, and in no less measure, the women, were moved. In San Javier it was a time when no one, even the infirm, got by without at least moving their lips [to drink]: everyone, willing or no, was obliged to participate in the fandango, but above all, the element of the town traditionally called the "cholitas," those who best moved their hips and most often waved their handkerchiefs [that is, they danced the cueca].
>
> These cholitas worked the year around in order to compete in the days of Carnaval, in their luxurious lambskin leggings, and in the elegance of their polleras and ample shawls. It was an almost liturgical point of honor that these cholitas should unveil a completely new outfit, from the blouse to the shoes, during the eight days that the constant dancing lasted, fifteen days in extreme cases.

> *Each social class had its place for its dances and feasts...the last, the highest level, was that of the "cholas decentes" (cholas of the town), who, due to the particular circumstances of the place, enjoyed the greatest control [mando] over the men. Because of her economic fortitude, she had more money; she managed the town's economy and commerce at a level equal to that of the cholas of the highlands [cocanis]. She bought, sold, bartered, and traveled to the nearby mines, carrying the region's products, and products from Oruro, and then returned with goods to fill the shelves of her store. She was a market genius, and, at least in the rural hamlet, and in the home, the person who directed the domestic economy.*
>
> *While their husbands and lovers—tailors, cobblers, shirt makers, or in the majority of cases, layabouts without a job or positive attribute— passed the time arguing over politics and drinking chicha in the hovels [chujllas] and chicherías of the outskirts of town, the women courageously conquered league upon league, tirelessly following their beasts of burden, challenging the dangers of the fords and the rigors of the storms, and in sum, fighting energetically for life. To live in San Javier de Chirca was to live in an authoritarian matriarchy. These cacicas [adapting cacique, female "strongmen"] were the cholitas, with control over everything, and decisive influence in the política criolla. [Medinaceli 1981 (1929):104–105]*

This account reads like a son's paean to the matriarchal woman de pollera (as both market woman and mother) in her productive mode. Here again it is the chola, and in particular her costume, that animates the frame of the fiesta. Medinaceli's novel, still a standard part of the Bolivian public school curriculum, equates the traditional provincial Carnival with the chola. Quillacolleños in fact sometimes used the term *Chaskañawi* to refer to a particularly striking cholita.

In Medinaceli's panegyrics, she is also intimately associated with the chichería, as we shall see, a regional space of political mediation par excellence. The chola in fact indirectly defines the contexts of political intrigue. As represented in the folkloric fiestas, it is precisely this traditional productivity that mediates the political engagement of provincial men, who make frequent rounds of the chicherías, by way of a matriarchal but masculine creole politics. One former town councilman even penned a series of "semblances" of well-known figures of Quillacollo's recent past, including a sketch of "La Koyu Ñawi"—named for a large birthmark on her right cheek (Rojas Delboy 1996:103–106). La Koyu Ñawi was a well-known purveyor of chicha and supporter of the popular Republican Party in the early twentieth century who, as the story goes, single-handedly drove out of her establishment a group of thugs from the rival and elite Liberal Party by flinging hot ashes on them. The very aggressive independence of this folkloric and matriarchal chola, as a florid regional figure, also served as a timely reminder of regional autonomy during the era of political decentralization.

The Cholita as Erotic Object

The chola's ubiquitous presence as part of Quillacollo's public cultural events, now reinforced by the regularity of provincial folklore festivals, has inspired a new round of writing by cultural activists with the chola as a protagonist. This literature weaves together the multiple cultural themes associated with the chola—her agricultural productivity, incarnation as a patron saint, and erotic energy—always in a close, often reinforcing, relation to each other. A typically sentimentalizing sample, written in a Harlequin Romance style, is provided to us by the organizer of the apple festival in Vinto. His story tells a tale of love blooming and dying between a provincial youth and a cholita. As is explained, they meet during a fiesta:

> I met her in the fiesta of the virgencita of Rosario, where the pueblo lessens its sorrows and expands its gaiety. I saw her for the first time as she blessed herself next to the Virgin. Upon comparing her, she seemed prettier, satanically beautiful. Her grenadine lips shone with the flickering of the candles. For a moment time stopped, and the angels, the flowers, and the candles faded, and my heart sang. [García Canedo 1995:45]

The young man expounds upon the cholita's beauty with romantic descriptions that focus increasingly on the pollera: "Florinda, with her ardent multicolor pollera, went tracing flaming shapes through the paths of the countryside [campiña]." And again: "Her pollera formed of rose petals enveloped me in its turns, and I could drink your essence, Florinda, my candid flower." And finally: "Very quickly upon seeing Florinda, my eyes were adorned with the most beautiful of cholas, arising from the cornfields [maizales], with her sensual face projected onto the infinite and resplendent sky, and passion embedded in her multicolor pollera" (García Canedo 1995:45–49). The romance fades only when Florinda, supposing her lover would want her to, changes her pollera for pants (becoming a chota).

The chola is an essential protagonist in the performative traditions of regional politics and folklore. In her incarnation as a "cholita," she is intimately associated with traditional patronal fiestas, as well as increasingly frequent regional folkloric festivals, which are typically organized by provincial municipalities throughout Cochabamba's valleys.[11] The *entrada* of folkloric dance groups during the fiesta of Urkupiña features a variety of dances that are considered stylized performances of Andean cultural practice.[12] Perhaps most notable are the groups of mostly city girls who don "*mini-polleras*" to dance in the popular *caporales* fraternities. These mini-polleras, worn by women who would normally be de vestido, are festive costume versions of the everyday pollera, worn only when dancing.

Some female fraternity organizers felt strongly that this trend toward increasingly *mini* mini-polleras was little more than the "cult of the body" and represented the "exploitation of feminine beauty." They felt this distorted the solemn and religious nature of the fiesta, which some scoffingly suggested should be renamed "Urku-pierna" (with *pierna* being Spanish for "leg"), to emphasize the increasingly exposed and sensual bodies of the female folkloric dancers themselves. Writing about Quillacollo, Maria Lagos (1993) has emphasized that these city girls are best understood to be imitating and appropriating the dress of more authentic cholas, in the process subjecting Andean culture to a folkloric performance of a mestizo-ized Bolivian national identity. But we can also understand the occasional donning of even stylized polleras as one way people of Andean descent living in more urban contexts maintain an active connection to an indigenous heritage. Criticism of apparently inauthentic cholitas also ignores the role played by this eroticized and stylized incarnation of the cholita in the public performance of local politics.

During the entradas I witnessed, local and national authorities often came out of the crowd to dance with these cholitas. Important populist políticos also commonly sponsor dance fraternities to perform during their regional visits. During a rally I attended for then–UCS party leader Max Fernandez in 1995, a line of caporales literally followed the politician's entourage from the airport to the rally site several miles away! The act of a político and chola dancing a cueca was an obligatory and routine part of almost any sort of public and festive occasion attended by municipal authorities. Dancing the cueca is thought to promote a spontaneous "affection" (*cariño*) between the leader and the assembled crowd. On several occasions, I have seen women decline to dance with some local authority, perhaps not wanting to be the object of public attention but claiming that he should find a "real chola" with whom to dance. This performed flirtation between político and cholita is a reminder that the secret love affair, in the colonialist account productive of racial mixture, is integral to the public, folkloric, and political identity of the urban indigenous woman in Quillacollo.

An old standard of the Quillacollo Carnival entrada, which pronouncedly equates the cholita with ribaldry, is the "chola k'alincha and her compadre." A satirical feminine figure, described by friends as "mischievous," a "jokester," and "brusque," the chola k'alincha always appears in the company of her upper-class lover. Again, we encounter the illicit love affair. K'alinchear, recall, is an idiomatic verb that refers to the male propensity for womanizing.[13] In reference to the Feria de la Manzana (Apple Fair) in nearby Vinto, one columnist wrote effusively about a "coctelito dubbed the imilla kjalincha, prepared appropriately from apples, which illuminated the eyes and whetted the tongue of those who tasted it. I judge the spirit of this delicious liquor to be none other than that of Eve, revived and primal, in the fronds of the apple trees of Vinto" (Urbano Campos 1995). Here, imilla (Quechua for "young unmarried woman," but also "servant girl") functioned as a synonym for cholita.[14] Notable as well is the pervasive association of the chola with nature's agricultural gifts and with the cult of the Virgin. This relation takes on particular force in the historically productive region of Cochabamba, commonly referred to as Bolivia's "breadbasket." In the context of fiestas, the Virgin and the chola are earthly incarnations of each other (Figure 4.2).

As a central protagonist of the celebrations associated with Quillacollo's politics and folklore, the k'alincha unambiguously suggests a sexual intimacy.[15] The expressive underside of this is a somewhat lurid local tabloid fascination with cholitas as unwitting victims of sexual predation. These include apocryphal stories with racy titles like "Cholitas: Sexual Slaves," telling about innocent young girls hired as cooks but forced into prostitution. Or they are stories of police tracking down the source of bootleg pornographic videos found in the weekly market with titles like Cholitas XXX. Commenting on a report of one such illicit cholita porno ring, an outraged official from the mayor's office of the city of Cochabamba declared, "It is not possible for the dignity of the woman de pollera to be compromised" (Osorio 2005). But the festive, public, and illicit elaboration of these trysts (whether a product of upward or downward mobility), goes the suggestion, creates among men the ability and increasing desire to locate a woman de pollera somewhere in their past. The love affair, the intimacy of such an illicit encounter, carries colonial echoes of mestizaje while it redefines the terms of inclusion in the popular.

The Productive Chola

In conversation with one young municipal official, politically active and then one of three staffing Quillacollo's Department of Culture, I was offered

Figure 4.2. The annual chicha festival: A poster featuring a "come hither" image of a regional qhochala or cholita in nearby Tiquipaya.

this heartfelt commentary on the perceived increase in women opting to dress de vestido:

> It's part of the alienation. It amounts to denying your own heritage, your own ways. What happens? They think that to wear skirts [faldas, instead of the pollera] means to be better than other women. But seeing a woman de pollera do twice that of those de vestido, I know that these

others feel much more incapable than the woman de pollera. And this is demonstrable, because she has a much greater capacity through her community, her simplicity, to be able to produce much more than those de vestido. At times the women de vestido don't even produce. They do nothing to help their families grow economically.

This also underlies the importance of the woman within the house, because in terms of women today, for some time we've seen an evolutionary process of the working woman. The majority of women no longer work but have become homemakers. They wait for the man's salary to arrive and invest it but don't, themselves, produce. But cholas produce. They're active. They're workers. They have creativity. They produce. They go to their fields, and take care of business. They sell things. They trade [rescate] potatoes, sell food. That is the true chola, and the real woman, producing and seeing to the economic development of their families. And so, there's a big difference. The chola speaks three languages—Aymara, Quechua, and Spanish—something the woman de vestido can't do. Sometimes those de vestido feel embarrassed to speak Quechua. She thinks, "I'm no Indian [india]!" There's a total confusion of identity.

In this extemporaneous lecture by a young man, whose mother is de pollera and makes a living as a street vendor (*vivandera*), one detects the repeated theme of chola productivity. This comment is typical of the recent and positive revaluation of the chola in Quillacollo. In this young man's view, such production (in the market, the field, or the home) is essentially female and creative and is defined by the chola's multiple roles and skills, as the fulcrum of Cochabamba's agrarian and informal economies. In contrast, modern women, who adopt modern skirts and who wrongheadedly stigmatize manual labor and are thereby themselves unproductive, deeply perturbed this young political and cultural activist.

The association of the chola with agricultural fecundity in fiesta contexts was most apparent in the annual fiesta of the Virgin of Urkupiña, the town's patron saint and the focus of one of Bolivia's largest and internationally prominent annual festivals.[16] As both the Virgin María and *mamita* Urkupiña, this potent figure condenses popular folk Catholic beliefs about saints with Andean conceptions of vital and gendered telluric forces. The fiesta's popularity skyrocketed in the 1970s, just as the ongoing parcelization of agricultural land in the valley was becoming an acute problem and rural families were busy finding options other than small-hold farming. During the fiesta devotees enter the mines of the Virgin built into her Calvario, where they work, striking the rock veins with a sledgehammer until removing a chunk. Faith in the Virgin is demonstrated by this productive work, first symbolically in the mines, then throughout the year to follow. This stone is then made the basis of an elaborate ch'alla, as a ritual act of supplication and affinity carried out for the Virgin (see figures 4.3 and 4.4).

Just as the chola is the productive "engine of man," the Virgin is considered "the señora of the home, of the fields, of the mountains, and of the vital cycle of men" (Rocha 1990:74). In a social strategy reminiscent of the prebenda, mamita Urkupiña (as the Pachamama) is propitiated and "fed" with a ritual libation of cigarettes, beer and chicha, streamers, fireworks, confetti, coca leaves, an aromatic burnt offering (q'oa), and sometimes prepared dishes of food. If properly sated, she will in turn attend to the well-being of the supplicant. This traditionally includes ensuring the continuity and equilibrium of reproductive forces, which in the past meant success in agricultural production and human procreation. Particularly in her incarnation as the Virgin María, Urkupiña brokers the supplicant's relation with God, interceding positively on the supplicant's behalf by putting in a good word to ensure that his or her petition is addressed. Nowadays, success might mean anything from the purchase of a new truck to a new laptop computer. If incorrectly propitiated, or left unsated, she might also become malignant and cause "bad luck," including death, which is considered a "punishment" (castigo) of the Virgin.

Many commentators on the Andes have stressed that the term Pachamama contains the Quechua root pacha, which means at once the world, the earth, and time. Hence the Pachamama has been conceived as the "ancient space-time concept immanent in the earth" (Nash 1979:121–122), or defined as the "creator of time" (Girault 1988:9), a circumstance embodied in preconquest agricultural rites. I want to draw out one implication of the equation of the Pachamama, and the Virgin of Urkupiña, with time. In a region increasingly characterized by urbanization, a scarcity of fertile land, and the decline in importance of agriculture as a subsistence strategy and prevailing way of life, libations to the Pachamama also signify a ritualized and temporal displacement, a temporary return to a mostly gone and utopian time of traditional agricultural lifeways now registered primarily through local folklore festivals. Devotees engage in relations of reciprocal exchange with the Pachamama, who mediates their access to this rapidly vanishing world. Here self-consciously traditional cultural and engendered concepts of productivity frame the logic of the regional market economy. And the exchanges characteristic both of development and of politics are transacted within this frame. The Virgin, in short, keys this productively cultural frame within which men in politics traditionally operate.

Figure 4.3. Quillacollo's patroness: A girl lights votive candles to the Virgin of Urkupiña in Quillacollo's San Ildefonso Church.

Figure 4.4. Pasantes: Sponsors of Quillacollo's patroness, the Virgin of Urkupiña, during her annual celebration.

Writing largely about Cochabamba, Marta Irurozqui Victoriano (1995) also has discussed the role of a "rural utopia" in the literary imagination of early- and mid-twentieth-century Bolivian writers and the ways this literary utopia was taken up in prerevolutionary provincial politics. For these writers, the specter of the cholo was responsible for "all Bolivia's defects and vices" (1995:359), making a functional democratic nation impossible. Their solution was to opt for a morally positive alternative from the past to the flawed hybrid present, by constant reference to "the cult of the legendary and now lost greatness of the Quechuas and Aymaras" (1995:360). This faded greatness was yet dimly reflected in "the values of the simple life, full of sincerity and innocence, in contrast to an urban life characterized by deceit, fraud and insidiousness." Important for this utopia was that it was typically expressed as a "profound localist sentiment" (1995:379), where consideration of the Bolivian nation as a whole, the *patria grande*, was excluded in favor of romantic elaborations of the patria chica. Irurozqui Victoriano's analysis provides the historical depth of this male literary and political imagination, still active in the efforts of contemporary local folklorists. Now, however, it is a basis for something very different: the still evident indigenous undercurrents of provincial but urbanizing life in places like Quillacollo.

This development is best illustrated by the emergence of regional folklore festivals, in conjunction with the policies of neoliberal structural adjustment in Bolivia. As part of a regional cultural renaissance, they first began to be organized in 1986 and have since grown in number (see Carpio San Miguel 2001a). There are currently at least a dozen such regional festivals, creating a yearlong festival calendar. The themes are resolutely agricultural and invested in the "mysteries and enchantments of the provinces" (Gonzales 1991), with festivals devoted to chicha, corn, apples, peaches, trout, and *huarapo*, a regional fermented beverage, among others. They take place over several days in different towns and promote a carnivalesque atmosphere designed to attract families from the nearby city. Employing a neo-indigenist logic, organizers of these festivals maintain that their popularity proves that diverse urban sectors still have identifiably "provincial roots" as Qhochalas, that is, native Cochabambinos, and that urbanites still wish to maintain rural "customs interred by false modernity" (Gonzales 1991). Each festival features an abundance of regional cuisine (platos típicos), live concerts by folkloric bands, performances by dance fraternities, games, and different special features, such as a cholas-only bicycle race or a contest among cholitas to crown the "Queen of the Festival."

These festivals are also referred to as *ferias* (fairs or markets), which connects them by inspiration to the agricultural market (called *ferias agrícolas*), on which they are loosely modeled. These compose a regional network of markets, greatly expanded after 1952, where basic perishable goods not only from the valleys but also from the highland regions beyond are bought and sold on a rotating weekly basis. The folkloric version, sponsored by the municipality and with the support of local NGOs and international organizations, evokes the bustling atmosphere of the genuine agricultural market, where the figure of the chola as a key transactor predominates. When explaining the rationale for the festivals, organizers emphasized the familiar necessity of "recalling" or "rescuing" the "traditions most associated with the valley" but also the goal of investing in the local economy. They talked of tourism and the need to revitalize a flagging agricultural market, colonial in origin, in which the newly autonomous alcaldías have an important economic stake. In these festivals the municipality works together with the small-scale agriculturalist to promote their shared interests. For example, Quillacollo's first Feria del Maíz in 1986 sought to "revalorize the culture of maíz, demonstrating its productive capacity, as well as its nutritional value." To this end, the festival promoted the many traditional uses of corn in regional cuisine: in soups (lawas), on the cob (choclo), off the cob (moti), as an alcoholic beverage (chicha), and in baked goods (humintas, "cornbread"). During the festival, colloquia were held for chicha producers, in which "experts" offered detailed suggestions to better rationalize the still "inefficient" chicha industry.

These festivals have a straightforward economic goal of stimulating the consumption of regional agricultural produce, as an important regional patrimony, in the neoliberal context. As a regional journalist and folklorist stated the issue, these festivals are designed to encourage "the enrichment of Cochabamba's gastronomic and gastroethyl [referring to the elaboration of chicha] culture" but are also a means "to become aware that Cochabamba will be initiated on the solid road of progress only when it takes advantage of its farming and cattle industries in the most optimal way." In this manner, the cultural idiom of folkloric festivals converges with a serious attempt to meet the regional economic challenge at the level of the municipality by likewise focusing on the productive transformation of a diminishing agricultural sector. This approach at the level of the municipality parallels that of Caritas at the level of the household. Both constitute local efforts to generate productive private enterprise by maximizing available cultural resources. And the symbolic appeal for economic stability is made primarily through the woman de pollera, now in her neoliberal guise as a calculating market woman, who provides potential consumers with commercial access to the folkloric renegotiation of traditional identity.

This idea of chola productivity, as it circulates in the regional development context, can also be used by men for co-optive political ends. In 1994 I would daily walk by a photography exhibit in the Department of Culture, accompanied by folkloric music and featuring the town's mayor, that documented the many "communal projects" (faenas) carried out and "public works" (obras) delivered during the mayor's self-described "communal administration." The mayor was presented in the recurrent role of material benefactor and town patron, but there was a special section devoted to his relation with local mothers' clubs. This included numerous photos of the alcalde lending a hand in different ongoing work projects while surrounded by women de pollera, also working. Among these was a photo of him handing out baskets of food to women in honor of Mother's Day. Below ran the following caption:

> The communal government has initiated action within a model of shared work and with the particular presence of women's clubs. With the characteristic beauty of the women, accustomed to responsible work, and the beauty of the valluna.... The presence of the woman in this task especially marks the consequential nature of such everyday work.

The colorful costume of the chola jibes well with the expected image of Third and Fourth World women maintained by development NGOs as the expected recipients of development aid.[17] This is comparable to a similar scenario among market women de pollera, who are viewed as more authentic by prospective customers (Buechler and Buechler 1996:171; Paulson 1996:88; Peredo Beltrán 1992:36; Seligmann 2004). Here the productive woman de pollera, as the traditional basis of the household economy, is viewed as the logical collaborator and exchange partner for the productive activities of the municipality. As the primary symbolic complement to the mayor's largesse, native women de pollera, in their several capacities, bolstered his public image as a selfless benefactor to the mothers, and so families, of the region's popular sectors. And these women are, to repeat, ostensibly a composite public semblance of the mayor's own female ancestors, a point further emphasized by the imposing chola's hat—a campaign image—painted on the front of his house.

Conspicuous both in the city and in the rural province are flyers circulated to publicize these folklore festivals, which always feature a cholita. As in the political propaganda, she is depicted wearing a shortened stovepipe hat and mini-pollera, with a red-lipped sensuous expression and ample bosom. She is also shown in association with the festival's agricultural theme—holding a bushel of corn, or a tutuma of chicha, biting an apple, or offering a toast with a glass of huarapo. Festival organizers offer a variety of reasons for why the cholita has become the poster girl for these festivals. One organizer noted the need to "maintain this social category [of the chola] as a dignified tradition." Another festival organizer, and writer of romantic regionalist literature in his spare time, claimed the chola's image was used "to make the feria more authentic because the chola is a very typical personage...and the woman is the pollera." The chola cochabambina is also "more colorful and provocative" than cholas from other regions, and she represents the social class that is "closest to nature and most involved in agriculture." He concluded, "The earth [tierra] is her richness." Yet another organizer noted that her accentuated physiognomy attracts attention and recalls Eve's role leading Adam into sin. The cholita displays, in his words, a "great capacity for work" and is traditionally responsible for "inviting" people to fiestas.[18] And in fact girls—usually students enrolled in the University of San Simón in the nearby city but dressed for the day in the pollera—are often on hand to welcome people to the festival.

These cholita posters facilitate public awareness of and symbolic access to self-consciously traditional festival spaces. In fact, active participation in dance fraternities, with the concomitant need to don the expensive festive costume, has been cited as a strategy employed by women de vestido who wish to switch permanently to the pollera (Buechler and Buechler 1996:183). As the role of the chola's image in the region's folklore festivals makes clear, the chola organizes, advertises, and invites participation in regional cultural events. And while cholas organize fiestas, at the same time fiestas quite literally produce and promote cholas, as privileged political and folkloric currency.

The Chola and Brokerage

The most common surrounding for the chola k'alincha, it seems, is the chichería. In the folkloric mode, it is in the drinking context that she becomes especially libidinous—a virtual exhibitionist. The cholita of Medinaceli's novel, herself a chichera, dances the cueca with particular passion in the chichería: "with a licentious grace, voluptuously wiggling her behind [nalgueando], and waving her handkerchief in the air" (1981[1929]:58). In fact, in Quillacollo conversation among men about cholas often quickly shifted to bawdy innuendo with marked double entendre. Asked by the ethnographer to describe the "typical chola valluna," one friend ticked off her braids, pollera, her k'epi (woven carrying sack), and stovepipe hat. Unsolicited, he then characterized her unique personality. The chola valluna is identified with "mischievousness" (picardía) and "pride" (in that she does not change class). A companion broke in, laughing, "With her milk cows [*vacas lecheras*]!" referring to her breasts. Now in the spirit, my friend continued, she is also "masculine" (*varonil*) and "sentimental." Beginning to laugh as well, he concluded, "She feels and loves strongly. With this love, she'll kill you if you cross her. She'll yank you by your plumbing [*pichula*]!" This sort of ribald wordplay, characteristic of drinking companions talking about womanizing, was quite common. In fact, I spent significant energy during fieldwork extricating myself from attempts by friends to set me up with supposedly interested, and I suspect mythical, cholitas.

As her antics during Carnival attest, the figure of the chola k'alincha is by now quite institutionalized in Quillacollo's chicherías. A case in point is the local legend associated with the town's popular watering hole, the chichería Chola Milagrosa (Miraculous Chola). In one version of the story, the establishment is named after its owner, now an old woman and ironically de vestido. As a young cholita, she jealously shot and killed her lover, erected a cross over the spot, and eventually started up her chichería there. The fame of the establishment has persisted due to its consequently "miraculous" chicha. Another case of the institutionalization of the chola cult is the recently renovated tradition of the *wallunk'a* (Quechua: "swing"), also usually performed in chicherías, which now traditionally accompanies the celebration of the Day of the Dead (Todos Santos) in November throughout the region. Although it is historically unclear whether the wallunk'a was traditionally typical of the region (say, prior to 1952), it is an important expression of the regional cultural renaissance of the last several decades and an evident example of the local invention of tradition for political ends (see *Los Tiempos* 1994). As one activist, also a journalist, pronounced, "Despite what many insist to the contrary, the festival [of the wallunk'a] now forms a part of Quillacollo's patrimony, which has surpassed local frontiers."

A local folklorist who published an authoritative account of regional agricultural ritual—written in a timeless ethnographic present—described the wallunk'a in the following terms:

> During Todos Santos the fiesta of the wayllunk'as begins, which lasts until the day of San Andrés, November 30. On the 2nd of November the first swings are built, many of them several hundred meters from the cemetery.... In each swing there is music (of accordions, guitars, and bands). Different sorts seek to be pushed on the swing, but above all it is the cholitas who stand out. One accedes to her requests [pedidos] with the condition that she sing a few couplets [coplas]. If she

> *does not carry out her promise, she is pushed even harder and is not permitted to get off until she begins with the first verses.... Everything unfolds in an ambiance of enjoyment, laughter, whistles, and catcalls. [Rocha 1990:64–65]*

At the apex of her swing, the cholita is supposed to try and seize with her feet one of several baskets of flowers and foodstuffs suspended in front of the swing. In the past, I was told, these baskets were adorned with real money and the cholitas could win livestock as prizes. I was also told, by a guffawing former mayor no less, that "innocent" cholitas sometimes swung without undergarments, causing quite a spectacle. Sung in Quechua and "interpreted by pretty cholitas [*simpáticas cholitas*] and young men [*jovenzuelos*]," the couplets are resolutely lewd in character, referring to amorous and often illicit relations between the sexes and utilizing double entendre almost exclusively. The wallunk'a, then, enlists familiarly erotic and pastoral characteristics of the chola's image to the end of social reproduction.

One such wallunk'a I attended was advertised throughout Quillacollo with the following flyer: "Popular artists of the Cochabamba valley. Platos típicos and the best chicha. Festival of the wallunk'a and couplets of the Day of the Dead. Homage to Encarnación Lazarte [a famous couplet singer and cholita of Cochabamba]. Organized by the cultural group Itapallu." Encarnación Lazarte is the best known and earliest of such "couplet cholas," getting her start in the late 1960s. According to reports, she never "rejects invitations to cultural and culinary festivals dedicated to revive or to maintain our culture" (Carrillo 2003). The chichería that served as host for the event, on the town's outskirts and in a zone densely covered by agricultural plots, was owned by the sister of the founder of this local cultural movement. Her brother, whose influence was apparent in the electoral propaganda adorning the town's adobe walls, was an ardent backer and client of the then-mayor of the town. In recent years, he had also made an unsuccessful foray into the regional political arena as the local candidate for a small and inconsequential socialist party of the reconstituted political Left.

Another notable feature of this particular wallunk'a was the presence of the regional writer and journalist Ramón Rocha Monroy, who cheerfully gave away copies of his novella *El run run de la calavera*. Although written in a magical realist style, the novella seeks to authentically depict the peculiar popular beliefs associated with the region's celebration of the Day of the Dead. As part of a literary corpus on regional cultural identity and with indigenist content, the novella is thematically continuous with the earlier works of Medinaceli and others. Throughout the event, Rocha Monroy drank with cholas who we are to understand would otherwise be found busily selling, trading, harvesting, and managing their families somewhere in the region's three valleys.

The couple who owned the chichería offered me their views on wa-llunk'as. For them, this was not a custom inspired by literary convention. Rather, the wallunk'a has been practiced at least "from the time of the *tata-abuelos* [Quechua: "great-grandparents"] and the Inca, as a custom of the ancestors." In a familiar refrain, they also asserted, "The principal motive is to rescue and maintain the traditions of the *llakta* [town, but also region], but not to profit from it." And as a symbol, the swinging chola represents "the alternations of life and death." Themselves de vestido, the owners insisted that the wallunk'a should be performed only with "pure cholitas," since the couplets impart "something of romance," of "mischievousness" (picardía), and of "obscenity." They added that originally those who prac-ticed the wallunk'a were not de vestido, as the upper class (*alta estrata*) was prejudiced against it. The cholitas "liked these customs more. They are by nature happier, from more rustic parts [*tierra adentro*], more aggressive, open,…a symbol of the valley." Indeed, during the wallunk'a, cholita after cholita was called up to mount the swing to try for the baskets, while a folk-loric group performed their innuendo-rich couplets and, between songs, drank heavily.

This event was attended by several town VIPs, including the mayor himself, who was made the subject of a satirical carnivalesque couplet in which a cholita openly surmised about his sexual potency over the micro-phone. During the event the mayor was uncharacteristically referred to as *jilakata* (a Quechua term for an indigenous local leader rarely used in Quillacollo) rather than the more standard Spanish term *alcalde*. He was then predictably implored to dance a cueca with this cholita, a request he obliged. Given that the Day of the Dead takes place mere days before bian-nual regional elections, in past years this particular wallunk'a has been heav-ily attended by local authorities. The owners of the chichería recalled how the different candidates came "with their people" and dressed in the "caps and T-shirts" of their respective political parties. Party members also handed out political flyers to the attendees, encouraging people to vote for their can-didate. As a regional cultural event, the wallunk'a was one part folklore fes-tival and one part politics.

The politicization of these folkloric venues has become so standard that it is a frequent cause for complaint. One folkloric festival organizer lamented to me the necessity of having to, in his words, "prostitute culture" in order to bring off the festival at all. Consider this representative complaint by an out-raged woman, herself uninvolved in local politics, which appeared in a sec-tion of the regional newspaper dedicated to news from the provinces:

The rural markets [ferias] and fiestas are one of the few opportunities in which the inhabitants of communities can come together: friends, compadres, relatives, authorities, etc., in order to share and converse together, around a provocative pitcher of chicha, or around a succulent chicharrón *[a regional dish of deep fat fried pork parts], gossiping about conceptions that reflect at once religion, the national reality [read: politics], and other peculiarities, confined to the daily tasks in the furrows: planting, care of crops, and harvest.*

But, given the nearness of the elections, very curious things take place. It is a different environment, with a strange flurry of activity.

One Sunday, I met with the members of a community in order to participate with them in a religious event, prepared for this date. There appeared suddenly a small vehicle, up until now unknown by the locals. From the vehicle descended three persons. And then, Oh, pre-electoral magic! In the blink of an eye, they inundated us with political propaganda. And we, stupefied, asked ourselves: "But how did they know to find us meeting here?" Then, one of the group responded, "These types have eyes everywhere…"

Yes, the above tale is nothing but a paradox, given the amount of times that those sorts are seen in these parts. But something important that should deserve the attention of all who aspire to arrive at the precious seat of power is, without doubt, whether those who look for aid or support in order to rise to their political offices [cargos políticos] *also know how to respond from above to the needs of the forgotten areas of our territory. [Colque 1993]*

This is an all-too-familiar parable of the "ambush," as the article put it, of rural festive occasions by political parties. Note the idealized portrait of provincial fiestas as moments of collective communitas that form the backdrop for political meddling. This perceived politicization of regional folklore was part of the decadence many feel threatens the region's cultural integrity. When clumsily done, indeed it might depersonalize political efforts to promote intimate cultural ties that, as symbolic currency, depend for their effectiveness upon a conviction of the presence of that very intimacy (compare Herzfeld 1997:1–36).

Not everyone approved of the revival of the wallunk'a. This traditional practice, they felt, has been "given over to electrified musical groups and the sale of chicha." It has been reduced to little more than advertisement. Exclaimed one disenchanted local, "All they do is teach a few cholitas to attract people to the establishment." In the case of the wallunk'a, in fact, a similarly decadent machination can be said to culturally inform the work of politics. In point of fact, a client of the mayor used his sister's establishment to provide a public forum for his political patron. In so doing, the cholita, as a ubiquitous folkloric figure, functioned as the medium for the accomplishment of political work. Politicians seek out the presence of the woman de pollera as a symbol of the llakta, as self-consciously traditional, and as a key to the intimate political backstage of the household and of the chichería. Despite the accusations of prostitution, events such as the wallunk'as generate political surplus value through the access they provide, courtesy of the mediatory role of the chola, to a traditional cultural identity.

The Chola's Decadence

Nowadays in and around Quillacollo people entertain a looming pessimism about the future cultural integrity of the traditional figure of the chola. One hears a widely uttered conviction that she might soon disappear entirely from view, trading in her pollera for pants or modern skirts. This in part explains the nostalgic tone often adopted when considering the chola's plight, detectable in the social alienation identified with the perceived trend of women opting out of the pollera, voiced earlier in this chapter. Complaints varied. But they included concern that the shrinking hemline of the pollera in the festival entradas amounts to a gross distortion of traditional values. Returning to Quillacollo for a visit in 2001, the man who had been the town's mayor in the mid-1990s lamented to me at length the decline of its weekly market—still an important way station for agricultural products. Women who once carried potatoes in woven shawls (called *awayos*) are now more likely to use plastic bags. Now vendors are too engrossed in their telenovelas to bother with offering a yapa, neglecting their responsibilities to their caseros.[19] This, to his mind, is the negative consequence of "modernity."

The sense of things out of joint is comparable to local rhetoric about political corruption, such as the use of the prebenda. I even met with such talk when attending a town beauty pageant. The complaint was that the girls competing were no longer all from Quillacollo itself. As one founder of a local dance fraternity, a woman, stated the problem, "If we talk about the current chola cochabambina, now with her short pollera, high heels, and makeup, she is no longer authentic." This woman, de vestido, who worked as a hair stylist, had sought to counter this, striving to "move against the principle of exhibitionism" and to "not treat the woman as a commodity," by founding a fraternity that promotes the "costume of the authentic Qhochala." With increasing regularity, such authentic Qhochalas are on public display only during moments of folkloric performance. But I have explored some of the ways that this can also be understood as a renewed expression of urban indigenous identity, which in fact incorporates the felt crisis of the potential disappearance of traditional lifeways.

Commenting on the omnipresent political propaganda, with which I began this discussion, a friend who has worked with various political parties in Quillacollo over the years offered me some choice words about the decadence of traditional regional identities:

> [The political parties] wanted to identify themselves with this symbol of the valley. But well-adorned cholas, with earrings and hat…are no more! She [the chola of political propaganda] is a fictitious chola. She no longer exists. There has been a change in costume, in colors, with polleras designed in Europe. It's a transformation of fashion. Now we have the modern chola. There's an evolution in the form of dress. Her undergarments of the past are no more [laughing]! There aren't any more plain handwoven polleras. Her hat is no longer of the stovepipe variety. Now it is lighter and made in Panamá. She sports a sweater made in Brazil.... I believe that there is a conflict. This [the political propaganda] will distort matters. The original chola is no longer.

A notable characteristic of these criticisms about the chola garb giving way to modern dress styles is that what counts as modern is the dispersion of the local into the global, and so, the perceived loss of regional cultural fixity. Notable as well is the fact that these criticisms were all voiced by men and women, de vestido to be sure, in variously close and active relations to the local political arena. It is, in short, the people who are most politically active in Quillacollo who seem most concerned about the possibility that the chola might disappear into the global flux. This is odd, in a sense, given that it is also this same political class that most doggedly adheres to a local rhetoric of development and modernization for the town. But then we have to remind ourselves what sorts of cultural resources popular politicians utilize to be successful in the provincial electoral context.

A permanent problem in Quillacollo's politics is the relationship of cultural self-identity and social status to political representation. In part, this chapter has been concerned with what it means to represent Bolivia's various increasingly urban indigenous-descended popular sectors throughout the period of neoliberal democratization. The twinned national policies of privatization and decentralization have encouraged the blossoming of an elaborate yearlong calendar of folklore festivals in Quillacollo, with the chola cult at its center. If the administration of Evo Morales has ushered in a new era of indigenous empowerment, the experience of indigenous peoples, moving to cities, working in the informal economy, and living on the urban margin, is still significantly neoliberal in shape. Charles Hale's (2006) discussion of indigenous cultural rights in Guatemala makes clear the extent to which "neoliberal multiculturalism" has opened up important spaces of indigenous empowerment, even as it is also a form of governmentality designed to shape indigenous concerns in keeping with dominant state-driven concerns and policy. Nancy Postero (2007b) has effectively demonstrated for Bolivia how collective efforts to organize among indigenous Guaranís in Santa Cruz are powerfully shaped in the terms of an "indigenous citizenship" that encourages indigenous peoples to act as neoliberal subjects. To this set of concerns I have added a closer focus upon the cultural mediatory channels that traverse traditional and neoliberal technologies of the self and the extent to which what it means to be "indigenous" has been actively transformed and expanded in the process. In peri-urban Quillacollo this has happened through the mobilization and revival of recognized and local cultural resources, such as the industrious and enterprising traditional and neoliberal chola.

In my experience politically engaged individuals in Quillacollo constantly sought to demonstrate access to the interior spaces of regional popular culture. Hence they pursued intimate but public relationships with those women who traditionally control and mediate the interior recesses of cultural identity, in the home, the marketplace, and the chichería, as a way to build up political networks among themselves. As I have explored, male políticos frequently delivered economic staples to women's groups, as half of an exchange typical of the regional political and development contexts. These exchange relationships were made the basis for the popular spectacularization of intimacy. Organized by local male political representatives, these theaters of exchange are one way that they can become political clients of the regional leaders who provide the goods and services to the zone. While goods pertaining to the domestic economy visibly changed hands from men to women, in fact, these were really exchanges among men.[20]

Across the various cultural frames of reference we have considered—the matriarchal domestic economy, the cult of the Virgin, fiesta libations, folkloric parades, agricultural and folkloric festivals, indigenist regional literature, the wallunk'a, different traditional forms of Andean reciprocal exchange, and so on—I have emphasized the woman de pollera as a protagonist and cultural shifter in the mediation between popular and indigenous identities in peri-urban Quillacollo. In short, she both constitutes the traditional frames of reference within which political events happen and provides men with a means of personal attachment to the indigenous world, while also embracing social mobility, by way of the pastoral field, market, fiesta, romance, and drinking establishment. This is the case even as such politics were talked about by women themselves as a kind of adultery and as an excellent example of the Machiavellian duplicity that both women and men freely associate with the política criolla. In fact, the very ubiquity of the chola's image in politics stands in inverse relation to the participation of women from indigenous and popular backgrounds in Quillacollo's municipal politics.

However, we are now in a better position, I think, to appreciate the anxiety especially voiced by political types over the apparently inevitable passing of the traditional chola from the social landscape. They were anxious about a potential loss of access to such sources of attachment and the opportunities for cultural intimacy they provide. They recognized the chola as popular currency and cultural capital. If the chola indeed "modernizes," políticos will have that much less to hang their hats on and perhaps even find themselves politically cut off from the interior spaces of regional popular culture that are the sources of arguments about the changing terms of indigenous and popular belonging. There would thus be fewer avenues for popular legitimation in other than the most transparently and stereotypically folkloric terms.

5 Patrimonial Pendejadas

Self-Prospecting and Cultural Estrangement

The taxi ride from Cota to the chichería, past zigzagging fields of alfalfa, corn, and pasturing cows, was cramped and bumpy. I had accompanied three leaders of Quillacollo's federation of street traders—composed primarily of families of recent in-migrants and ex-miners—to this semirural periphery as part of a fact-finding trip with five town councilmen to confirm that the federation's purchase of 6 hectares of land in Cota had been legal. Illegal land speculation was rampant in this sparsely settled zone. And despite lengthy negotiations the location of the tract so close to the chapel of the town's patroness, the Virgin of Urkupiña, was unpopular with the councilmen. The municipality wanted no interference with the Virgin's yearly fiesta, which was a lucrative source of public revenue. At the same time, the town's rapidly increasing population over the past two decades had precipitated the hasty and largely unregulated settlement of the nearby periphery.[1] The street traders, in their turn, suspected personal motives on the part of at least one councilman, Santos Rojas, who, rumor had it, wanted them to buy a nearby plot of land from him instead.

After a walking inspection by the councilmen, which included frequent mention of the need for further "technical study," the *dirigentes* managed to persuade their counterparts to accept an invitation to drink. A night spent drinking might help to establish the mutual trust (confianza) they needed to work out a compromise and finally to extract the long-delayed municipal blessing recognizing their "right of ownership" to land they had in fact already paid for and that would be used to build homes for families of six-teen unions currently without. As the taxi wended its way to the chichería, the three leaders debated. What drink should they offer? One suggested beer. Why not chicha? I asked. He made a tie-knotting motion, adding, "Now they don't drink it." As is true throughout the Andes, even seemingly casual public drinking in Quillacollo, especially of chicha, can quickly become a ritualized affair, during which social hierarchies are asserted, polit-ical relationships are solidified, conviviality can be converted into reciprocal obligations, community can be confirmed, and popular-indigenous cultural belonging can be negotiated.[2] What to offer merits careful consideration.

Once assembled at the chichería the councilmen sat arrayed on one side of the table, with the traders on the other. Bottles of beer and glasses were brought but only for the municipal officials. A bucket of chicha, meanwhile, was placed on the end of the table nearest the traders. One of the dirigentes hastily served beer to each of the councilmen in a glass, while they them-selves served each other chicha out of bowls (tutumas). Not far into the evening, the traders "invited" their counterparts to chicha. Three accepted the invitation straightaway, downing their tutumas in a few draughts, as is the expectation. Two declined, including Rojas, citing recent surgery and a sore throat, respectively. They sipped cokes. There was discussion of the chicha's quality. As the night drew on, food was eventually served, and peo-ple continued to invite one another and to tip their bowls to the Pachamama. The traders and councilmen then got down to business, with free-flowing discussion of present and related concerns. These included the problem of the increasing number of street traders clogging Quillacollo's main arteries who would have to be displaced during the days of the fiesta of Urkupiña—a controversial issue, since these are the days during which people stand to profit the most. (In fact three months later, and just days prior to the event, the municipality's attempt to remove sellers' kiosks from the town center precipitated a riot.)

Three buckets of chicha were emptied—a modest total. One of the traders explained that he never drank beer but exclusively chicha, especially (and pointedly, considering Rojas) when he was not feeling well or had a sore throat, "to cure myself." (In fact I often heard people attribute medici-nal properties to chicha.) One of the councilmen playfully berated Rojas for his refusal of chicha, particularly given that I was drinking it, so he eventu-ally grudgingly accepted a bowl only to sip it. Jokes were shared, the major-ity in Quechua, and only by the municipal representatives. Always sensitive to impressions, at one point Rojas directed a humorous Quechua harangue in my direction, which I could not follow, to put me in my place, to the

Figure 5.1. The entrance to one of Quillacollo's many drinking establishments advertising its good chicha.

general mirth of all present. Traders and councilmen alike commented on the "sweet" and "pretty" qualities of Quechua and on its expressive superiority to Spanish. After several hours of this, the local officials contrived to exit the scene, over mild protests from the traders, who stayed on to drink for some time afterward.

Negotiations of this sort are commonplace in Quillacollo's politics. They are one of the ways that functional political relationships are built and maintained. Drinking together is a promising moment of "sharing" (*convivencia*) (Figure 5.1). The ambience of the chichería, too, is, a privileged cultural space within which interpersonal politics are conducted. The reciprocal invitations to drink, gradual switch from beer to chicha, telling of jokes, and pointed discussions of the traditional value of chicha and Quechua all emphasized that the "ample democracy" (Rodriguez and Solares 1990:142) of the chichería provides people with the expressive opportunity to take up a popular Andean identity, on the basis of which they can actively facilitate political relationships. If a circumstantial or situational conviviality, such moments are opportunities to effectively orient cultural heritage to political ends.

Viewed by the street traders as the major obstructor on the town council to their plans for Cota, Santos Rojas was often criticized by the leadership of the traders' unions during the many months this process dragged on. His equivocation at the chichería appeared to validate their concerns. One of them described his conduct on the council toward them as patronizing. Another complained Rojas acted as if he were "king of Quillacollo." He was quick to add that Rojas "used to wear sandals"; that is, despite his attitude he comes from "peasant" (campesino) stock. Around this time, too, Rojas often appeared in public in suit and tie, briefcase in hand, and sporting embroidered leather cowboy boots. At another moment the same dirigente volunteered that Rojas used to be "poorer than we are now" but that he has become a "*desclasado*"—someone who rejects his own past. The individual who sold the land at Cota to the traders, a potential Rojas competitor, was also very critical. He labeled Rojas "aggressive," a "robber," and a "hick" (*rústico*). Santos Rojas, he categorically asserted, "no longer cares about the humble folk." What it means to be "humble" was a basic matter of contention in the relationship between the street traders and the municipal authorities, as it often is in Quillacollo. And it was, in part, the negotiation of the recognition of a shared humble background that the original night of reciprocal invitations to drink had been about.

Family and Patrimony

Such attention to the recognition of the particulars of relatedness, heritage, and descent is part of a broader cultural argument in Quillacollo about identity, which we might describe as concerned with the implications of *patrimony*.[3] The concept of patrimony in this context, as concerned with ancestry and heritage, is a formulation with historical specificity in Latin America. Typically patrimonies are discussed throughout the region as birthrights "inherited from our parents [*padres*]" (Zelada 2001), variously mobilized often to dramatize the eternal verities of national origins presented as a fixed, timeless, and even spiritual essence (for Latin America, see Alonso 1988; Rowe and Schelling 1991). Such national patrimonies are regularly archived in museums, represented by sacred objects, the subject of *costumbrista* national arts and letters, recorded and performed as folklore, or presented as the rationale for public festivals. Perhaps above all else, national patrimonies provide a cultural genealogy of the sources of nationhood.

As Javier Sanjinés's (2004:35) excellent discussion of early-twentieth-century modernist and liberal Bolivian nation builders makes clear, these men tended to exhibit a "combination of pride, nostalgia and fascination with the Indian, while at the same time demonstrating repugnance for any breaking of racial boundaries." The Indian race, therefore, was to be "studied, disciplined, and exalted under an enlightened, paternalistic, and authoritarian political order."[4] In the context of the formation of national identity, the "Indian question" was most often folded into the national patrimony as a noble cultural heritage of the distant past best represented by the civilizational legacies of the Inca and of Tiwanaku and ambivalently expressed through the many-stranded midcentury discourse of indigenismo. Meanwhile, the "degenerate" indigenous peoples of the present had no place in the future of the nation and were to be culturally incorporated into the national mestizo ideal. Conceived and critiqued in such terms, however, the relevance of patrimony is constrained to the space of the nation. Here, I am concerned instead with the relevance of patrimony as part of a more boundary-transgressing and everyday popular experience in Quillacollo.

García Canclini has productively criticized this fixing of national patrimonies, insisting that patrimonies are neither settled nor principally about the establishment of national authenticity. He has suggested, instead, that more attention be given to the social uses of patrimony now reformulated in the terms of cultural capital. This means not representing it as a set of stable values or meanings "but rather as a social process that, like the other kind of capital, is accumulated, reconverted, produces yields, and is appropriated" (1995:136). This chapter is concerned with how Quillacollo's urban indigenous and popular classes, in García Canclini's (1995:133) words, reconstitute their own patrimony through the "memory of what was lost and reconquered." This is particularly characteristic of so-called cholos, people like Santos Rojas (and the street traders for that matter), who arguably compose a majority of the town's population and who are often described as people conspicuous for having "no firm definition" and having "forgotten their past" or who are accused of being "desclasados." These are people publicly criticized for their dubious or unreliable relationship to representations of their own origins and status, as they are accused of actively seeking to suppress a stigmatized indigenous descent. And yet, as I pursue here, it is this same cholo population that, at least in Quillacollo, is also actively engaged in renegotiating its own circumstances and, in so doing, the terms of reference of an increasingly urban indigenous experience.

Patrimony, as I am concerned with it, is primarily an everyday political process: constituted by public performances; political discourse composed of debate, criticism, rumor, hearsay, anecdote, and humor; and the substance of narrations of self and acts of strategic forgetting, which participate in the construction of political relationships (Figure 5.2).[5] If the political style of cholos—problematically mobile betwixt and between the Indian and mestizo worlds—taxes our descriptive powers in categorical or definitional terms, this chapter explores the construction of the public relevance of ancestry or cultural heritage, as patrimony, produced in the ubiquitous disjunctions or interstices between generations, in particular between fathers and sons. The sharp estrangement of personal displacement and loss is here entangled with active reference to the past, and to family origins, for the contemporary construction of popular and indigenous cultural belonging. This is at once an arena of partial recognition, which also helps to enable the possibility for collaboration and alliance building in the political context.

My focus on questions of patrimony is not casual. The term has become increasingly publicly legible in Bolivia of late. One expression of this is its growing legal usage in national legislation, as an extension of a steady departure from the discourse of mestizaje, including Bolivia's most recent constitutional reform recognizing the country's "pluricultural and multiethnic" identity. The Ley Orgánica de Municipalidades, revised in 1985 as part of a package of decentralization measures, defines municipal resources as patrimony (patrimonio)—as collective inheritance and property. This measure was further enhanced by 1994's Popular Participation Law, which consolidated the category of cultural patrimony or heritage as a basis for local political claim making. In part on the basis of such national legislation, throughout the early and mid-2000s indigenous and grassroots social movement activists opted for the language of patrimony to claim their collective rights to such resources as water and gas (see Albro 2005b). Finally, Bolivia's new Constitution, approved by its constitutional assembly in late 2007 and by Bolivia's legislature in early 2009, refers to the term some thirty times. Patrimonial references to "humble" and other kinds of ancestry were regular occurrences in Quillacollo during my fieldwork, providing a readily recognizable frame of reference within which the personal and the intimate were brought together with the public and the categorical.

Patrimony is an overdetermined preoccupation among Quillacolleños of all sorts. If I am examining the explicitly political implications of patrimony, there are many other illustrations of its importance for the significantly transient population of this town. Ancestry and heritage are central subjects of regular family-level ritual events in Quillacollo. Remembrance of the dead

Figure 5.2. Politics and heritage: Quillacollo's mayor participating in a practice session with a local fraternity of *tinku* dancers.

is most widely celebrated during Todos Santos, or All Saints, the first three days of November.[6] This is a ceremony of public recognition of immediate relatives who have recently passed away. People construct "tombs" (called *mast'akus*) in the family room of the house or in the cemetery itself for at least three years after the death of a loved one, called a *mosoq aya* (recently dead). During Todos Santos the spirits of the dead are lured back home with the food and drink they most enjoyed in life, which is prepared and left for them on the altar, along with traditional baked goods in the shapes of animals, angels, and babies. Family members, nearby relatives, fictive kin, friends, and acquaintances all stop by to share in the food and drink and to reminisce. The following day the family makes a trip to the cemetery to chase the wandering soul back into the grave. Along with Todos Santos are many family-level rituals, usually called misachikus, celebrated six months and one year after someone dies, where people again convene to eat, drink, mourn, and recall the dead. These collective ritual events foreground death and public memory of the dead. They also emphasize the extension and maintenance of kinship with dead relatives as an active relationship that requires regular attention.

And as I have explored in much greater detail elsewhere (see Albro 2000), cultural activists in Quillacollo, including journalists, writers, teachers, politicians, and folkloric performers of various sorts, have in different ways and over an almost twenty-five-year period circulated many dozens of short sketches of illustrious local citizens as well as biographies of lesser-known people. Most recently, and often coordinated with the work of the municipality's three-person Department of Culture,[7] these short biographical sketches have appeared in the regional newspaper, *Los Tiempos*, as well as in a variety of more local circulars, in order to communicate, in the words of the activists themselves, the many "untold stories" or "little-known facts" of Quillacollo's history through its popular protagonists and as a way to cure the region's "cultural rheumatism." These efforts have self-consciously been intended to invite people to reacquaint themselves with their own—apparently displaced—cultural legacy. The discourse and practice of patrimony, in several registers, is a publicly available means to actively assert a cultural affiliation.

Marilyn Ivy (1995) has written compellingly and in similar terms about the active memorialization of ancestors on Mount Osore in Japan. In addition to allowing people to work through their grief, she explains, the rituals on Mount Osore facilitate the process of settling the dead into their status as beneficial ancestors. If in a different way, people in Quillacollo also engage in self-consciously traditional efforts to transform their ancestral relationships into "objects of positive knowledge" (Ivy 1995:181). In these and other ways, many of which I describe throughout this book, everyday forms of public patrimonial claim making have in the past quarter century come to be a basic idiom for the negotiation of the overlapping and expanding cultural boundaries of popular and indigenous cultural belonging in local politics.

Indigenous Identity and the Desclasado

People often volunteered to me accounts of their own humble beginnings. Typical was the reminiscence of one former local authority who watched his father cry in embarrassment and shame because his family had for years been reduced to eating only "flour, freeze-dried potatoes, broad beans, and animal fat." These accounts—images of past suffering crystallized in telling anecdotes—were ruefully offered up by many as concise justifications for their current political investments. When invited to reflect upon the sources of his long-term political activism, a local municipal authority offered the following:

> I lost my father when I was three. We had to work together, myself from
> about eight or nine years of age,...in selling. We sold anything, any-
> thing that we had, from pastries, to sweets, to gum.... Perhaps it's
> good—all that happened to me—because this stage of life gave me, as
> a kid, a certain maturity to undertake the correct road for my future.
> We were six people, three boys and three girls. All siblings. At first, I
> sold sweets. I sold cups of gelatin in the streets.... Sometimes we shared
> in a lot of suffering, when children in better economic straits insulted
> us, humilliated us, offended us. It was a very sad moment.... For that
> reason I feel happy and proud of the past.

During years of fieldwork, I was told and recorded many dozens of such anecdotes, presented as tales of growing up in the informal economy. The above story, told by someone new to politics, projected his humble beginnings onto a memory of loss, the death of his father—a ubiquitous source of estrangement among Quillacollo's politically active class. His father's sudden absence precipitated family disaster. But as recalled—a time of difficulty *and* of opportunity—the anecdote also displays a characteristic ambivalence about a past that is instrumental for this individual's current political pursuits: a pride in the past and success in the long road taken at significant personal cost. These humble beginnings are perhaps the most important explanation offered for his role as a local authority representing a popular and indigenous constituency hard hit by chronic poverty and job insecurity, circumstances that have been exacerbated throughout Bolivia's neoliberal era.

When asked to talk about his own origins, another political acquaintance and town councilman recalled his childhood in the Potosí mines, where "life punished us." When pushed, he elaborated:

> Well, we all hope to improve things. It's normal, natural.... But that
> doesn't mean that you forget what you've always been.... I'm proud of

who I am, of what I do, of what I think, of what I feel. I feel very iden-
tified with myself, with all that I have. If I have defects, magnificent!
Like any human, I accept it. Poorly founded pride is when one lives
superficially. Well-founded pride is when one accepts his reality as a
person, as a man. And this is translated into personality.... But, with
myself, I don't change because I don't forget my origins. I don't forget
my ancestors. It's something I keep within, which I have for myself. And
on the outside I can change twenty thousand times.

These sorts of reminiscences, common enough, make it clear that social and cultural origins are treated as the product of heaped-up experience that—as recalled experiences of gender and of kinship—correspond to and provide the representative authority of identity. Recognizing these ancestral debts means accepting one's "reality as a person." As examples of what Debbora Battaglia (1995:93), in her discussion of urban Trobriand politicians, has called self-prospecting, these kinds of accounts amount to a cultural "extension toward sources." As "humble" patrimonial claims, they have a culturally connective purpose in a context of regular social displacement.

The work of political networking I described at the outset of this chapter is an important part of the ways that indigenous inclusion is expanding in urban Bolivia in relation to these humble sources of identification and in proximity to the work of provincial and municipal politics. But consider the example of Cassio Buenavides. Though he was born in the city of Cochabamba, he explained, his parents were from the nearby highlands of Tapacarí, a onetime haven of the provincial elite but now an isolated and primarily "Indian town." In fact Quillacollo's cemetery is dominated by the mausoleums of former gente decente families who once upon a time composed the pre-1952 oligarchic and landowning elite, with many from Tapacarí, the provincial seat until 1901, after which the honor switched to Quillacollo. He called his father a "small landowner" (*terrateniente pequeño*), and Buenavides even exclaimed to me once that he enjoyed the benefits of "Indian servants" (*pongueaje*) as a child. But then the 1953 Agrarian Reform expropriated his parents' land, and the family relocated to a peripheral barrio of the city. His father became a "petty merchant" (*comerciante*), selling *muñapo*, used in the elaboration of chicha, to the mining centers of the interior while also maintaining a small milk farm on one hectare, which Buenavides still owns and works.

He asserted that this allowed his family to keep a tenuous hold on the "middle class," despite their fall from grace, and enabled Cassio to study, though he never finished. Buenavides is currently a schoolteacher, studying at night to be a lawyer and living a simple and spartan bachelor's life on the unfinished second floor of a brick building in Quillacollo's colonial-era center. He often regaled me with tales of the many chances he has passed up to climb aboard the lunch wagon, including his direct access as a client to national-level political figures like the former populist dictator René Barrientos, opting instead for his political service to the folk of "humble origin." This rhetoric of service appeared calculated in part to distance himself from the figure of the llunk'u, the debased and fawning political client and pervasive cholo type that was the subject of chapter 2.

Cassio Buenavides is a raconteur. But many others were blunt in suggesting that the man does not match the story. Numerous people claim to have been patrones, they added, when they are really de origen humilde and when they are confident their bluff cannot be called. They pointed to Buenavides's "error-ridden" popular Spanish vernacular as proof that his father never spoke Spanish, let alone properly.[8] They also pointed to his idiomatic Quechua and extensive familiarity with, among other things, popular drinking customs—all characteristics that make him a very able provincial político. There was even the suggestion that his last name has been changed to a more "noble" Spanish one. His local nickname, Enano (Dwarf), not only associates Cassio with often malevolent creatures of popular folklore but also works as a racial jab at his pretensions, implicitly identifying him with the small-built Andean male.

In short, many concluded that he is most likely one or another sort of *campesino desclasado*. In fact Buenavides's own raucous accounts of political proselytizing have him chewing (*p'ischar*) coca, drinking chicha, and cagily manipulating diverse Andean relations of exchange in ways comparable to the cultural strategies of reciprocal obligation identified as characteristic of rural market traders (see Lagos 1994), all facts that undercut or at least qualify his claim to be a product of the bottom end of a now-fallen provincial elite. If details vary, Buenavides's is a not atypical kind of local and urban political career, reliant upon intimate familiarity with indigenous and popular cultural capital, however derived, rather than in the familiar mode of populist-type patronage.

In Quillacollo—and elsewhere in Bolivia—one of the ways the experience of estrangement is publicly expressed is through rejection and suppression of an underprivileged or indigenous past, epitomized by the figure of the *cholo desclasado*. This is a term—often employed—that does not sharply distinguish ethnicity from class but makes explicit the ways that, if not simply overlapping, class and ethnicity are often mutually constitutive.[9] The desclasado, people explained, is understood to relentlessly pursue upward social mobility, including its ethnic and cultural trappings, in the process actively abandoning or forgetting prior family and friends. The controversial desclasado was described by one acquaintance to me this way:

The desclasado is that person who, being humble, of humble origins, a simple man, a person who has always been part of the goings-on in the pueblo,...suddenly from night to day appears in a respectable situation. Yesterday that person shared in a conversation, in an institution, a fiesta, a social happening. Suddenly he appears not to know the people with whom one day, at least, he shared a drink. He feels contempt for these same friends, compañeros, who are below.

A desclasado, then, removes himself from traditional—explicitly Andean—cultural contexts and pointedly denies any involvement with the social obligations potentially imposed by such contexts. Another person added, "If one is talking of desclasados, they are those who, when they have money or some profession, forget who they were." He continued:

I say, and ratify, that if years pass I must remain the same person! Definitively, there can be no change, because that would be to leave behind who you are [desclasarse]. Whatever other change, it would automatically be to forget yourself.... Some professionals who sprang from humble people, of humble origin, or poor, and known in town by people of their age, thanks to life have had the luck of studying to become a professional. But once professionals, they have forgotten their class, their origin, their point of departure. Now they believe themselves superior to people and do not recognize the humble folk, the people from whom they sprang. These are people who forget themselves. I believe there are many such types here in Quillacollo.

As this commentary suggests, poverty and humble origins are not always the same. The former implies economic straits, whereas the latter is connected to a cultural legacy. For yet someone else, desclasados "come from our ancestral culture." He elaborated:

We have an origin, a past, in which we should found our lives.... The most Indian [morenito], the ugliest, feels humiliated, offended, and so intends to hide his origins, wearing fashionable clothes, and intending to be what he is not.... But upon acquiring these new things, what this does not permit you to do is to reject your past, your origin.

Those who do not want "to recognize their own identity...put on a mask and afterward come out against this same identity." To be a desclasado, then, is to exhibit an antagonistic relation to one's own past, as both an economic and a cultural condition, and a desire to publicly erase it. This includes a circumspect estrangement from an ostensibly "humble" past expressed as evasiveness about one's family background. We might say the desclasado is accused of practicing a daily strategy of what Nietzsche (1967:58) once called "active forgetfulness."

Trivial acts like rejecting an invitation to chicha in favor of a bottle of beer are interpreted as acts of desclasado types. Drinking chicha is an archetypical cultural act in and around Quillacollo and throughout Bolivia. People in Quillacollo refer to chicha as the "elixir of the Inca." One local cultural activist noted that "despite the many centuries," it is something that has "been maintained," and it is "a drink that is ours." A refusal to imbibe is a rejection of popular ancestry. While elaborating upon the behavior of desclasados, several people made use of the well-known aphorism "Un indio que se refina se desafina," loosely translated, "When an Indian puts on airs he is off-tune." Desclasados, then, expose themselves despite their efforts to the contrary.

People constantly reminded one another of this. When told, for example, of a rival's complaint about his lack of professionalism on the town council, a largely self-educated former councilman simply laughed and commented, "As if he never carried buckets of water for the butchers!" As the criticisms of the street traders made clear earlier in this chapter, Santos Rojas certainly seemed to exhibit the attitude of the desclasado. And the accusation worked to put him in his place, as it were, by reintroducing his humble beginnings. And yet despite such accusations, as we will see, Rojas himself was not shy about his deprived upbringing or his cultural connections to an indigenous ancestry. In Quillacollo's popular-indigenous urban environment, the discourse of the desclasado is, increasingly often, part of a pervasive political strategy of humble origins. That is, from the point of view of the accuser or the critic, it is a foil for active acceptance (rather than rejection) of the virtues (rather than stigma) of indigenous ancestry as cultural and political capital. The apparent ubiquity of desclasados is one way that indigenous concerns are reintroduced into the politics of urban Quillacollo by those seeking to claim more authentic ground as popular figures.

Family and Estrangement

In the simplest terms, the years since 1952 have seen the near-total disintegration of provincial oligarchic privilege alongside a notable urbanization and mobility among families from indigenous and popular backgrounds. Since the period of structural adjustment beginning in 1985, the peripheral urban and political context of Quillacollo has continued to be characterized by an exponentially expanding informal economy (and the informalization of society as a whole), in-migration,[10] social mobility, the confounding of sharp distinctions of class and ethnicity, and an emerging urban indigenous experience. Nor is social mobility simply upward. It is also increasingly sideways and down. Quillacollo's political space contains as many stories of fallen elites as of upwardly mobile people of indigenous descent or ex-workers from impoverished backgrounds. If once reliable, distinctions between town and country, the peasantry, the workers, and the artisanal and traditional political classes no longer describe the political scene of this small city particularly well. "Indigenous" is now a category variably inhabited by professionals, factory workers, traders, and campesinos alike, if in different ways and not without conflicts. And these people, from a variety of family and work settings, find common ground in the idioms and practices of the everyday negotiation of patrimony.

Despite their diverse backgrounds and regardless of whether their patrimonial inheritance is cast in positive or negative terms, politically engaged people constantly remind themselves and others that "we shouldn't reject, or forget, our origins." This injunction is often voiced as the demand of memory: "I continue communicating with, continue seeing, this previous life that I've lived." Such sentiments reflect the tension introduced by the need to address the question of personal continuity *through* diverse experiences of displacement and social mobility.[11] As recalled, daily bread, a house with no door, a bowl of chicha, Todos Santos altars, freeze-dried potatoes, and cups of gelatin all become personal and cultural points of reference incorporated into often striking self-representional efforts, as examples of what James Fernandez (1986:236) has called "images predicated upon the inchoate"[12]—in this case the estrangement that is a part of urban indigenous experience.

These experiences also include the increasingly ubiquitous social fact, even more pervasive throughout the neoliberal period, of displaced ancestry. In particular, people often never come to know their fathers well or share the same social space with them. Participation in the regional labor circuit as a seller, buyer, or transporter; high rates of semipermanent male out-migration in search of work, mostly to the cities of Argentina; or significant periods when the children are sent to live with more prosperous relatives all mean that fathers often become intermittent and transient social facts of their children's formative years. As well, a significant number of locally active políticos have come to Quillacollo from elsewhere, leaving their families (and family histories) behind. Instances of this last sort have increased dramatically with the recent wave of itinerant and mostly Aymara-speaking ex-miners (*relocalizados*), represented in Quillacollo by the growing population of street traders, as well-publicized casualties of structural adjustment. All of this has meant that a person's family history, particularly in the public but intimate forum of politics, was a frequent source of speculation throughout my research.

Despite the evident regional preoccupation with family relations as determinant of social status and cultural identity, the exact relationship between father and son—as represented by the many intergenerational details of heritage ostensibly linking them—was in the majority of cases murky at best and often actively and jealously kept in the shadows. This became apparent in an uncomfortable situation I created for myself with a clumsy attempt to chat up a former neighbor of Quillacollo's most important political authority, local UCS head Caesar Buendía, for details about his family history. Later I was confronted by one of Buendía's brothers (having been apprised by the neighbor), who warned me in no uncertain terms to stop asking questions.[13]

If inadvertent on my part, the family perceived my work as potentially negative press. Even their political associates agreed that Buendía's family has always been "very closed" (*muy cerrado*) to outsiders. This is not just because of the specter of corruption.[14] It is also because the impression management of family history, in terms of the particularities of social experience and ethnic identity, is a critical part of politics in Quillacollo. These undeniably unhappy experiences of hardship are also public accounts of the relative absence of an elaborated corporate or categorical class standing and ethnic or cultural belonging among political operators. Instead, a well-known and self-evident public genealogy is displaced in the work of impression management by the many details of diverse projects of social mobility.

These details of family history inform, in turn, a set of public arguments about the political relevance of cultural heritage or patrimony in Quillacollo, including the ways people inherit and represent the interests of multiple constituencies: professionals, the popular laboring sectors, members of the informal economy, and small landholding or indigenous peoples. And as the relative proportion of people in Quillacollo has tilted steadily toward people with more recent roots in diverse rural, indigenous, and popular contexts, as well as extensive experience within the laboring and informal economies, political participation in urban and indigenous terms is becoming a status quo.

The Story of Politics as Have-Not

To better understand Santos Rojas's own patrimonial claims we need to touch ethnographic ground with his life in the context of the ubiquitous poverty that has figured in the early years of the lives of so many políticos from "humble origins" in and around Quillacollo. The following fragment of a more extensive life history I recorded with Rojas, as an up-and-coming politician, is a graphic illustration of the often-turbulent, deeply ambivalent, and—I want to emphasize—productively culturally murky status of fathers in the dynamics of local family life.[15] Rather than a simple retrospective, this account is evidently self-constitutive, at once "history and fairytale," to borrow from Vincent Crapanzano's (1980:6) apt description of the interpretive strategies of life histories. Rojas's tale of his father's antics and eventual disappearance is itself a representation of his estrangement. And as Rojas's life history account makes apparent, his father's disappearing act is also critical to his own "desire for recognition" (Crapanzano 1980:10). If exceptional in its many details, Rojas's story of his family's origins is at the same time a negotiation of the local terms of recognition, which actively and publicly develop the contours of his own career as a hard-won claim to a collective cultural patrimony. It was Rojas who invited me to record his life history, and who hoped to publicize it, rather than the other way around. And this narrative fragment is a representation of his self-conscious pursuit of a popular-indigenous political career in urban Quillacollo.[16]

As Rojas told the story, after his father squandered money on drinking without himself earning a cent, eventually absconding with most of the family's economic resources, Rojas's family, never well-off, was reduced to a hardscrabble life. This was epitomized by his image of the house they lived in—a tiny ramshackle house not even of adobe but of dried brambles and straw cut from the nearby hills, with "no floor, no door, no walls, and no bathroom." As a child, Rojas lived hand to mouth, rarely if ever eating meat. He grew up as a street urchin, running the streets and roving the nearby hills of Quillacollo. He volunteered stories of stealing from others' livestock, orchards, and fields to survive. Rojas's account is a particularly graphic illustration of the extremes in the relations of fathers and mothers to their children's lives. During our first interview he tells of his family's beginnings:

> I would have to take up the origin of how this family is born, because it's something important. If you don't look for the roots, only with difficulty are you going to arrive at the tip. It's in this sense that I want to indicate that my ancestors, that is, my grandparents, have a rich tradition [emphasis mine] in that they took their nuptials without first having known each other. That is, my great-grandparents took note that my grandfather was of a family of merchants in horses and cattle. Therefore, they arranged a marriage. My grandfather was from around Molle-Molle, Saucerancho, and the like. And my grandmother

was from here, from Quillacollo, where we have our house at present. And so, as arranged, the hour for their nuptials arrived, and they knew each other for the first time in the bed! And this was the marriage.

    And since they never before had any relations, they simply came to know each other all at once in the bedroom. As fruit of this a son was soon on its way to being born. But it always was the custom that arranged marriages should be respected, since it was the decision and the desire of the parents. And it was the custom [emphasis mine], no, of the entire community at that time.... And since they didn't know each other before, there existed an incompatibility of characters. So in the end they did not live together. My grandmother lived in one place, and my grandfather in another. My grandmother took the decision of living with my aunt and uncle. Now my grandmother was accustomed to drinking, since her ancestors had owned a chichería. But my grandfather was of another family, who didn't like to drink. It was fruit of this that they separated. There was a schism, no. My grandmother took two children, and my grandfather took two children. From this, I have two uncles who are big drinkers, alcoholics, and two who don't like drinking at all, hardly ever tasting a drop. The first two, who lived with my grandmother, are gregarious folk, who like fiestas. The others, they don't. That is, there's an influence, no.

    In her youth, my mother dedicated herself to commerce. And since at that time the mining centers were in their apogee, and the sale of tin was the peak of the economy... [in her commercial activities] she came to possess a determined quantity of money. Though she was of the age that by custom my grandparents were married,... my mother, with this rigid character [not drinking] rejected many offers of matrimony. There were very good men, from here, from Quillacollo, Quillacolleños, who offered her marriage. But she rejected them. You see, she was already of age, almost thirty-five or thirty-six years old. And so she was going to be too old. At this time my father appeared, more or less in 1955. My parents formalized the marriage. But my father was one of those great hunters after money. He saw that my mother had money. For this, he married out of self-interest [interés]. He was light-skinned [rubio], my father, whether good-looking or not I couldn't say, but of Chilean descent.

Of note in Rojas's account is his explicit emphasis upon the traditional or customary status of arranged marriage in the grandparental generation. The scene is set in terms of a fateful relation of people to established customary practices, from which he is an eventual issue. Note, as well, that Rojas emphasizes the activities of his mother—de pollera—as an industrious and self-made market woman. She represents a traditional—even notorious—cultural figure. The political implications of the evidently gendered qualities of patrimonial inheritance figured prominently in chapter 4. Finally, note the sundering of the family on drinking grounds as well as the contrast between the customary marriage of Rojas's grandparents and the self-interested marriage of his father. These are two of many such narrative disjunctions that emphasize Rojas's problematic relationship to cultural inheritance. He continues:

> Once the marriage was formalized, with the monies she had saved in her commercial activities, my mother soon bought a truck. In Quillacollo at that time, there were barely two people with trucks. We are talking around 1960. No one else had one in Quillacollo, according to the information given me by my mother. So then, my father, since it hadn't been his sacrifice in the purchase of the truck—it hadn't been his money, he hadn't wasted his lungs—seizes it like it was the lottery! He began to take to the road with the truck, forgetting about my mother, going from chichería to chichería. "Look, I have a truck," and so on. And on one of these trips occurred a disgrace. He ran over a child. And since it was one of the first trucks, any kind of accident with a truck was, well, big news.... Since it was a case of just two trucks, the entire population took note of the tragedy. And, as an anecdote in addition, when [my father] went to pay the indemnization for the child who had died, they wanted to take my younger brother with them. "Now you must give up a son. I don't want your money," they said.
>
> Things went along this way, but the fights were born a little from this. My older brother and I came along. My mother is dark-skinned [morenita]. And, you see, my father had never worked, never done anything. He was simply throwing everything away on the truck, which was the fruit of the sacrifice, effort, and self-denial on the part of my mother, who had not been able to make use of those monies. And upon making them available and trusting in my papá, this one was throwing it away all over the place! My mother hit him often. She hit him. You see, he was a person who didn't understand. He came to the house drunk. My mother said to him, "You have to work! You have to work! What are your children going to eat?" The day arrives when he answers her, "Why should I work? Do you want me to swallow my lungs [tragar mis pulmones]?[17] Carajo, I'm not going to work! It's you who has to work! To each his own, since it's the sacrifice of his lungs." "But we have children." "And what do I care about the children?" That is, he showed

no interest in us. "And what's more, they aren't even my children! Because these are dark! My children are light-skinned [literally, joveros]." Since it was my mamá with the dominant gene, I came out the color of my mother and not him. "They're dark, they're ugly," he said.

Set amid a story of social mobility, Rojas makes it clear that his hereditary ancestry is derived not from his father but from his valiant mother. And this identity is "dark," that is, exhibiting indigenous descent. The "grandparents" in his explanation of the family's origin are from her side of the family, while very little is said—or known, one suspects—about the father's family background. Rojas uses his father's ostensibly "whiter" ancestry as a basis not for his own mobility but for separating himself from his father's trajectory. Santos Rojas in fact now lives in his mother's mother's house. He, too, is dark. He also dramatizes the schism between mother and father, the two ancestral lines, as incipient estrangement and in terms of his father's refusal to "work." Rojas's own claim as a *padre de familia*—his narrative of a poor boy who has made good—is meaningfully contingent upon his own father's aggressive rejection of just this role.

As the narrative unfolds, his father's behavior becomes increasingly problematic:

> So things developed in this way. And before this there came a day when my father hit my mother. And my uncle, who was plenty strong—my uncle terrified my father because he always hit him—when he saw him hitting my mother, he tied him up. He grabbed him while he was hitting her. They tied his hands and feet, and garroted, he beat him. And my father cried for help. I remember. "Santos! Santos! I want you to free me, Santos!" He asked for help, saying these things, no. And I, being a sentimentalist, walked over and watched him. In front were my brothers. "Hahahahaha!" they laughed. But I felt pity that he was in this situation. And while I looked, some other people stirred up a small riot and freed him, no.
>
> One time I even ran away from home. Because [my father] lived separated, in the house of his mother. His mother had already died. I was already with my uncle, and I was hungry. I had this uncle, but he was screwed up [fregado]. He didn't give me food. And when one is small, he needs to eat all the time, right. You can't stand hunger, no. When small, you need things. Whatever you can get, you eat. So I climbed up for this coahada [unprocessed cheese], which is for preparing kisillu. I was hungry and wanted to eat the coahada. But the entire container fell on top of me. Out of fear, I fled to the house of papá. I was with my

papá. And I remember he carried me from chichería to chichería. He made me go to all the chicherías. I ate chips, or whatever he gave me.

Then my mother came. I was scared to come to my mother, so that she could punish me for what I had made fall. "Come hijo. You're going to go," she said. My father, saying, "Your son is suffering a lot." But I didn't want to go, saying, "Papi, Papi, my mother's going to come..." So I didn't go. But immediately afterward I began to think, and I returned. When I got home, I arrived in the middle of the night and without shoes. My mother received me nicely. She embraced me nicely. Sunday came, and she bought clothes for my brothers. But for me she bought nothing. I wanted to go with them as well. "No. You stay as punishment. Since you looked for your father, you have to remain in this state. I won't bring you anything." So I cried.

Rojas continues to emphasize the schism between mother and father. While it is clear that his mother's house is where he knows he belongs, it is his father who takes him on the road, from watering hole to watering hole—characteristically popular settings for political networking. From the outset, the theme of drinking is prominent in his account. The family is divided between drinkers and nondrinkers. In other opportunities, he related some of his drinking excesses as a younger man. But, at least at present, Rojas conspicuously does not drink. If, as he noted in another conversation, his brother "follows in my father's footsteps" by drinking chicha hard and often, Rojas is firm that he does not drink or at least rarely drinks. When he makes an exception for chicha, it has a traditional purpose. His comment: "Yes, there are customs. We always invite one another. And I don't lose the customs." An appropriate ch'alla, he noted, provides "a little sustenance to the Pachamama." During fiesta contexts where such expectations are pervasive, he explained to me, he drinks "a little" until he detects the slightest alcoholic effect and then stops. If his personal experience with the chichería has been intimate and if he is conversant with the reciprocal obligations imposed by drinking (particularly as connected to successfully managing one's social relations in the popular milieu more generally), Rojas avoids drunkenness while embracing—even discoursing at length on—the cultural significance of chicha among the popular and indigenous sectors. If he has rejected his father's excesses, he accepts and locates himself within the encompassing cultural world in which they were carried out, although one is reminded of his performance that night drinking with the traders.

Rojas concludes his story of his father:

In this way we lived a constant problem. We continued growing, and one day...my mother carried my father to the police several times, to make him work. But he didn't want to work. He was lazy. Since she knew it was a marriage of convenience and she didn't love him at all, my mother, therefore she cited him because of these problems.... Time passes and they decide to separate. And one day my father arrived. We were sleeping at night. And you see, such was his hatred that he grabbed a stick of dynamite and threw it. The dynamite blew up. My mother left the house, with luck, right when there was the spark [of the fuse]. You see, my father waited the entire night for my mother to come outside to relieve herself. Our house was an open-air type. There was no place to take cover. So he grabbed the dynamite and threw it, for revenge. But my mother saw the spark. She had been headed there, but she didn't go near and the dynamite detonated, throwing her to one side. And afterward my father ran off. That was the last thing he did. From then on he never came back again. I didn't even know where to go to see him. Never again did he come. Afterward he disappeared. I was three, four, or five years old. Small. It was at that time.

This was the path when we were small. There were always people who teased us. That is, they insulted us, because of the poverty in which we lived. Our humble conditions. We had no house.... Once established in school, and my father having forgotten us, my mother made trips to Morochata, to the campo, the rural hamlets. And she bartered [hacía trueque]. She might bring clothes and exchange it for a calf. Or she would bring potatoes. In this way we maintained ourselves. I remember one time, when my mother traveled there, my father carried us off from here, the three siblings. He carried us off and beat us. He was a type, I think, who was sick in the head. From where does his disappointment spring?

Rojas's father came and went as the mood took him. As depicted by the son, his father was shiftless, unreliable, unpredictable, and even violent. His indefatigable mother, on the other hand, served as the family rock and moral compass. Despite the violent tension between husband and wife, his mother worked doggedly for the family's survival, while his father wasted what she earned on failed schemes of upward mobility. Rojas claimed to have taken little from his father except the legacy of paternal abuse, early departure, and extreme economic hardship. These are the key features, however, of his "humble" social origins, even if forced on the family by his father's irresponsibility.

In a later interview, Rojas reflected on his childhood years with his father and emphasized how he has repressed these experiences as a public aspect of his self-identity. As an adult, he can only "cry within" (*llorar por adentro*). Rojas now gives little thought to his father, talking little about him. And yet the "rancor" he harbors about these years is what he offered as the principal reason for his present political commitments. Along with other políticos I worked with who suffered father abandonment while young children, this life-defining experience is also a linchpin for a self story told in an explicitly cultural register and emphasizing his humble origins, indigenous racial background, and personal experience with the local vernacular of traditional practices. However problematic an example of "rueful self-recognition," in the words of Michael Herzfeld (1997:4), nevertheless, recognition it is of Rojas's intimate and varied connections to Quillacollo's urban Andean social space. And yet all of this was most often publicly registered in the discourse of the desclasado, which nevertheless locates his indigenous heritage in a different way.

Paters and Patrimony

If clearly not the case for Santos Rojas, many men active in politics, who were also born and raised in Quillacollo, extolled their fathers as virtuous models. In 1994 the father of a town councilman—an "important leader" in his day—had been dead five years since Christmas. This had turned the holiday for him into something more akin to a day of mourning. His father, nicknamed Pepito, had been a Manaco union leader and a footballer on both the Tomás Bata and Wilstermann clubs—the latter the most celebrated club of the city of Cochabamba. The councilman fondly recalled having grown up in this "paternal bubble" and attributed his leftist tendencies to his "parents," which included the antecedent generation of men—fathers and uncles both—composing his extended family. As he put it to me, "I grew up in this environment, and it is to this that I owe my formation as a person." Patrimonial inheritance constantly played in the background of politics in this way, as part of the public self-prospecting of cultural identity in Quillacollo.

But most politically active people in Quillacollo were estranged from their fathers, who either died or abandoned the nuclear family very early in their childhood. These men lacked a dominant male role model throughout their lives. In fact, the cynical truth is that this pattern of conjugal fragility often appeared to reproduce itself in their own lives, visible in their precarious relations with women and eventual departure from their own families. Many políticos flatly insisted to me that their political activities were largely responsible for undermining the stability of their family life, as a source of chronic friction between spouses. Comparing this situation to the subject of chapter 4, cultural patrimony, then, is evidently gendered. And políticos draw differently on their respective inheritances from often absent fathers and typically present mothers.

The marriages of a majority of those prominent in town politics during my time there, for example, have already ended badly. The wife of one político has left him and moved to another country. Another is divorced and has relocated to Quillacollo, in self-imposed exile from his previous life. A third has a stormy and distant relationship with his wife, who has left him for extended periods and lives in another house, though nearby. The wife of a fourth has also repeatedly left him, only to grudgingly return. A fifth lives alone and is often held up as a pathetic figure of local pity, since his family abandoned him. And several other men, though middle-aged, have never married despite a strong cultural preference to the contrary—living alone in sparsely decorated rented rooms. Still others are married but without children since they devote too much time to politics. Finally, even in relatively harmonious cases, men confided that their wives strongly disapproved of their political activities and discouraged them. This disapproval can fester, forestalling the arrival of children and eventually fueling a rocky marriage that typically ends in divorce.

A second category of people recounted similarly tragic tales but in which the father did not immediately disappear, though his role was actively and corrosively negative. A councilman and member of a musicians' clan claimed his father—a widely known and admired figure of local history— was an "important negative influence" whose severe parenting style left him with "internal traumas." "He traumatized me," claimed the son. He was a "suicidal dictator" as a father, saying "I still have psychological problems" because of it. Most typical were the cases of a tension-ridden father-son relationship, emerging from the social contradiction between the family's attempts to exploit their son's labor, usually in farming, and the son's own strong desire to escape from these same family pressures. In the narrative of the son, held in thrall to the "family business" and trapped in a "subordinate" status (usually referred to by the term *lloqhalla*, or youngster), he eventually deserted his nuclear household in early adulthood—a break facilitated by the mandatory year of military service. More graphic were tales of drunkard fathers who squandered their lives and scant family resources in chicherías, were violent and abusive, and were sometimes in and out of jail. On the one hand, then, the relative social disadvantage of being fatherless or deeply estranged from their fathers was often a cause for ridicule and served as motivation to many of these men. Their political careers—told as heroic narratives of cheating despair and upward mobility—were explained as self-validation obtained through a successful life of accomplishment (*una vida realizada*).

A third category betrayed an essential ambivalence about their fathers' circumstances, which took shape in the divergences, inconsistencies, and reinventions, often plausible, of políticos' own social and cultural backgrounds, as compared with the accounts of others. I will have more to say about this case. Hence we can specify several different ways that patrimonial legacies inform political careers. If each case presents different generational relationships, they are unified by the relative absence of the flesh-and-blood pater.

Throughout this chapter I have been most concerned with the public negotiation of social estrangement as a productively exploitable if controversial type of cultural capital in the political trenches, a kind of capital that helps to compose political careers, to build political relationships, and to maintain plausible relationships with the popular or indigenous world. This is epitomized by the ubiquity of father abandonment as one unexpected linchpin of a patrimonial process and as promoting public specu-lation about and negotiation of people's absent personal histories.[18] Fully two-thirds of the thirty-five or so leaders with whom I worked most closely and who dominated Quillacollo's political life either never knew their fathers, lost them at a young age, or left them behind in coming to Quillacollo. But the displaced ancestry and genealogical anonymity enjoyed by local leaders allowed them imaginative and plausible latitude for public reinventions of their lives and for ongoing impression management through the idiom of cultural heritage.

Santos Rojas's life history account, along with the arguments over Cassio Buenavides's past and social status, is an example of everyday public performances of identity where, as Suzanne Langer (1979[1942]:310) has put it, "dramatic action is a semblance of action so constructed that a whole, indivisible piece of virtual history is implicit in it." The historian David Lowenthal (2006) reminds us, too, that ancestral claims to heritage are best understood not as invocations of history so much as attempts to create history. The very term *de origen humilde* directs attention to connections between the circumstances of ancestry and self-identity, even as it suggests that this relation is itself a process that is bracketed and negotiated in the space of perceived differences between family origins and present status through what is publicly known and unknowable. Lowenthal (2006:4) also emphasizes, "We all have a stake in each other's history." In Quillacollo, this is very literally the case, as people mobilize cultural capital by publicly and contentiously filling in absent family histories, which are at the same time part of the construction of political networks.

This is not, of course, an altogether unfamiliar fact of politics. We can certainly note comparative precedents for such plausible if fictional genealogical manipulations in the effort to gain "legitimate" access to available political resources. Clifford Geertz (1980:31), for example, makes the following point about the competition for kingship in Bali: "As in other descent-based political systems, genealogies could be, and continually were, manipulated in order to rationalize current power realities and justify current prestige claims." While in Quillacollo politics is certainly not descent based in the sense that anthropologists typically use this term, there is no doubt that who one is perceived to be and what one's political relationships are significantly depend upon public assumptions about ancestry and social origins, which, in turn, partially determine who one can credibly aspire to represent.[19]

Patrimonial Counterinventions

I want to dwell still further on the cultural reconversion of patrimony for the consolidation of political representation in cases where the father's role is essentially mysterious or problematic. One illustrative case is Pancho Sánchez, who has been called many different things by friends and rivals alike, including "swarthy" (negro), "unpolished" (sin preparación), "a brute Indian" (indio bruto), "a donkey" (burro), "semiliterate," "a bootlicker" (adulador), "alienated" (un resentido) but also an autodidact, audacious, "crafty" (taimado), "very astute" (muy vivo), and "assertive" (muy pendejo). In his own words, his mother is "of campesino extraction." But, he quickly stressed, there are "different types of campesinos," and he wouldn't call her a "true campesino." As an ally explained, in his early life Sánchez "was given low esteem, treated badly."

Pancho is said to have been born in a mining camp to a woman de pollera from an extramarital affair with a man of modest means from Oruro. His parents separated, and with his mother he came to Quillacollo when he was four. His mother worked as a chichera and as a corn trader (rescatista de maíz). Pancho often helped with her trading circuits through the countryside. According to others, he soon lived as a "street urchin" (polilla), rarely if ever attending school. He himself lamented to me that he was only able to complete "primary school." He eventually became an assistant in a bicycle shop, then owned by another politically active individual, where he was "treated very badly, often walking the streets without shoes and in filthy rags." Pancho can now most often be found at his key-making shop, a street kiosk, which, comparable to a chichería, also regularly serves as a gathering place for exchanging news and information, a great boon for politics.

Pancho Sánchez mentioned none of this. When pointedly asked, he explained offhandedly that his father ran a "supply store" (pulpería) in the distant mining camp and later worked for the railroad. His mother also put pressure on him to work while he was still only a boy. When an adolescent, and tired of his mother's desire "to control" him, Sánchez sought recognition of paternity from his father, hoping perhaps to publicly legitimate his status as this man's son. But, as others tell the story, Pancho's father physically attacked him and threatened to kill him if he showed his face again. There was little trace of the violence and rejection in this father-son relationship in Pancho's own narrative, however. Even though Pancho admitted that his father has "never helped" him, he appeared not to bear much of a grudge and viewed the man in a positive light, calling him a "capable man" and someone "from the middle class."

This contrasted with his "illiterate" mother, who "lacked formation," lived nearby, and whom he routinely visited until her recent death. Similar to the case of Santos Rojas, Pancho's family's poverty was in large part a result of the separation of his father and mother, his father's refusal to recognize his own child, and the fact of his mother having to bear the burden of the family's survival alone. In his own words, this meant that when a young child, they "lived like campesinos, without any comforts." These circumstances precipitated something of an identity crisis. Pancho Sánchez told a humorous and revelatory, if perhaps apocryphal, story about his birthday. His mother had always celebrated his birthday around Corpus Christi, until one day his father appeared with Pancho's official birth certificate. To his surprise, he learned that he was born on another day and year; and to his shock, he learned that his mother had been calling him by the wrong name!

But Pancho Sánchez has forged a political career by being particularly astute (vivo), a personal characteristic essential to the patrimonial counter-inventions foregrounded in this chapter. Illustrations of his astuteness were also typically tangled up with a more general effort in pursuit of economic survival and social mobility. In these accounts, his personal and public lives were hard to distinguish from each other.

His marriage is a case in point. As a close friend of Pancho's noted, "The way he grabbed his wife was also a strategy." The two have been unhappily married. And she has left him twice for others. But in the first place, Pancho made himself "her savior." She became ill and required surgery, which was too expensive for her family to afford. As her situation worsened, no one could come up with the money. Seeing his opportunity Pancho stepped forward to put up the cash. When she recovered, she asked him how she might be able to repay him, whereupon he revealed that he was "in love with her." As was observed, "How could she deny her savior?" So they were married. She works in the town's main market, selling beef, and is a member of the local market sellers' union. In his own right Pancho "could not aspire to be a political leader." But once married, he quickly became very active in his wife's trade union. Although not a seller himself, he eventually maneuvered himself into a key role as a union leader, commanding a sizable "following" (*convocatoria*). With his marriage, Sánchez gained access to an important political constituency he could actively represent in public forums and in the corridors of the mayor's office.

Pancho's entrance into municipal politics turned on a similar act of "astuteness" (*viveza*). Prior to the first elections in 1985, the political party he was with, the ADN (Nationalist Democratic Action), approved its list of candidates in a consensus vote of the local membership. This list of thirteen or so names was then sent along to the departmental seat for ratification. Pancho Sánchez's name was not on the list. But he was an "intimate friend" of the secretary of the local party apparatus, Cassio Buenavides. In keeping with his duties, the secretary had to deliver the list. Inviting him to chicha and "on his knees" (*de rodillas*), Pancho persuaded Buenavides to add his name and to remove another's. The local party head, "carelessly" and "without his glasses," signed the list, which was then filed in Cochabamba. Once it was returned from the departmental higher-ups and others saw Pancho's name there, they assumed that it had been added in Cochabamba and that Pancho must be a valuable client of someone, and so, have some merit as a candidate. The upshot was that Pancho entered the town council by the back door as his party's alternate for the winning candidate (who had become mayor), without actually having been elected, appearing on the public ballot, or even having enjoyed the knowing support of the local party membership.

Pancho Sánchez conspicuously used a patronymic linking him to a well-known clan of nouveau riche businessmen in Quillacollo. He called them his "cousins" (*primos*). When pressed, he explained that his mother's brother is a *primo hermano* to the clan's head, Aurelio Escobar, a relationship he correctly defined as a "son between brothers," that is, a first cousin. But the kinship suggested by the patronymic is not quite what it seems, since Escobar's children would be at best Pancho Sánchez's second cousins, a much more tenuous kinship tie. Furthermore, even if true, that would mean his patronymic would ultimately be derived from his mother's extended family and not that of his father. Here, Sánchez has transposed a distant kin tie from his mother's side to his father's, perhaps pressing a nonexistent claim of relatedness. There was, however, little contact between Pancho and the clan to whom he claims an affiliation. And in fact, there was considerable animosity expressed on their side toward Pancho, whom they scoffingly called a "bruto indio."

In other circumstances, when not dedicated to the work of political self-prospecting, Pancho in fact explicitly acknowledged the substantial antagonism and political rivalries that existed between himself and Aurelio Escobar, the clan's head. As rivals within the same local political party and organization, Pancho agreed that Escobar "hates me, since I've shadowed him" (hacerse sombra). In Quillacollo to "shadow" someone in political terms means to successfully usurp his political role or standing. Pancho was willing to admit backstage that his patronymic claim was in fact part of his long-term strategy of upward political mobility from humble origins. Pancho also disparaged Aurelio Escobar's standing as a prosperous mestizo businessman. As Pancho told it, "Escobar is married to the daughter of an *hacendado*.... But his parents were rescatistas of potatoes, barley, and corn. He isn't even middle class." Aurelio Escobar's in-laws, Pancho insisted, gave the couple their large house and set him up in business.

In another moment, he recounted how Aurelio Escobar once tried to publicly provoke and insult him, yelling across the street, "Hey, key maker!" Sánchez approached the group Escobar was with and invited them to drink. He then indirectly returned the insult, saying to no one in particular, "If I'm a key maker, I admit it with pride. I prefer to earn my money honestly than as a pichikhatero." Escobar, he suggested, came by his money in the illegal trafficking of coca leaf for the cocaine industry. He was also little more, went the suggestion, than the humble trader his mother was, dealing in coca leaf rather than corn. The difference between the two—at least for Pancho—was that Pancho publicly embraced his humble past while Escobar attempted to conceal his as a desclasado. These personal swipes against Escobar in other circumstances inadvertently undermined Pancho's use of the Escobar surname as a means of implying his own middle-class origins through his absent father. They also emphasized the extent to which such patrimonial genealogies compose the stuff of factional politics and network building.

This relationship to patrimony is by far the most politically common in Quillacollo and best exemplifies, I would argue, the process of creating effective networks through the shared historical experience of estrangement. These affinities operate minimally at two levels. At the level of dyads (clusters of which become key parts of provincial political fronts), they are spontaneously expressed, for example, in the cultural atmosphere of informal political work, including invitations to drink in chicherías or the jokes and shared idiomatic slang used during drinking bouts, where fragments of personal origin myths are recounted and debated and where the intimacy productive of trust (confianza), often discussed as an essential ingredient for political cooperation, is built up. Such affinities, in turn, reinforce the transient solidarities of a given provincial party apparatus. A shared background as "de origen humilde" establishes effective communication among políticos as the basis for ongoing working relationships.

We have here a collectively told public biography, multiply authored and discrepant, largely produced through conspicuous disagreements generated by public speculations about the absent fathers and cultural displacements of people like Pancho, Santos, and Cassio. Part of political work in Quillacollo, as self-prospecting, is comparable to what Susan Gal (1991) has described for the funeral of the Hungarian composer Bartók: a public political process of the negotiation of identity composed of argumentative exchanges over multiple biographical claims. People like Caesar Buendía were very discreet about their origins, a trait many associate with the cholo desclasado, always striving to sublimate the "Indian" within and to erase any sign of his humble origins. But, as I have been detailing, the discourse of the desclasado is, too, a claim highlighting proximity to an indigenous heritage. And it would be unfair to Buendía not to recognize this. Despite his sunglasses, suit, and tie, he at least paid lip service to his popular status. And yet it is precisely the obscurity of these biographical facts that increases political maneuverability, providing a critical social margin of flexible accommodation to reconvert cultural capital to popular and indigenous ends when necessary.

Substantial patrimonial details are ambivalently and purposefully subject to the play of the local political imagination, as a virtual absence, while conflicting social claims and counterclaims keep the question of identity up in the air. The facts of these sorts of personal histories, diverse products of an increasingly typical social mutability in Bolivia, are not fully public domain even as they are publicized. Provincial authorities in Quillacollo by and large embraced this, since such informational lacks have become a basis to negotiate political space and a recognizable popular and indigenous style, which people routinely gloss in conversation as "de origen humilde."

Politics and Counterinvention

As an effort to explore ethnographically Bailey's (1988:168; 1991) insistence upon deceit as a quality intrinsic to political success, this chapter has been concerned with at least one way in which local-level Bolivian políticos are, in his words, "metacultural virtuosi." This is also an avenue for understanding the expressions of Bolivian neopopulism most conspicuously represented by the UCS and CONDEPA throughout the 1990s—described at the time as the spread of a "new Indian consciousness" (Ströbele-Gregor 1994:107)—as this laid the groundwork for the plural and popular-indigenous coalitions in the 2000s, as well as the current successes of Evo

Morales and the MAS (see Albro 2006a; Lazar 2008; Postero 2007a). In her study of provincial politics in nearby Tiraque, María Lagos has noted that while provincial factions seemed to cohere along ideological lines—nationalist versus leftist—upon closer inspection these rhetorical differences were superficial when compared to more immediately salient factors. She concluded, "The internal cohesion of factions tends to be based more on leaders' shared experiences than on the sharing of a well-defined political ideology" (1994:138). I would take this yet further to suggest that factional cohesion in Quillacollo builds upon the cultural *construction* of such shared experiences, which takes place in part through everyday negotiations of patrimony in the mode of political self-prospecting.

The possibilities for the recasting of tradition through multiply authored selective personal histories are captured in Herzfeld's apt phrase "counterinventions of tradition." As he notes, "Rethinking the tangle of multiple pasts often happens in the intimate spaces of culture" (1997:12), such as the relationship of gendered claims to family ancestry as cultural patrimony. Savvy políticos worked to convincingly insert themselves into regional history, and the intimate spaces of urban indigenous identity, with productive uses of paternal signs. This chapter has sought to capture precisely these circumstances, where cultural patrimony is important capital to be confirmed, disconfirmed, elaborated, repressed, or supplemented but in an urban environment of disjointed generational ties amid rapid social change. One way this is accomplished is through the negotiation of the intimacies of social estrangement, where the shared experience of estrangement brings political allies together in culturally defined working relationships. This has been augmented in significant ways by the experiences of the neoliberal era, including the growth of the informal economy and in-migration, which has created stress for extended families, separated fathers from children, and sent people to Quillacollo from multiple points distant.

José Limón's (1994:108–116) insightful treatment of Mexican American cultural poetics in South Texas makes a point of the generational disjunctions increasingly typical of emergent postmodernity. To his mind, the working-class subjects of his ethnography carry on in a world characterized by a spectrum of "negations of a historically and seemingly relatively stable cultural past." The author equates the younger generation's ignorance of its own family history with the lack of a narrative frame that helps them to make sense of their lives. Instead, they are left struggling to weave together a fragmentary popular cultural world mostly made up of "textualized surface images," in this way becoming something less than "active bearers of tradition." But things are different for Quillacollo.

In Quillacollo estrangement also has a political purpose. We might ask:

How can narratives of self-estrangement help to articulate popular political sensibilities? Gastón Gordillo (2002) has used Adorno's notion of a "negative dialectic" to describe how estrangement has been culturally productive among the Toba in Argentina—as a crucial source of meaning generated by the negation of what one is not[20]—while in Quillacollo multiply authored and selective life historical accounts represented differences between the past and the present as well as between displaced social origins and present self-identity and patrimony. As public patrimonial performances, displaced ancestry could become productive disjunctions for political work.

The productive relationship of estrangement to patrimony, as I have described it and as encapsulated by the intimacies of "humble origins," amounts to a cultural pragmatics that presupposes spatial disjunction, distinct implications for gendered inheritance, displaced and possibly unknowable ancestral referents, and the transportability of cultural forms in the construction of political relationships. In the ongoing description of indigenous movements in Latin America, this is a less recognized expression of the relationship between the indigenous and the nonindigenous. For Bolivia, such peri-urban spaces as Quillacollo expose the fragility and failure of an erstwhile national narrative of racial, cultural, and class mixture (or mestizaje), even as they provide the contours of an emergent and distinct kind of urban indigenous political experience. In this case I have explored how the generational transference of patrimony variously wanders through public efforts of self-prospecting. In Quillacollo it has been this very lack that has pragmatically formed the basis of public political self-narratives and which in fact has helped to *produce* political relations. At least in politics this play of paternal shadows is a process that involves the cultural manipulation of deprivation, mobility, gender, absence, and displacement as a basis for emergent cultural claims.

6 Recognition and Realpolitik
Spectacle, Career, and Factional Genealogies

In this chapter I describe the role of ritual libations, called ch'allas, as a kind of political spectacle. Ch'allas are a widespread, everyday, and traditional ritual fact of the Andean highlands, and their role in mostly rural and indigenous settings has received substantial ethnographic attention over the years in Bolivia and elsewhere (see Allen 1988; Bastien 1978; Girault 1988; Van den Berg 1989).[1] Descriptions of ch'allas in more urban settings, however, have typically only accompanied the discussion of larger periodic or calendric fiesta or folkloric events (see Albó and Preiswerk 1986; Albro 1998b; Buechler 1980; Buechler and Buechler 1996; Nash 1993) and so have not considered their more everyday political implications. In the period of the intensification of local municipal politics throughout the late 1980s and 1990s in Quillacollo, these explicitly political ch'allas became regular occurrences as part of municipal politics and as individual opportunities for the cultural performance of representative political personhood by local authorities.

In Quillacollo the activities of newly empowered municipal authorities have become a litmus test and basis for public contestation over the direction of the province throughout the era of neoliberal democratization. And the actions of the alcalde, in particular, have become a factional lightning rod as the subject of close public scrutiny and debate. Since the restoration of local elections for mayor, several mayors have become the focus of intense factional struggles and the subject of charges of "irregularities" in the management of the municipality and, as recently as 2007, have been forced to resign.

In one of the many ch'allas that I witnessed in Quillacollo, Mayor Luis Martínez publicly aspersed and delivered two pieces of heavy machinery to the town. This was only one of a series of ch'allas performed by the mayor on an almost weekly basis to inaugurate a new water well or a recently paved road, deliver newly purchased machinery, draw attention to the ongoing modernization of the municipality's services, or do some other "work" of the mayor's office. The road machines had been obtained with loans from Toyota's South American company, to be paid for in installments by the alcaldía. In this case the road machines were ostensibly to be used to help pave the town's mostly dirt streets. Sponsors direct their libations to what they assume to be prevailing public understandings of accepted cultural truths. But often against their will, or simply unintentionally, the self-images they project through these libation spectacles can also generate contradictory responses, produced from variable local perceptions of their own prior careers. This chapter is concerned in particular with the fallout from this ch'alla carried out by Quillacollo's then mayor, who was at the time subject to growing factional pressures.[2]

The Mayor's Ch'alla

For this ch'alla—held in mid-October 1994—the bright yellow Caterpillar machines were parked in the central plaza, awaiting the event, garlanded with flowers (a tradition called t'ikanchay, typical of the fiesta of San Juan where people adorn their livestock). Each machine bore the newly painted, conspicuous label "The Term of Office of Luis Martínez." The mayor's father, wife, and elder brother were on hand, and a band played traditional Bolivian folkloric music while the mayor bantered with the crowd. The organization of this event had rubbed some council members the wrong way, since it marginalized them and gave the impression that Lucho alone, as mayor, had been responsible for the acquisition of the machines. These people, some of whom were his allies, were conspicuously absent. The ch'alla got under way when a priest from the church housing the town's patroness, the Virgin of Urkupiña, offered a blessing asking the Virgin's protection for the town's authorities. The priest's blessing involved the sprinkling of holy water onto the road machines. And while people typically differentiated between the bendición (blessing) of the priest and the ch'alla, the two acts of aspersion were clearly parallel parts of the encompassing libation.[3] Next, an underling of the mayor handed him two traditional ceremonial vessels filled with chicha, called *aypuritas* (from the Quechua verb *aypuriy*, meaning "to partake with" or "to invite").[4]

As the town's first political authority, Lucho (Martínez's nickname) then offered a rousing speech to those assembled, itemizing the works in progress for the town and giving a list of past and future personal achievements. His comments were populist in tenor (for example, "We're among you on a daily basis!"and "We've made the bureaucrats come out from behind their desks!"), and he emphasized the congruence of his goals as an authority with those of the community. Though not the case here, a ch'alla of this sort would at this point typically include recognition of the quota paid and the work contributed by the neighborhood committee (junta vecinal) and mothers' club of the barrio in question.

Referring to the delivery of the machines, Lucho boomed, "I believe we've fulfilled our obligation" ("Creo que hemos cumplido"), echoing the cultural logic of saint supplication. Such a relation is mediated by frequent ritualized exchanges. And the alcalde's efforts of public accountability here approximated the recognizable terms of a public civil-religious obligation in ways comparable to the burdens undertaken by pasantes—couples who sponsor and finance, often at considerable cost, different parts of saint's day festivities.[5] Townsfolk, too, regularly take on the burdens of sponsorship for saint's day festivals, dance fraternities, and public works projects. The timing of ch'allas to coincide with popular saints' days or national holidays, frequent public accounting of how public monies are spent, and repeated requests to forgive leaders' inadequacies all nurture the impression that local authorities are fulfilling their expected communal responsibilities rather than behaving like self-interested and professional politicians.

Lucho also addressed the crowd in a stylized Quechuañol, equal parts recognizable political speak and local popular vernacular.[6] Typical of this regional Spanish, inflected by ample code switching, was his frequent reference to all present as *llaktamasis* (loosely, "fellows"). The Quechua noun *llakta* refers to Quillacollo in terms of an Andean union of a localized place-deity (the town's Virgin), its territory (the municipality), and its population (regional vallunos). Despite Quillacollo's exceptional origin as a Spanish parish rather than an indigenous reducción (see Sánchez-Albornóz 1978), Lucho rhetorically proceeded as if it had always been an Indian town. In its mayor's account, Quillacollo's peculiar history was displaced to assert an older and more pervasive indigenous claim.[7]

He also addressed the crowd as "dear *q'otus*," a term with particularly local connotations. The Quechua term *q'otu* translates literally as "goiter." As the story goes, before potable water was available locals were obliged to drink from a nearby and "contaminated" spring. People from around

Quillacollo became identified with the goiter that gradually developed from years of drinking this water. But the water was also rumored to increase sexual potency in men. The source of much humor, as is told, q'otus acquired a reputation for "grabbing" women and carrying them off. The image of the q'otu, then, is a playful reference in Quillacollo to their particular indigenous "wild man" within (see Taussig 1987), as a humorous and visible index of local identity. Both terms, then, convey a particularly local intimacy and imply the mayor's socially reciprocal entanglements with Quillacollo as a set of ongoing obligations.

Upon finishing his speech, the mayor dramatically grasped the bowls to carry out the *ch'allaku*, as he pointedly called it by adding the Quechua suffix. Calling the act one of "patrimony and custom" for Quillacollo, he then smashed each aypurita down upon the machines. As a finale, the alcalde enthusiastically danced a cueca, a traditional creole dance, with a representatively local woman (in this case, a chola from the crowd—a woman wearing the traditional gathered skirt). Such a public display of his dexterity with this deceptively difficult dance (the coordination of minute footwork with distance from the woman and the movements of hand, kerchief, and torso) is one of the many intangibles of popular identity, which in this case is the demonstration of embodied or tacit knowledge (Polanyi 1969), which people in Quillacollo might readily recognize as typical of a local man from humble origins.

Afterward, and perspiring, he quickly moved to help municipal employees methodically serve chicha to the crowd. One is supposed to consume the first serving in a single draught and pass it along, inviting the next person (Quechua: *Tomaykuy!* literally, "Drink!"). Ideally everyone should drink from the same vessel, as at least a momentary indication of solidarity and a gesture consistent with the etiquette of local watering holes. By inviting the crowd to partake, the alcalde reinforced his formal role as ritual sponsor or padrino (as the event's "godfather"). It is particularly important to make sure enough chicha is on hand, since sponsors are sharply criticized for being stingy if the food and drink are found wanting. While the chicha made the rounds, others in the crowd offered their own spontaneous ch'allas to the machines, spilling more chicha on the ground. With this, the alcalde began to give interviews to the assembled radio reporters, bringing the formal act to a close, though people continued to drink for some time afterward.

Publicity and the Cholo

At first glance, such libation spectacles are readily recognizable as staged political artifice. One is witness to a typical bit of political stumping, with the mayor—a nattily dressed urbanite in suit and tie—speaking primarily a politician's Spanish over amplification to a mostly Quechua-speaking crowd. With evident sincerity, he has gone through the motions of a ritual act recognized as an archaic practice throughout the Andes since before the Inca and with relevance to a fading agricultural world, performed on heavy road machinery no less. But at the same time, this affair is typical of the culturally hybrid and urban provincial arena of the so-called post-peasant (see García Canclini 1995; Kearney 1996:171–186; Warren 1998:68), an arena often historically obscured in the ethnography of Bolivia (see Albó 1990, 1997; Rivera 1993a). As such, these explicitly political libations iconoclastically fly in the face of conventional ethnographic renderings of collective Andean cultural practice and ethnic identity.

Even so, the apparent incongruity between the man and the act—his urbane social skin and the rustic agricultural ritual—seems to confirm the demagoguery about which locals are so eloquent. After all, how can this admittedly ambitious and upwardly mobile político sincerely (particularly when clever insincerity is the expectation) employ an indigenous cultural idiom of reciprocal exchange without provoking skepticism from a justifiably cynical population? If it is quite likely a put-on, why doesn't the libation just backfire? My analysis of this ch'alla considers the risks of failure accompanying ritual performance in ways reminiscent of Geertz's (1973) well-known interpretation of a disastrous Javanese funeral ceremony. Geertz (1973:169) identified the source of the problem as "an incongruity between the cultural framework of meaning and the patterning of social interaction," introduced by rapid social change and the movement of people into a more urban context, which caused the religious significance and political significance of the rite to come into conflict, in turn, confounding any consensus about the ritual's basic meaning for participants. But in addition to examining how the present ch'alla became problematic as an expression of Quillacollo's urbanizing and factional political environment, rather than simply writing this event off as inauthentic and as a failure, I examine how apparent incongruities associated with these political ch'allas in fact participate in generating changing expectations about the cultural identities of their sponsors.

As I explore in the following discussion, the public debate the mayor's schedule of ch'allas unleashed in Quillacollo attests that these acts are much more than just shallow electioneering stunts by politicians mostly removed from traditional Andean cultural practice. In fact, amid the pronounced fluidity of provincial cultural identities, I understand these libations as a vital part of local native experience, if now much less discernible through visible signs of self-presentation than in the past, and as concerned with the accommodation of indigenous identity to a popular and urban political space. As rituals of marked tradition in Quillacollo, ch'allas are decisive contexts where the recognizable boundaries within and between contemporary popular and indigenous identities are publicly and plausibly defined, disputed, debated, and redefined. Ch'allas are opportunities to evaluate the ritual sponsor's responsibilities toward the greater community, where the sponsor serves as a foil for the talk of public accountability.[8]

Though *cholo* is a historically pejorative term, recent cultural activism in Quillacollo has made an effort to publicly project the cholo's social and cultural traits in a more positive light. This effort has been commensurate with an increasingly dramatic shift in national cultural policy, from a 1990s emphasis upon Bolivia's "variegated" (*abigarrado*) (Toranzo Roca 1991) or "*pluri-multi*" (ILDIS 1993) identity, informed by the multicultural trappings of neoliberal reform (Kohl and Farthing 2006:125–148), to the Evo era's more explicit platform of indigenous rights. Nevertheless, the problematically fluid social and moral characteristics of the cholo have been historically employed to mark the boundaries of social difference and conflict and to invite a referential indeterminacy intrinsic to this volatile cultural category.

Despite efforts among Quillacolleño activists to revalue regional *valluno* culture, public discourse still stigmatizes cholos. For this reason, although "Quillacollo as a whole is almost completely made up of cholos," as I was told, "We don't call each other cholos." In moments of so-called traditional performance, the attributes of regional popular culture are thus carefully separated out from their ostensible cholo agents. In contrast to the humble campesino, then, Quillacolleños will often describe cholos as "mean, aggressive, vulgar," "bullying" (*prepotente*), "more troublesome" (más pícaro), and "rude" (*malcriado*). Cholos might better themselves and then spitefully "turn on their own class." As one friend—himself considered a cholo by many allies and rivals—explained, "Styling themselves as famous leaders within their own small circle, cholos turn on their own station in life. They consider themselves superior. They participate selfishly, as an 'I,' nothing more." For local political authorities, the label "cholo" implied a self-serving hyper-egotist, a person who has forsaken the social obligations of his milieu and as such is unlikely to represent a popular constituency in good faith.

This makes Quillacollo's political arena comparable to the practice of politics in other peripheral urban communities of Bolivia. Sian Lazar (2008:195), for example, characterizes the dilemmas facing trade union leaders in El Alto in the following terms: "Leadership is the terrain for struggles between collectivity as an ideal and the practice of self-interested action by individuals." As elsewhere in Bolivia (see Postero 2007b), in Quillacollo these struggles are often explicitly framed in terms of the impositions of an almost quarter-century-long regime of neoliberal citizenship, where political authorities are often accused of behaving like utility-maximizing individuals. As a municipal authority and ritual sponsor, Lucho was subject to precisely this charge. But if neoliberal state reforms are a readily available idiom of public censure, I do not treat them as necessarily determinant of the erosion, say, of collective accountability. Instead, critiques emphasizing the negative effects of individual autonomy, rent-seeking behavior, and self-governance feed easily into, and reconstitute, prevailing criticisms of self-interest already closely associated with diverse forms of social mobility available to people at least throughout the second half of the twentieth century—and often epitomized by the figure of the cholo—even as these are now reconstituted as condemnation of the neoliberal present.

Not surprisingly, then, those in attendance at such political libations often seemed unsure of what they were seeing: demagogue or genuine article, national politician or traditional provincial authority, a dramatization of the Indian within or a superficial electoral farce. Often equivocating, they at once characterized these performances as "traditions of our ancestors" and as "parts of our culture" and at other times dismissed them as "clownish acts" (*payasadas*) expressing the "whim" (*capricho*) of self-aggrandizing políticos who "don't know what gods" they are really addressing and just want a piece of the recently baked political pie. This ambivalence was intimately nurtured by the Janus-faced view of the cholo as both pejorative and popular. It was also carried over to the credibility of políticos' claims about themselves, that is, the ritually projected public identities of people whom other people might choose to call a cholo in private.

Public Careers

In an urbanizing province, where ideas about cultural identity are unsettled and wariness about the motives of political types readily detectable, not everyone can legitimately hope to represent the increasing heterogeneity of Quillacollo's popular sectors. Public figures are far from enjoying the liberty simply to make themselves up. Political plausibility—the cultural authority to represent a local popular constituency—turns on many factors, including the negotiation of questions like racial appearance, dress, the social origins of one's parents, how one makes a living, perceived competence in agricultural techniques, fluency in the popular regional dialect, whether and how one drinks chicha, a capacity for and comfort with manual labor, and fluency with the historical idiom of union politics, among others.[9]

But there is no particular rule of thumb to judge such plausibility. And, increasingly, popular traits are intangibly expressed and not visible in any definitive way. While especially in the rural Andes dress styles have been used as signs of ethnic standing or regional identity (see Murra 1975), over the past several decades and commensurate with increased social mobility, popular male dress has lost its clear distinctiveness in Quillacollo. Until fairly recently, a typical valluno could be recognized by his black or brown broad-brimmed hat, white button-down shirt, dark vest and pants, and *abarcas* or *ojotas* (tire-tread sandals). Such an appearance was often ascribed to the typical cholo, who came "from the countryside." But as one follower of the mayor explained to me, now cholos "no longer wear abarcas or home-spun pants. They prefer blue jeans. They stopped wearing the *ch'ullu* [woven cap]." This is in notable contrast to traditional women of popular descent, who are still identified by their colorful polleras, white stovepipe hats, embroidered blouses, braids, tassels, and black heeled shoes—a fact with political implications explored in depth in chapter 4.

People also usually did not self-identify as cholos, given the term's pejorative history. People affably agreed, "We're cholos, descendants of the mixture," or, "We are all mestizos, of mixed blood." But this does not change the fact that, as a friend observed, "it is difficult to recognize cholos walking down the street." As he explained to me, often "they are blonder than you, and with blue eyes." Though you would never know it, he continued, many apparent professionals "with their suits, cars, and shining shoes" are in fact "sons of peasants." Instead, identity has become a process of assessments made by others, claims, and counterclaims, if possible based on years of association and built-up knowledge. Of course this is not always possible.

If cholos notoriously "put on masks," the differences people did insist upon are not superficial, if they are intangible. Since previously reliable means, such as dress, phenotypic variation, or language, were no sure gauges, perceived behavioral attributes (such as being "vulgar," "rude," "troublesome," and so forth) and other discriminating skills such as literacy have become more decisive. People often insisted that cholos "can neither read nor write." Or they were at best "semiliterate." But such facts assume more than a passing knowledge of another's career. The efficacy of the present ch'alla boiled down to the mayor's relative success laminating his public image to his career. Political performances are a question of whether the implied claims of an authority's ritualized self-image are in fact adequately confirmed by the working knowledge, or assumptions, others possess about the history of a given sponsor's career.

Rather than foreground cultural identity, in this chapter I emphasize the importance of public careers as a way to focus attention upon the contested trajectories of personal histories in their social contexts. I am concerned with the public negotiation of self, that is, how careers are publicly constituted as they circulate throughout the political arena. This usually happens in piece-meal fashion, combining such mutually implicated sources as inherited knowledge, personal experience, hearsay, local radio reportage, public speeches, and the character assassination accompanying factional politics. In the context of the ch'alla, with its spectacle of self-presentation, the mayor's self-image was potentially markedly at odds with what people might insist are established facts of his career. And in a context of substantial mestizaje, there was ample room to question whether the cultural contours of self and career effectively support each other.

People in Quillacollo almost obsessively rated the plausibility of others in terms of their relative "personality" (*personalidad*), a fleeting quality emergent from the combined cut and thrust of a career, as we saw in chapter 2. In public discourse the question of personality has come to syncopate shades of popular and indigenous identity. To illustrate their cultural malaise, traditionalists gestured to the encroaching city and lamented, "We've made ourselves depersonalized." Those accused of having "fragile personalities" were thought to "lack formation" or not to exhibit "transparent behavior." Such people have "lost their essence." That is, "There is affinity neither through family tradition nor through ideology." Recall, such people were characterized as practicing llunk'erío, the two-facedness of veiled self-interest often associated with political clients or the manipulative compadre. As implausible leaders, they are "big talkers" or "people who put on airs" (Quechua: *ch'ajwaku*; Spanish: *figurón*), people who overdramatize and so misrepresent their checkered or undistinguished pasts. Inflationary or sycophantic rhetoric was widely excoriated as typical of the cholo. About cholos, a político friend expounded, "Their attitudes are tremendous! They'll try to sell you bridges where there aren't any rivers!"

Political libations are public efforts to assert the contrary. Rather than men without definition, authorities are staking a claim as established leaders, as people who are "known" (conocidos). Quillacolleños recognized that a successful libation was both an act of public accountability and, as Bill Hanks (1984:148) makes the point for Mayan shamanic performances, a "highly condensed autobiography of the performer." When addressing an audience during a ch'alla, sponsors typically began by reminding the assembled, "All of you know me." Being "known" meant several things: recognition of one's status as a legitimate public functionary, one's investment of time and effort, one's effectiveness as a political intermediary, one's status as local, trust, and one's career as significantly public knowledge. More specifically, the ch'alla itself was understood to express a person's "authentic personality," since people are assumed to speak frankly and from the heart under chicha's influence. For this reason, delicate egos often avoid chicherías, fearing they might run into too much bluntness. The transparency of chicha-saturated words, then, was one register of the autobiographical claims advanced as part of political libations.

Ruth Behar's (1993, 1995) writing about the life history genre is useful here. Behar dwells upon the creative "world-making" capacities of the protagonist. She seeks to elaborate "the relationship between history and its textual representation" (1995:151), that is, how a particular account is negotiated and constituted in and through narrative. In Behar's hands the life history is a situated encounter, neither whole cloth nor self-evident. And for her, the life historical text is primarily constituted in its reading. As such, in Quillacollo ch'alla sponsors made themselves vulnerable to often conflicting, if entirely plausible, local critiques. In what follows I examine the factional playing out of the aftermath of the mayor's ch'alla, paying particular attention to how these tensions served as the basis for the development of culturally persuasive alternatives used to mount challenges to the convictions of his own political performance.

In a political arena informed by a colonial legacy that loosely correlates social origin with status (see Rivera 1993b), the mayor's career was also understood in the broader generational context of his family's exploits. To borrow Kay Warren's (1998:193) apt words in reference to pan-Mayan activists, the mayor's critics were focused upon "the social relations of generational change as a mediator of political struggle." Particularly in an environment of factional politics, then, in Quillacollo public accounts of the mayor's ch'alla took a genealogical turn.[10] And as Foucault (1972:86) has put it, "The role of genealogy is to record its history."[11] The ch'alla event unintentionally foregrounded the fact of the public circulation of multiple and often opposed, if also potentially plausible, self-images. In this sense, local debate energized by the mayor's ch'alla included assertions intended to fill in the details of his career, in the process dwelling on his apparent self-promotion and the contradictions and misrepresentations it generated.[12]

As we saw in chapter 5, the diverse experiences of estrangement can become productive cultural capital in provincial politics, providing exploitable latitude for public and appropriate reinventions of self, for building political relationships, and for the urban expansion of the possibilities of indigenous belonging. And if the present chapter also trains our attention upon questions of patrimony and the relationship of kinship to ancestry, the genealogical quality of debate associated with the mayor's ch'alla instead effectively fills in the details of his contentious career. This process, therefore, tends in another less productive and more factional direction, highlighting identity claims as "unstable assemblages," to use Foucault's (1972:82) language, significantly composed of faults, fissures, and dissension. In this environment, reinventions are in permanent tension with their potential collapse.

Libations and Politics

Quillacolleños readily conceive of ch'allas as prototypically traditional acts (see Peredo Antezana 1990). Local cultural activists viewed the ch'alla in even more essentialist terms, as a "sign of one's Andean blood" (*sangre andina*). When I asked people about the mayor's ritual libation, they first emphasized that it was "traditional." Lurking behind the Virgin María, as her Quechua moniker Urkupiña suggests, is the presence of the Pachamama, the female chthonic agricultural deity. In local explanations the object of a ch'alla was invariably the Pachamama. As was repeatedly described to me, the ch'alla was understood to be part of the town's "ancestral culture," an act that has survived from the "time of the Inca" (*el incaico*). Chicha, as well, was often euphemistically referred to as the "elixir of the Inca." As a marked cultural act, I was told, the ch'alla was assumed to be "just custom, what else?" (*"es costumbre pués"*) and to come "from the Quechuas and Aymaras." Along the lines of "just custom," an ally of the mayor pointed out, "If you were to ask someone here why the mayor is offering a libation, he would say to you, 'Because this is what we do, and I do it as well.'" Abercrombie (1993) has detailed how the ch'alla is a means to assert the common basis, remembered continuity, and sharedness of a specific local community. And even for people raised in the politics of the historical Left in Quillacollo, ch'allas provided opportunities for political authorities to interact directly and sincerely with their "bases" as "comrades" through a planned moment of the ritual erasure of distinctions of class.

Whether just a casual flick of the wrist, or more expansively choreographed like the mayor's rally, ritual libations in Quillacollo were both signs and performances of the specifically *Andean*. Within this ritual frame, additional distinctions were drawn about this act of "collective communication," as one friend labeled the ch'alla. One such distinction is an emphasis upon the province's agricultural heritage (for example, Albro 1998b). In this urbanizing province, agriculture remains economically relevant. But even more, it looms as a vital ground for the cultural imagination. As a performance of the continuity of tradition, the ch'alla is "done with a drink that is ours" (*de lo nuestro*). Although Quillacollo is said to "lack much tradition," chicha, brewed from corn, comes "from the earth" as a "primordial part" of regional culture. About chicha, one local authority explained, "Maize and man have always lived together." Chicha, in his words, is a "unifying brew." And so the ch'alla "reminds us that we come from the earth and to the earth we will return."

There are varying degrees of complexity of a ch'alla in and around Quillacollo. Typically, whenever alcohol was consumed—at a fiesta or in a chichería—the first drops were reflexively offered to the Pachamama "for luck" (*para suerte*). On saints' days or during the Martes de Ch'alla of Carnival, more complicated and formal ch'allas are done in the fields and home; these involve streamers, confetti, a ritual table (*misa*), chicha, and firecrackers, as well as a ritual meal (see Rocha 1990). Born and raised Quillacolleños sometimes commented on the differences between the ch'allas traditionally performed in the province and ch'allas more recently brought to Quillacollo by Aymara migrants, which often employed a ritual specialist, included other elements, and were rumored to be done "with blood" rather than chicha (which was not the case). But such rumors emphasize that ch'allas are also acts of cultural discrimination. Ch'alla performances can also highlight social pretensions in the choice of alcohol for the libation. In addition to chicha, beer or champagne was often used, with both considered to be "more refined" (*más culto*). However, most people I talked with felt the elitism of champagne ran counter to the basic point of the libation as a moment of collective "sharing" (convivencia). Many people considered a ch'alla performed with champagne to be illegitimate and to be an example of "mere politics."

But almost everyone insisted that a reason for all libations is to mediate exchange relations with potent human or cosmic forces, in this case between the community and the Pachamama, the mayor and his electorate, the municipality and Toyota. In a public context of drinking reciprocities, Lucho's term, *llaktamasis*, suggested the import of such exchanges. The suffix *-masi* is added to nouns to connote spatial proximity or intimacy. A simple definition might be "neighbor." But this suffix carries more complex connotations of the sharing of trust (confianza) or of a person with whom one is likely to cooperate in small daily favors (yanapa). The offering of chicha by political authorities is a kind of masi-like action that Quillacolleños thought of as comparable to a t'inka, a "little gift" (*regalito*). Such t'inkas "grease the wheel" (*aceitear*) or initiate a dialogue (such as a proposal of marriage), or they can function as signs of sincere respect and congeniality (*simpatía*). As such, t'inkas effectively "open the heart."

In offering a ch'alla, petitioners interact with the Virgin María (or Pachamama) so that she might intercede on their behalf. People strive to coax the reciprocal potential from their ritual investment. During the fiesta to the town's patron saint, a pilgrim explained, "One gives her a ch'alla in order that she fulfill [*cumplir*] her obligations." The general idea, as put to me, is "to share [*compartir*] with the gods." In a different twist, another felt a ch'alla is meant "to offer tribute [*pleito*] to the earth, to nourish [*alimentar*] her with a spiritual inducement." In a further variation, the ch'alla was described as "a toast [brindis]; it's like irrigating [regar], to thank the Mother Earth and at the same time apportion [dotar] her with chicha." Ch'allas were often done in the hope that something desired "be made a reality," "that it bring good fortune" ("que sea en buena hora"), and, furthermore, that it "last" (see figures 6.1 and 6.2). The beneficent mediation of the Pachamama requires repeated ch'allas, for these are "her sustenance."

Political ch'allas like the mayor's—with their subtext of pasante obligations, shared drinking, and daily exchange relations—were carried out as evidence for an authority's ongoing commitment to the needs of the community. They were one way to express enduring alliances in the popular arena through repeated exchanges. Social intimacy was conveyed through the diverse obligations incurred through ritual exchange: to apportion, share, offer tribute, nourish, give thanks, irrigate, and fulfill obligations. As one local official explained it, in this libation to inaugurate the road machinery the emphasis was one of "redistribution for what we have received," as part of the process of provincial modernization. The ch'alla gave recognition to "the work done and delivered." When I seemed perplexed, he explained that one could offer a libation for the road machines the same as the Pachamama, because after all both are "productive municipal instruments."

In the course of conversations with me during my fieldwork, people negotiated the myriad apparent differences between this consciously traditionalist idiom and rapidly diverging present urban practicalities through recourse to such analogies and as a way to perpetuate the importance of cultural tradition as politically salient. The mayor, for example, described his own ch'alla to me this way:

> One does it in the most ample and spontaneous manner and it lets this wealth [of local custom] shine through. Now you've seen.... The affection [cariño] of the people was such that they gave a ch'alla in various places even when they should have done it in only one place.... What have we done? We've given a ch'alla to the Pachamama, linked with the earth, although it's no longer earth but pavement [laughs]! But it's still a part.

In the mayor's view, the spontaneity of the audience's unscripted ch'allas, which followed the official act, revealed the "affection" (cariño) shared between himself and the community. Whatever differences might have existed, went the reasoning, these were superficial in comparison to a shared obligation and to a shared background of humble origins. But at the same time his comment made plain the fact of a lingering historical rupture.

As customary acts ch'allas also register some obvious and potential

Figure 6.1. Hopes of social mobility: A man prepares his ch'alla, which features a hoped-for new home in miniature, during Quillacollo's fiesta of Urkupiña.

Figure 6.2. Blessing a truck: A family concludes a ch'alla for their vehicle to ensure hoped-for safe travel.

differences between the past and the present. Even for locals, the mayor's ch'alla made sense largely by way of analogy. As one longtime political figure put it, "The townspeople [vecinos] have every right to be happy that their alcalde is preoccupied with their well-being. In the same way, a good harvest is ch'allaed, since it is thought the Pachamama has been benevolent. If a ch'alla isn't done, people think the matter will turn out badly." And as a local activist noted, "Despite the many centuries [chicha] has been maintained. It symbolizes revolt.... It is a drink of collective communication, despite the differences in social class.... For me, it's a political symbol also, of the recuperation [reivindicación] of the people." Beyond direct analogy, the fact of historical rupture informs the importance of custom, precisely because of the revolts, emergent class differences, and evident need for cultural recuperation, which for many accentuated the diminishment of local tradition.[13] If ch'allas had been a part of the activities internal to local agrarian or worker union life, expressly political ch'allas were assumed to be relatively recent additions to the scene simultaneous with the national decentralization measures that increased the relevance of provincial alcaldías and that began only in the mid-1980s.

Debates over the cultural implications of the mayor's career took place because of and within the acute awareness of rupture, also epitomized by the social mobility evident in the careers of most political authorities. This background of the lack of continuity of tradition informed interpretations of potential genealogical discontinuities within the mayor's family. Comparative research on ritual libations in Bolivia has emphasized their role in promoting a local historical consciousness by relating the past to the present through the management of genealogical "paths of memory" (see Abercrombie 1993, 1998; Arnold 1992; Orta 2002). However, this work has taken place in overwhelmingly rural highland settings, where corporate ethnic identity predominates and where libation performances typically "transcend the immediate interests of the family" (Abercrombie 1993:156). In such semiurban borderland towns as Quillacollo, however, identity is much more of a family matter. Ch'allas in Quillacollo stir up genealogical memories less mapped upon a long-term Andean colonial history (compare Rivera 1984) so much as part of the contentious family histories and factional politics in which individual sponsors are engaged. This, in turn, can become a point of departure for alternative interpretations of the ritual event.

In Quillacollo, as I have noted, the expressive power of reference to matters of family and descent was extensive. The ch'alla, recall, is an example of "ancestral culture." Likewise, people often defined culture to me as "all that was achieved by our ancestors [*antepasados*]." Valluno identity included consideration of whether someone is truly a "son of the town." Provincial economic, cultural, or religious assets were typically discussed by the town's authorities as its patrimony and also must be understood as creative manipulations of the cultural terms of family inheritance, as previously discussed. To say, "It's just custom," then, is to draw a moral equation between then and now, based on kinship.[14] And if reference to the family did not preclude still prevalent usages from the pre-1952 feudal patriarchal world, where the patrón was addressed as *tatay* (Quechua: "father"),[15] despite the obvious fiction authorities often described the town as like "one big family," with the mayor in the role of "father" or "older brother."

This metaphor is in fact grounded in the concrete realities of local livelihoods. After all, most key economic relations are conducted at the level of diversified households (Dandler 1987a:681). And, except for the relatively rare instances of more involved public display, as with the mayor's libation, families are the most significant ritual unit in Quillacollo, conducting their own weekly ch'allas "for good luck." Of the four or so different recognized ritual tables (misas) used for ch'allas and sold daily in the local market, all were intended for use by families. Given the expressive power of reference to family, public comparison of the careers of father and son in the libation's aftermath was thus very much to be expected.

For all his political success, in a formulaic turn of phrase I heard many times from political authorities in Quillacollo, the mayor wanted to justify his claim that "I am still who I am" ("Sigo siendo lo que soy"). With his libation, then, he intended to address public suspicions that he was a self-serving and unrepresentative politician and to reemphasize that he was working for Quillacollo. His comment: "I don't have the MNR's discourse[16] but that of the lifestyle [*vivienda*] of Quillacollo. I can dance our cueca. I drink the chicha from here.... We want to feel ourselves [*sentirnos a nosotros*]. We have to define ourselves, with our own patrimony." This self-identity was promoted by the drinking reciprocities typical of the ch'alla. As one person concisely put it, "I'm giving something of myself with the ch'alla."[17] The performative frame of the ritual event encouraged an understanding of the mayor's career as an authentic expression of a representatively collective self. Describing the alcalde's role, one of his core followers observed, "[The mayor] is sending a message to the public that he still shares what it means to be someone from Quillacollo. From his high position, he also moves closer to the people...showing affection [cariño]. He is closing the gap, the distance, between himself and them." His public reciprocity with chicha was offered as a negation of the alcalde's social mobility (his national political contacts, suit and tie, and level of education), as a testament to a kind of provincial upbringing, ostensibly with many youthful nights spent drinking in chicherías under his belt.

But those on hand for these ch'allas did not simply or uncritically accept these rhetorical figures and surface images. Friends and enemies alike subjected them to scrutiny, as both a critique of the mayor's spectacular self as "just talk" and as "mere politics." The mayor himself inadvertently opened the door during the ch'alla event by criticizing nameless rivals for their apparent rumormongering. In the aftermath of his libation, and as an extension of the act's autobiographical register, others interpretively set the mayor's ritual performance amid his family's history and ongoing factional arguments by appealing to contours of local experience beyond the power of words either to confirm or to deny. A detour, then, through local contentions about Lucho's family history might put some plausible flesh on the bones of his identity as a libation sponsor.

A Genealogy of Saints and Clients

As the political-ritual sponsor of public works in Quillacollo and as a prominent and influential local authority in an era of decentralization, the mayor and his post have become a site of convergence for overlapping axes of meaning that address the question of political legitimacy and personhood in ways comparable to, if distinct from, other resonant cultural shifters, such as the "populist chola" of chapter 4. These include such salient cultural matters as sponsorship, drinking etiquette, reciprocal exchange, a regional vernacular, the fecund powers of the saints, regional traditions of planting and harvesting, and, of course, the local relevance of family. The libation suggested a popular primus inter pares as the characterological shape of a mayor who is trustworthy, faithful, reciprocal, sincere, transparent, an effective intercessor, and locally productive. As the ch'alla act itself illustrated, this account was meaningfully developed through frequent analogies between the spiritual religious-folkloric and human political arenas.

Especially vital analogies between the spiritual and the political—a bundle of equivalences ideally embodied in local authority—in particular turn on notions of intercession. Such analogies inform the region's particular cultural logic of brokerage. But while there might be a contested set of ideals, as factional rivals insisted, the actual person of the mayor might fall well short of expectations. Factional enmities exploited the tensions within these analogies, playing up the possibility of historical rupture—ritual as a performance of *mere* analogies—by questioning the accuracy of ritual claims. These analogies were unpacked as part of the public construction of Lucho's political genealogy. As with Foucault's (1972, 1984a, 1984b) genealogical method, local factional talk, then, pursued the dissension within specific claims to truth.

Lucho's family can refer to a history of intensive involvement in local political affairs. Small built but proactive and often combative, the mayor's father, Abundio Martínez, still boasts of a prominent and somewhat controversial political career. Born to a hat maker and raised in the town, Abundio married a woman from Oruro in 1943. In his words, he had gone there, probably to the mines, "looking for work." Abundio explained to me that *his* father, Lucho's grandfather, was of the popular and interstitial mestizo artisan class. Such artisans provided essential services to the landowning elite and filled out the turn-of-the-century population of the town. At that time only a few thousand souls were divided among landowners, artisans or smallholding agriculturalists (piqueros) independent of the patrón, and Indian peones who worked on the haciendas under feudal conditions. Abundio's family lived, and continues to live, in a one-story adobe house (since added on to) on what was once the edge of town, next to the train tracks laid down in 1917.

At the turn of the century such artisans as the mayor's grandfather, though thought of as provincial vallunos, were largely indistinguishable in dress, demeanor, speech style, and other cultural attributes from the piqueros, peasant agriculturalists, and indentured estate workers of the surrounding valley. In fact they were typically small-scale agriculturalists at the same time (Larson 1998). The biggest difference was that in some cases piqueros were literate. Whereas the artisan had a trade, and might also send his children to school, both mestizo and campesino could be found working their or others' land and operating in the agricultural market. Today distinctions are still occasionally drawn between these statuses. "Vecinos" (town dwellers) are still sometimes set off from "vallunos" (country or hamlet dwellers in the valleys), and both are categorically contrasted with *laris* (a derogatory term for non-Spanish-speaking indigenous agriculturalists from the nearby highlands).

This shared orientation has facilitated frequent cultural collusion among both vallunos and their peasant counterparts, based on extended relationships of reciprocal exchange, for political or economic ends (see Lagos 1994). During my years in Quillacollo, Abundio—as a self-described *quechuista* (Quechua speaker)—was in the habit of dressing very simply, "like a peasant." And he could often be seen riding his beaten-up Phoenix brand bicycle through town in a dusty brown broad-brimmed hat and rubber sandals (abarcas), all typical of the campesinado of Cochabamba's lower valley. His wife—dark complected, craggy faced, and de pollera— owned and ran a chichería that for many years catered to rural traders and peasants who came into town to buy and sell their agricultural produce on market days.

Abundio told me that he became affiliated with the new "multiclass" and populist MNR as a young man while in Oruro. Upon returning to Quillacollo in 1948, he continued his father's artisanal path and went to work at the nearby Manaco shoe factory, which would become a national-level force in labor politics during the 1970s and 1980s. The Manaco factory had founded a workers' union as early as 1944, which by 1952 was firmly under the thumb of the victorious MNR. A member of Manaco's armed militia, Abundio was likely among those who scoured the countryside, threatening force to remove the remaining *gamonales* (white, or creole, landowners) from their soon-to-be-divided haciendas.

In Abundio's own account, the workers' union "made the revolution," fighting on behalf of "our campesino brothers" to release them from "the slavery of *pongueaje* [serfdom]." In short, from a rural and mestizo artisanal background, Abundio placed himself squarely in the center of the now-mythical revolutionary events bringing the populist MNR initially to power. Though he did so not as a campesino but as a worker. At Manaco he occupied several important positions as a dirigente (union leader), which included "secretary of acts" in 1950–52 and "organization secretary" in 1955–56. And throughout the mid-1950s, as a diehard member of the

MNR, Abundio was an active and well-established part of the factory union's leadership cadre.

Abundio was also a smallholding agriculturalist and was awarded multiple plots of land by the MNR government as part of the 1953 Agrarian Reform. Intermittently, part of his family's income since the 1950s has come from these and other plots, either directly or in a sharecropping arrangement. He also speculated in land, buying from and selling to campesinos. Although Abundio is a peasant leader of sorts, he told me, "I'm no peasant." But, he proudly insisted, a significant part of his livelihood has always come from the fields. As I will develop further, Abundio's family has indeed experienced upward mobility from the hat-making days of his father, a situation that clouds the family's clear-cut popular standing. And yet Abundio's factory job, political activities, possible graft, farming activities, occasional land speculations, and profits from chicha sales all formed part of a popular valluno strategy of household economic diversification, very typical of local families from popular rural backgrounds (Dandler 1987a). It is just such infamous economic "astuteness" (viveza) for which vallunos are particularly known in Bolivia (see Albó 1987b).

In 1955 Abundio left his Manaco job, deciding instead to concentrate on his agricultural plots (both granted and acquired) and the chichería. Despite his worker's background, politically, he moved out of the Manaco union and into the campesino arena, where he competed as one among several provincial *cabecillas*, a type of second-tier peasant leader, often with recognized party support (Dandler 1971). In 1965–66, during his years of active involvement in peasant politics, Abundio was also a leader of the provincial association of *chicheros* (chicha makers). One rival campesino dirigente claimed unflatteringly that he "fought for the peasants only in order to sell chicha." An important point, however, is that local distinctions between worker, peasant, and other sorts of union activities were far from sharply drawn.

Abundio claimed also to have been in the later opposition to Banzer (1971–77). For example, he told me about having marched in solidarity with Manaco's unionists against the dictator's massacre of peasants in 1974 (see Laserna 1994 for discussion of this event). During the earlier MNR era, Abundio also painted himself as a mortal enemy of the regional peasant cacique Sinforoso Rivas—the most powerful regional político during the years 1952 to 1962 who by all accounts fled to Argentina a millionaire—though other Quillacolleños insisted Abundio was instead Rivas's pinche (underling). Given Rivas's well-known autocratic reputation, one of Abundio's sons could thus plausibly assert to me years later that his family had always stood against the "tyranny of the strongmen," who sought only to "enrich themselves." In this sense, and despite his position as an MNR client, Abundio comes off as a popular fighter against corrupt political oppression. Such a characterization is at least as plausible as the less charitable though frequent description others offered of Abundio as in essence an acquisitive pawn of the regional MNR apparatus.

As I have stressed, one important dimension of the ch'alla is as a spectacle of culturally appropriate forms of intercession. Ideally, just as saints or the Pachamama are understood to intercede between humans and God, political authorities intercede between the saints or the national government and their own earthly communities. In recent history, an authority's "power capability" (Dandler 1976:344) has been measured in terms of his relative effectiveness as a broker, and so as an intercessor similar to a saint. Of course the mayor's ch'alla was, itself, meant as an illustration of such effectiveness. Public dramatizations of political intercession, as a direct extension of its saintly equivalent, include the Virgin's procession (romería), when local authorities carry her wooden image throughout the town. Just as with the more recently innovated political ch'allas, such folkloric acts publicly insert political authorities between a local electorate and spiritual powers. Políticos literally broker between religious supplicants, as political clients, and the Pachamama.

"Power capability" is illustrated by the delivery of concrete resources to one's community. Just as the Virgin of Urkupiña is treated as Quillacollo's spiritual benefactress (patrona), political leaders are the town's main human benefactors (patrones). Authorities conduct their relations with townsfolk by mobilizing explicit parallels between saintly power and their own political power. There are at least three senses in which the mayor is a "patrón." He is the ritual sponsor of municipal events like the libation. At the same time, he is a political patron, the head of a political machine and responsible for numerous clients (seguidores) who expect regular "handouts" (prebendas) from him. Characteristic powers of the saints accrue to the alcalde as well. The relative productivity of the Virgin, or any saint, in granting a good harvest or other "request" (pedido) is also the measure of a productive worldly leader. The alcalde, in his turn, must produce tangible works, such as the road construction machines, and more covertly though just as importantly line clients' pockets with political cachet. In contrast to the parallels with agricultural fecundity, which animate comparisons between the Virgin and cholas, here the emphasis is squarely upon the patronage-like delivery of material goods. Such parallels are further elaborated through the constant appearances of political authorities at saint's day festivities, where they typically inaugurate public works. An authority's "promise" of future works is paralleled by such activities as the yearly symbolic opening of the fields (*llank'ada*). During San Isidro oxen decorated with flowers—like the road machines—symbolically open the first furrows, followed by women planting seeds.

Effective political brokerage—analogous to saintly intercession—also requires "trust" (confianza). The relation of saint and supplicant is metaphorically comparable to the task of constructing political networks, where políticos must rely unconditionally on a core of backers intimately tied to the leader, called "intimate friends" or "friends of trust" (amigos de confianza). At the level of dyadic pairs, such confianza is typically established through sharing together in such social interactions as a long drinking bout in a chichería, where social masks come off and potential allies invite each other to jug after jug of chicha. As with the faith requiring that one make offerings to satiate the hungry saint, the initial step toward establishing confianza is the offering of chicha to a thirsty potential ally. As with the "punishments" (castigos) meted out by an ambivalent saint, political betrayal looms as a distinct possibility, if less likely under circumstances of confianza. Both religious faith and political trust represent ideals of stability and risk in social relations.

The career of Lucho's father has been shaped by his brokerage roles. Manaco factory workers were a type of Latin American rural proletariat (see Greaves 1972). As the famed water warrior Oscar Olivera, then Manaco union head, put it, the vast majority of factory workers were "sons of peasants." They were "people from around here, from the countryside, and not the city." Such individuals as Abundio, who came from an essentially rural background but went on to acquire political skills and an ability to navigate adroitly the national patronage hierarchy, proved to be invaluable to national leaders from the 1950s through the late 1970s (see Dandler 1983). In addition to their factory jobs, Manaco workers still maintained agricultural plots or engaged in other activities integrating them into the regional rural economy. Minimally effective political mediation in this environment required deft command, then, of the still mostly rural valluno cultural idiom, including fluent Quechua and Spanish code switching, familiarity with agricultural techniques, deft manipulation of the many relations of reciprocity and exchange, a capacity for manual labor, and significant time spent schmoozing in local drinking establishments, accompanied by the creative verbal jousting in the uniquely valluno Quechuañol idiom, as well as other subtleties of demeanor. Abundio, along with many of his rivals, proved to be a useful popular instrument for the MNR leadership and its need to maintain its grassroots hold on power.

For MNR higher-ups, Abundio was deemed sufficiently useful that in 1954, with the establishment of the Worker-Peasant Pact by the MNR (Soto

1994), he was tapped as an important provincial liaison between national caudillos, Manaco, and the provincial peasant agrarian union. By the early 1960s, as the MNR sought to marginalize the more independent-minded caciques like Sinforoso Rivas, it turned to loyal clients such as Abundio Martínez and began to actively promote them as peasant leaders. Even as late as 1982, with the restoration of democracy, Abundio was appointed subprefect of the province under the renovated MNR of Siles Zuazo. To be effective, in Abundio's words, a subprefect "has to know the campo [rural hinterland]." Befitting a life lived next to the train tracks, Abundio's career was one spent brokering between the rural and the urban, the peasant and the mestizo, the local and the regional. And despite the evident ambiguities of his political career, few Quillacolleños disagreed that, whatever his flaws, the public political legacy of their mayor's father provided a thoroughly popular and campesino context in which his son could potentially operate.

A Humble Patrimony?

During a visit to his hometown, Abundio's oldest son, who years earlier immigrated to Sweden and now runs a small import-export business, described his family as "close knit." The children lived at home through high school. And as a little boy, Lucho accompanied his father to union meetings, internalizing the styles of regional leaders, styles that would eventually serve him well in winning the alcaldía. In Lucho's account, the relationship between father and son was strict and autocratic, though they remained close. Lucho still lived in his father's house, and Abundio still made a point of attending most of his son's public appearances. In politics, Lucho's brother insisted, the sons have "followed in the footsteps" of their father. He emphasized to me that although "at times one might hide his origin, we can't forget who we were in the past." "Our family," he insisted, "will make people respect us," an attitude that irritates the "families of power." Nevertheless, "We continue to be humble. We won't inflate ourselves."

And yet Lucho's penchant for suits and ties, his social skin of choice, might give pause. Born in 1954, the youngest of the sons and described as relatively dark skinned (*moreno*), Lucho identified himself, in popular terms, as de origen humilde, often professing "pride" that his mother still wears the pollera. He could speak Quechua. But in my observation he did not do so often and rarely publicly. In addition to familiarity with his father's activities as a worker, farmer, and chichero, Lucho helped his mother run their chichería when he was a child and later worked odd jobs in the incipient local industry. Of those years he noted simply, "You did what they wanted you to do, what there was to do." But mostly, he went to school, something his father had not done. His father's school had been union life. This contrasted, too, with the experience of many children from a campesino background in his age cohort who were obligated to work grueling hours in the fields at a young age.

While his father's ties to agricultural production were varied, Lucho's relation to the rural context of work was much more tenuous. He himself admittedly never "worked" in the fields, nor did he bother to give that impression. In fact, given his intense political commitments, throughout his life he has not worked regularly at all. This is something that people were all too aware of. I heard one political enemy, for example, make a quip about Lucho's anticorruption campaign slogan (which read, "Lucho: The man with clean hands"), changing it to "hands clean of calluses." Lucho displayed scant firsthand knowledge of "oxen and plow," a widely recognized minimal characteristic of campesino status (see Lagos 1994:136–137). While I have seen him carry on with peasants in his minimalist Quechua about agriculture, Lucho was at a disadvantage in representing a provincial population whose livelihood still depends largely on the regional market in agricultural goods. Given his pig farm's modest size and his only occasional management of it, Lucho's claim of making a living from it, rather than directly from politics, was treated by critics as highly dubious.

In his words, as a young man Quillacollo's current mayor involved himself in politics "a little to the side, a little hidden from my father." As many former leftist comrades recalled, in the early 1970s it was "fashionable" for members of the "poorer classes" to become involved in covert leftist activities through the political exposure they received at the hands of an older generation of radical schoolteachers. In fact, for young men with a popular or indigenous background, it was a "capital sin" to be anything but a communist or a socialist. Despite Che's then-fresh failure, Lucho nevertheless soon became an active leader in Quillacollo's communist youth brigade, commonly called the Jota (short for the Juventud Comunista). By all accounts he did not just go through the motions. Friends and foes alike agreed that he was the main animus of the Jota during these opposition years, as a young but fiery "recalcitrant communist."

In strict ideological terms, then, the son broke with the strong convictions of the father, committing himself to another path with different popular and political implications. In the early years of Banzer, while Abundio continued his trajectory as a centrist MNR peasant leader, the young Lucho's politics conformed almost exactly to the image of the "extreme Left" that his father so disdained. But even so, there was consensus that the son had "the character of his father." Many folks recalled that during the resistance to Banzer, whenever a stick of dynamite was detonated townspeople simply figured "Lucho was to blame." And in a bit of probable mythmaking bespeaking Lucho's ambivalent public reception, he was often credited with having aided the escape from Bolivia of Inti Peredo, one of Che's lieutenants!

People reported that during the days of resistance to Banzer's regime, Lucho, unlike his father, was apparently taken to the nearby army barracks and tortured on at least one occasion. According to a former "comrade in arms," Lucho's respiratory condition—which keeps him from drinking alcohol, a serious breach of popular political etiquette—is owed to the beatings he received there. Though at the time married for several years, Lucho was atypically still without children. This fact was offered as proof of his "sterility" (and so, lack of paternal productivity), as a possible result of the torture.[18] Whatever his reasons, from popular points of view Lucho's constant public refusals to consume chicha (even on ritual occasions) together with his condemnations of this "golden elixir" as a vice made for an awkward and alienating public persona. In essence, people understood him to be publicly rejecting the traditional means for establishing the social intimacy needed for ongoing working relationships. Such an attitude was more usually ascribed to gringos, or to problematic locals, such as the zealously non-drinking Evangelicals.

But a fellow Jota member, who had worked closely with Lucho during these early years, felt he had "many virtues," which included an active but ascetic commitment to his beliefs as a "man of the Left, of the opposition." He characterized Lucho as a tireless fighter for the disenfranchised, totally and selflessly dedicated to the cause, to the point of continuing to live in his father's house, owning few possessions, sacrificing steady work, and putting off beginning a family. And yet Lucho is married to a relatively well-to-do mestiza de vestido (a woman of nonindigenous descent who wears Western skirts). Despite this antipopular fact, Lucho's energetic opposition to successive dictatorial regimes was thought by many to have been passionate and sincere.

In terms of the question of intercession, after a stint as a national student leader, Lucho returned to Quillacollo in 1990 to become president of its Comité Cívico (Civic Committee), a post he held until ascending to the mayoralty in 1993. As a civic leader, he addressed provincial crises by organizing protest marches, strikes, and sit-ins, strategies made prominent by the peasant coca growers in the nearby Chapare. In preparation for the provincial elections in 1993, Lucho then founded the Regional Civic Movement (MCR) with the express purpose of breaking with the "corrupt vertical politics" of the past. In his words, its founding was "spontaneous, personal, and against the state of chaos, without political aims." Cynics dismissed this organization as a blatantly "political trampoline."

But his movement did have roots in the popular protest politics of the epoch. It built upon the publicized successes of civic movements in other regions, which presented themselves as alternatives to discredited and often unpopular political parties as interlocutors between a disillusioned population and society (Calderón and Laserna 1983). This is a strategy that the social and indigenous movement activism of the 2000s would take even further and that has been celebrated as an emergent popular and indigenous political "horizontality," as typified by primarily indigenous associational politics (Gutiérrez, García, and Tapia 2000). This trend is illustrated by regular public rejections by the MAS of a return to patronage politics. Nevertheless, people casually noted that Lucho's political efforts, with their explicitly urban focus, were far afield from his father's career in worker and campesino union politics.

The MCR insisted it was "not a party" but meant to circumvent the necessity of party affiliation for active political engagement. It gave a place to go for former leftists now "in the street" as a result of the collapse of their own traditional options. The MCR also responded to the requirements of decentralization and the new political economic need for "regional power." It was a regionalist movement in a cultural sense as well, in that it self-consciously confronted the perceived loss of "valluno culture" as a result of the new influx of migrants from the highlands and worked to translate the valluno cultural idiom for a more urban frame of reference. Even so, Lucho's civic role allowed him only a slight power capability.[19] As a firebrand civic leader, Lucho found himself in a potential quandary. Though his political activism legitimated him as an intransigent member of the "opposition," it also ensured that, as a critic of representatives of the state, he was effectively barred from access to municipal resources. He was largely unable, therefore, to translate national patronage ties into concrete resources for Quillacollo. But this still might have been enough for Lucho to plausibly claim that he also operated as a political broker, mediating between a provincial tradition of leftist politics and a renovated civic politics, as well as between the celebration of traditional valluno culture and an increasingly urbanized Andean context.

Factional Politics

Since the reemergence of municipal party politics in the past twenty years or so, people have been all too aware of the politicization of traditional ritual, or as David Kertzer (1988:107) has nicely put it, the choreographing of "ritual in the battle for public support." As a local political operator admitted, "[Local authorities] want to appear to be great men [Quechua: *jatun runa*], who give things to the people. It's more than just a political campaign." A pervasive sentiment, this was typically carried over to criticisms of anyone perceived to be on the make as a political operator of one sort or another: "Each hungry soul founds a party.... The incursion [in politics] of the popular masses [*populacho*] is bad. They don't know what political doctrine is. For a pitcher of chicha, or a pollera, they attach themselves to the boss. They look to drink or eat for free." Critics, often dismissive of the economic straits motivating political involvement, emphasized that cholo sensibilities associated with a self-interested zeal have now pervaded the province's political arena, as individuals are drawn to the new promise of self-advancement and largesse during the era of decentralization. This self-interest, in turn, has threatened to turn traditional patterns of reciprocity, obligation, or intercession into shallow electioneering stunts. For such critics, the mayor's ch'alla was just that, mere humbug.

A political enemy of Lucho lamented to me how ubiquitous and trivial these ritual libations have recently become in the hands of local politicians:

> *This thing has become exaggerated. Many have taken advantage of the act in order to engage in demagoguery. And it has become customary. Whatever candidate, whatever politician, arrives at some place, grabs a tutuma of chicha or beer, and pours it on the ground in order to make an offering,...desiring something of the gods. And here's the rub. They don't even know what gods. If it's Christ, God, the father of Christ, or the Pachamama!*

A typical bit of political criticism, this comment suggests that politicians are not above disingenuously mimicking traditional and popular habits, neither knowing nor caring about any possible obligations or accountability. Indeed, as was so often said, "They make promises they don't keep." Such comments emphasized the absence of social investment in the community and the lack of reciprocal obligations, except as a cynical calculus of vote getting.

Criticisms of explicitly political ch'allas most often expressed the sentiment that they were carried out in bad faith, and so without sincere trust. Critics emphasized the deception of appearances (*figuración*), with such ch'allas an insincere and shallow masquerades where the candidate crudely hoped to buy public affection with "cup and pollera." A particularly frustrated observer dismissively insisted, "The ch'alla is a racket [*negocio*], nothing more!" To bolster such a reading, the mayor's political enemies began to offer other explanations, also plausible, built up from the same details of his family's political career, if counter to the representation of his performed image. Factional rivals strove to prize apart image and career and in so doing to ascribe less charitable intentions to the mayor.

This discussion of the factional disputes at the heart of Quillacollo's ritual politics and accompanying arguments over what constitutes the basis of authenticity of the public claims local authorities make about themselves begs more general questions about the status and grounds of authenticity, sincerity, and justification for the representation of popular sectors and indigenous peoples in Latin America and elsewhere. For example, the well-publicized debate over the relative transparency, and accuracy or truthfulness, of Rigoberta Menchú's claims about her own and her family's specific role in the politics of her natal community, and so her legitimacy in representing the predicaments and forms of self-representation of Maya Indians in Guatemala's counterinsurgency war, is comparable in form to the factional arguments here over Lucho's representativeness (see Arias 2001; Menchú 1984; Stoll 1999). Such modes of critique, at least in Bolivia, are not external to but increasingly implicated in evolving assumptions about who counts as indigenous.

If a highly polished orator, Lucho had a political grip on the town that was tenuous at best. Many uncharitable characterizations of Lucho's libation, which met with a chilly reception, drove this home. The following harangue by a UCS loyalist, half impromptu sermon on the abuses of ritual libations and half observation on Lucho's own career, was indicative:

> It's a thing that we sometimes do, not knowing what it is we're doing. It's paradoxical. For example, [Lucho] in good conscience, since he's areligious—he's not religious, he's never believed in religion—has always believed only in himself.... And we are demonstrating here that he is a figurón. He believes that he is God because the communists say: "I am God, I am the All, I am Man. What is important is not that people might die but that the idea triumph!" But I've had many communist friends. We've been living here. We aren't extraterrestrials you know. And we know of the wanderings of all those who act the fox amid the sheep, fabricating a series of things. In this understanding, he has identified himself with the popular idiosyncrasy of the pueblo, in order to say that he also is somewhat a believer, or to do the things that the pueblo does, or to get a little closer to them.... But what does he want to share hypothetically with the Pachamama? Absolutely nothing! Once again he is making a fool of the pueblo.... It's a form of trying to barter, of trying to bring other elements into his fold.

Lucho the popular leader is a fraud, this person insisted. The mayor lacked representative sensibilities precisely because his fundamental political allegiance forbade it. Indeed, the atheist Bolivian Communist Party has for years condemned chicha as an opiate of the masses, as an unenlightened and pagan religious practice, and has preached to its members to abstain. Former members in Quillacollo recalled to me their frustration at the cultural blindness of the party during that era, which ultimately alienated them from its ranks.

Recall that an alternative reason for Lucho's refusal to drink chicha was his deteriorated health, the battle scar of a fighter against dictatorship. Both health and ideology, however, were likely possibilities. Yet in this neoliberal moment, a characterization of Lucho's as the demagogic attitude of a backsliding communist can be the point of a counterfactual lance. In this view, given his prior leftist commitments, Lucho's libation was hypocritical. And the fact that his mayoral candidacy was with the MNR—the primary architect of sweeping neoliberal measures—clearly underscored his hypocrisy. It reminded people of the potential ideological compromising of Lucho having pragmatically thrown away years of allegiance to the Left to sell out, gaining the mayoralty as an MNR candidate. To unsympathetic local sensibilities, Lucho's apparent ideological waffling and his having "parachuted in" as a candidate proved he lacked personality.

A different strand of local commentary linked Lucho's eleventh-hour turn to the MNR to another kettle of fish, prompting people to reconsider the basic story of his father's career. Despite his own self-characterizations as a legitimate campesino leader, many—not privy to the internal wrangling of union politics—supposed that Abundio had been imposed from above. As opposed to the typical careers of most campesino leaders, he lacked a long history of engagement in peasant politics, which for local leaders of his generation dated back to the watershed peasant congress of 1945 in Ayopaya (Dandler 1987b). But Abundio constantly derided his competitors with a colorful bilingual rhetoric (in itself popularly legitimating, as a local vernacular), labeling them *vivillos* and *k'anchiris*, or clever profit seekers who "lived from bribes" and who "only came to visit us" at the union headquarters when they wanted something.

In turn, rivals freely tarred Abundio with the same brush. He was often critically appraised as a *tirasacu*, that is, as tugging on the coattails of MNR higher-ups. One rival referred to him as a *velapuco*, literally, a "church sacristan," someone who merely lights the candles in anticipation of the sanctioned authority. Still another blithely dismissed him as having been with "every government." The fact that Abundio had never been exiled, jailed, or beaten during his career tended to support this accusation in people's minds. His appointment as subprefect further supported a public reading that he was less local leader than client of national MNR politicians, a political errand boy for the real—and neoliberal—powers that be.

Lucho's unexpected swerve toward the MNR as its "invited" mayoral candidate, then, was also painted by critics as a return to the family fold.[20] From the point of view of his left-leaning career, Lucho sold out. Local perceptions of how he engineered this coup, even overcoming the strong internal opposition of the provincial MNR cell itself, further established this reading. Hearsay insisted that Lucho was able to go over the heads of the local cell by cashing in on political contacts in the city he had established at higher levels as a student leader. While causing acrimony, this gambit also made it clear that Lucho might harbor national aspirations, which made him untrustworthy as a local dirigente. To make matters worse for Lucho, on the campaign trail he vigorously denied a "militant" membership with the MNR, in an effort to preserve his political autonomy. But at the same time, as the party's invited candidate, he also began to deny that he had ever been an "official" member of the Communist Party. His stump speeches—with live folkloric music and dances—stressed his local identity as a q'otu even while touting then–MNR president Gonzalo Sanchez de Lozada's national platform called the Plan de Todos. For many, this was an incongruous admixture.

One former comrade mused that perhaps Lucho's damaged health had given him a desperate streak, since "he knows that at any moment he could go." And this accounted for his evident political sea change. Others were less forgiving, pointing out the presence of many of Abundio's old Manaco associates on his son's political team and the father's own long career in the MNR. In keeping with family tradition, for many Lucho, too, had become a self-serving local hatchet man for national interests, the representative of political outsiders to the province. In this reading, both the mayor and his father were conspicuous in lacking a healthy network of local political relationships. Instead, theirs was an imposed and thus illegitimate authority. This, in turn, made them inappropriate as local political brokers.

As the MNR's mayoral candidate, Lucho had been combative toward the provincial machine of the outgoing mayor, Caesar Buendía, himself from the nearby sierra and member of the locally dominant UCS party. This party commanded an efficient regional apparatus, which had informally controlled the town's political arena since at least 1985 and was composed of members of the informal economy, as well as transporters, petty merchants, relocalized miners, and people of indigenous descent (for extended discussion, see Mayorga 1991, 2002). In attempting to face down the UCS, Lucho stressed his background both as a "son of the town" and as an educated "professional," thinking to contrast his credentials with the largely uneducated and sometimes illiterate migrant and ex-campesino UCS leaders.

He characterized these men as "corrupt," "unpolished," and essentially "self-interested" políticos who were perpetrating a "joke" (burla) on the pueblo itself while treating it as their "private fiefdom." Lucho's older brother was more direct, referring to the UCS machine as filled out by "city peasants." In his view they were "vulgar, aggressive, rude cholos" who have "not stopped being peasants." But perhaps unexpectedly for him, the more manifestly popular and indigenous backgrounds of local UCS leaders, as practicing artisans, transporters, or factory workers and in many cases peasant leaders—men with dirt permanently under their fingernails—threw Lucho's own less visible and much more circuitously popular status into an even more ambivalent light, which the local UCS machine proceeded to exploit.

Wasting little time, they went on the attack. Lucho's identity as a valluno, insisted his rivals, was open to question. Their insinuations began with his ambiguous family status. Older UCS políticos referred to him as "this youngster [lloqhalla], this fraud, this boy without a personality." The mayor still lived in his father's house, possessed few agricultural or artisanal skills, and was known never to have worked a real job. If most people considered him "learned" (de preparación), his incomplete university career elicited mixed responses. Dedicated to politics, he spent considerably more time at the university than some deemed necessary, changing his course of study several times. Although married, he was not a father. Neither had he ever worked with his hands nor "earned the daily bread" (ganar el pan del día) as fathers are supposed to. In the prevalent machista idiom and in the view of the local UCS leadership, Lucho's manhood was yet to be established; he was not productive in several essential ways.

As a part of his goal to rationalize municipal bureaucracy, Lucho used the authority of office to rail against the intrigues of politics, particularly the use of chicha or cachet to establish personal loyalties (called prebendalismo), as well as a constant indulgence in "gossip" (chismes). Claiming, with some justification, to want to eliminate the rampant corruption of local municipal government, the alcalde frequently vilified traditional popular and indigenous norms for establishing personal relations of patronage and clientage, and so at the same time culturally legible modes of intercession. In terms of impression management, this attitude provided a further opening for his rivals.

From the point of view of the UCS people, Lucho's emphasis upon his professional identity, relatively extensive education, lack of routine exposure to local patterns of work, recent ideological waffling, machista deficiencies, apparently intact national political contacts, and extensive family history with the MNR—all known career factors—suggested someone with anything but a credible investment in Quillacollo. In their words, Lucho was nothing more than a cholo desclasado, someone of popular descent who seeks to hide and to deny his rural past and who wants to be a mestizo member of the middle class. We can compare such accusations to similar claims leveled against Santos Rojas, discussed in the previous chapter. A key subtext of their claim was the similarity of Lucho's behavior to that of the pre-1952 provincial elite. He was, in short, a person in whom little trust should be placed. At the same time, by calling attention to the machinations of desclasados, Lucho's enemies directed attention to potential differences of front stage and backstage in his ch'alla, as a public spectacle of self-prospecting.

But these broadsides were not the end of the mayor's troubles. Lucho had also alienated the other end of the local political spectrum, with whom he had forged the delicate pact that initially gave him the alcaldía. The ire on this end arose from a perception that the mayor had assumed too many executive powers, effectively marginalizing the other pact members. Rather than peasants or artisans, these men were mostly merchants, small businessmen, and professionals (often doctors, lawyers, or engineers). Mestizo provincials, usually with (now-muted) family ties to the once-dominant pre-1952 landowning class, their characterization of Lucho's libation and career was given a different though still negative spin; rather than a mestizo outsider molded by his experiences elsewhere, in their divergent account he was an upwardly mobile Indian fatally flawed by his close ties to an unfortunately unenlightened provincial history. Rather than a legitimate grassroots representative, or a disinterested national politician, went their argument, Lucho was the product of a corrupt, violent, and often tyrannical regional peasant politics.

One bitter councilman complained to me that, coming from a "poor family" as he does, Lucho's philosophy is summarized by the maxim: "He who triumphs is he who shouts." As I explored in chapter 2, empty but persuasive forms of talk are often treated as a cholo-type behavior. A former peasant cabecilla compared himself to Lucho's father this way: "For every one word I speak, Abundio would speak ten. Yet his son, Lucho, is worse still, averaging fifteen to every one!" A case in point was Lucho's conspicuous use of the title licenciado after his surname (meaning "degreed" and frequently used by lawyers). This was a conceit that many scoffed at, since he never finished a degree. The implication is that Lucho was a false professional.

For the mayor's former supporters, this sort of casuistry and deliberate self-misrepresentation simply brought home the man's ideological flip-flopping (again, the problem of the onetime communist turned MNR mayor). In their version this suggested Lucho's personal motives for seeking political office. In the words of one critic, having tasted the fruits of office, Lucho no longer wished to "recognize his origins" and simply "steps on people" in keeping company, as they say, "both with the Moors and the Christians." Another commented, "He wanted to arrive at a situation, be it with God or with the Devil." A son of a former hacendado and political rival was more explicit: "People who don't know how to manage money will always lose it. People who have never tasted of power, when they have it, go crazy.... Lucho heard the clink of money. I have a formation from childhood. Lucho never had anything. He's the son of his father, the son of a campesino leader. And the son of a cat is also a cat!" It was widely supposed that Abundio abused his role in the agrarian union to gain direct access to lands available through the Agrarian Reform, illegally speculating, and in the process making out like a bandit—which was true of many caciques. In this account Lucho took on the characteristics of a corrupt peasant Faust, with an ambiguous family status, overreaching his modest rural origins. As against the popular expectations of productivity and brokerage, here the mayor was associated with both political co-optation and graft. His personal acquisitiveness, people supposed, fatally compromised any potential local, collective productivity.

Many rivals of mestizo status viewed Lucho as an autocrat. For them, his indigenous ancestry was unintentionally revealed in attitudes comparable to onetime peasant strongmen like Sinforoso Rivas. One such person confided that Lucho "decides things arbitrarily," an attitude coming from his father, who encouraged his children "to be aggressive." And in fact years later, critics still called Abundio a "killer" (matón), claiming that during the 1950s he tortured militants of the Fascist Party, which drew its base from among the dwindling provincial elite. Abundio's local nickname, Ucureño, carries some dark implications, derived as it is from the name of a peasant hamlet in the upper valley that figured prominently in a rancorous war fought between 1959 and 1963 by rival peasant strongmen. During this so-called Ch'ampa Guerra (see Dandler 1984; Kohl 1982), the indigenous campesinos of Ucureña acquired a reputation for aggression, cruelty, and violence. And even though Lucho had gone to the university, he still hailed from a humble family. Echoing the earlier comparison to a cat, as was said of Lucho, "A monkey with tape is still a monkey."

Labeled by this mestizo rival—himself a former engineer—a "rude cholo," Lucho was assumed—like his father—to exhibit an evident cholo attitude of "pride, a self-interested conception, and a little jealousy." One close collaborator, a friend and admirer with a history in the Left, still admitted to having classified Lucho both as a "bully" (mandón) and as a "terrorist" (tirabombas) when he was leader of the Jota. For a merchant and head of a rival party, the mayor's "abusive" (prepotente) attitude ultimately "comes from the colonial era." Hence his evidently autocratic personal traits, with family roots in a peasant cacical politics, were ascribed by factional rivals to the potentially violent Indian within rather than to the regional and folkloric figure of the q'otu. The campesino origins of Lucho's career, epitomized in a corrupt and autocratic attitude, they suggested, would be his downfall. In the aftermath of his ch'alla and in the ongoing crossfire of slings and arrows between potentially more humble rivals and mestizo former allies, the mayor's pretension of a happy fit between image and career began to lose credibility and to crumble.

Hazarding the Self

Lucho's contested career resists easy assimilation into the racial or class categories of Bolivian colonial history. Rivera's (1993b) treatment of the different registers of "internal colonialism" in contemporary Bolivia is a case in point. For her, the violent, often coercive, basis of the Spanish colonial period remains the unresolved conflict at the heart of Bolivian society and continues to manifest itself in a series of dichotomous rifts in social relations. In her view, broad institutional matrices of the social and political, of ethnicity and citizenship, and of public and private spheres remain asymmetrically antagonistic and serve as the encompassing structural milieu of colonial identity formation, ultimately animated by the polarizing opposition of indigenous and occidental cultures.[21] But Lucho's checkered career, publicly informed by his father's prior exploits, only awkwardly straddles this colonial conjuncture, while circumventing it amid the ongoing recontextualization of urban indigenous legacies in Quillacollo.

Lucho's controversial public career has informed the fluid parameters of his ritual self-management. A successful political ch'alla must be able to subsume its contrary readings and to arrest the disjunctive sliding back and forth between public and private, which might easily jeopardize the desired outcome of this ritual spectacle as an effort of popular and indigenous self-prospecting. The factional confluences and contradictions among competing accounts of Lucho's identity are what ultimately determine the plausibility and representativeness of local authorities like the mayor. In this climate political ritual is very much a part of the quotidian politics of cultural life, where any publicized self-images are quickly drawn into the many "shadow conversations" (Irvine 1996:152) that engage them. The controversies or agreements over what was entailed by, suspected of, or should be concluded about Lucho's career promoted what were typically partial and partisan accounts of the mayor's credibility. This included the mayor's own account.

Webb Keane has explored, for the case of Indonesian political oratory, the hazards involved in self-representation. Keane's version of political performance is usefully agonistic. As Keane (1997:3) demonstrates, political events carry "disturbing undercurrents," and "potentials for slippage and conflict" are immanent in the ritual form. Such ritualized representations "hint at the nature and sources of potential failure as well" (1997:9). In the play of representational forms, for Keane—and as I have explored for political authorities in Quillacollo—effective agency is contentiously exercised in genealogical debates and problematically contingent upon "ancestral sources of authority" (1997:18). But these sources are read in various ways.

"Neither peasant nor white" (ni campesino ni q'ara), or as people say, "neither beer nor lemonade" (ni chicha ni limonada), Lucho's career was publicly and multiply authored, at once cholo and mestizo, not to mention variations on these unstable categories. Local arguments over Lucho's identity unfolded less in dichotomous ways and more in the provisional and interstitial spaces of transit between stable colonial or reified cultural identities characteristic of urban indigeneity. In the factional environment of Quillacollo's provincial politics the mayor was plausibly both insider and outsider, native son and cholo desclasado, autocrat and populist, provincial opposition leader and national party hack, populist fighter and mestizo client. In the terms of this array of distinctions, his standing in relation to widely recognized leadership ideals of trust, intercession, or productivity was vulnerable to persistent debate.[22] The unraveling of such multiplying and conflictual shades of Lucho's career, the tracing out of their contours in ritually intensified moments of factional encounter, suggests one way that cultural selves possess "alternative, cohabiting identities" (Battaglia 1995:93).

Despite his best efforts at spin control, during the next election in 1995 Lucho's career took a downward turn. He was roundly defeated by the combined efforts of the UCS's little machine he had briefly and so optimistically unseated and has so far failed to regain political office. And during the campaign, the luxurious official vehicle of the alcaldía, recently purchased by him while still mayor and "delivered" to the town in yet another ch'alla organized by the municipality later that year, was stolen, to be found abandoned and wrecked. People tended to understand the episode as a testament, for now, to the onetime mayor's failed political ambitions.

7 Conclusion
The Humble Politics
of Negative Solidarity

In a report on the thick airborne pollution above the nearby city of Cochabamba—surprisingly comparable in its density to much vaster Latin American metropolises—it came to light, to the understandable dismay of many, that none other than "fecal matter" (*heces fecales*) was one of the principal atmospheric pollutants contaminating the air people breathed (Urbano Campos 2000). The explanation given for this discordant fact was that the increasingly populated shantytowns and popular barrios on the city's expanding fringe—which conspicuously lack the infrastructure of "basic public services" like plumbing—oblige people to address the body's needs in the "open air." Apparently the contaminants are then swept up into the atmosphere by the gusts of dry winds that so often whip across the valley dustbowl within which both Quillacollo and Cochabamba are found.

But rather than the outcry of dismay with which one might have safely assumed such an alarm call would be met, this revelation generated more than a few wisecracking snickers in the local media, which wryly suggested that "it was as if the marginalized were taking their revenge" (Urbano Campos 2000:1). The revelation also unexpectedly provided some in the regional media a forum to exhibit a withering, though also tongue-in-cheek, self-critique. For at least one journalist, this cloacal crisis—in its way one facet of the broader *Crisis* of social upheaval intermittently afflicting Bolivia prior to, throughout, and after the neoliberal period—was a typical example of the ways that Cochabamba's underdevelopment sets it apart from those larger urbs, as the following editorialist's appraisal makes apparent:

> [In Cochabamba] there almost doesn't exist, in turn, industrial smog, which would be a parameter of productive economic growth. Cities like Mexico City, Santiago de Chile, or São Paulo can boast vainly of their catastrophic indices of pollution provoked by the smoke of their factories, while we breath, humbly and without any economic benefit, shit in the dust. [Urbano Campos 2000:1]

If Cochabambinos are collectively forced to breathe in what should stay expelled, this is connected with the department's underdevelopment, which in turn, in the estimation of many, makes it a particularly humble corner of Latin America.

In the colonial and republican periods, defined by such contradictions as those between the urban criollo and rural campesino worlds, oft-expressed phobias of hygiene were, for mostly urban elites, explicitly a question of the containment of potential popular and indigenous contaminants outside of "modern" urban spaces.[1] In the city of Cochabamba, one intermittent front of this campaign has been a well-documented effort to remove chicherías (and other vice-ridden signs of the city's past) from the city center to its peripheries.[2] In recent years, the municipality of Cochabamba has again taken up the clarion call, decrying the poor hygienic conditions of many of the city's nightspots and chicherías, which were claimed to "produce injurious effects upon one's health" (Contreras Baspineiro 2000:2). Setting aside inebriation as the problem, the article asserts, "It's a secret to no one that chicha, the most consumed drink, is not brewed in hygienic conditions. During its preparation chicha remains exposed to the elements [la intemperie] and its ingredients aren't guaranteed" (Contreras Baspineiro 2000:3). But of greatest concern were the unsettling results of a "microbiological analysis" conducted by experts from the regional University of San Simón, which revealed the unmistakable presence of "fecal matter" in the chicha served at some of these establishments. Typically, the chicherías of the city's margin or of the more rural hinterland lack roofing and sport mud-packed floors. And drinkers usually enjoy the company of stray dogs while sampling a local brew, which has sat fermenting in large open cisterns through rain, wind, and whatever else. Hygienic concerns are, therefore, by no means entirely misplaced.

If the nearby city treats the fermentation process of chicha as a "problem," it is at the same time at the center of popular provincial cultural practice. As a follow-up exposé in Los Tiempos explained, and as is well known in Quillacollo, many believe that chicheros sometimes drop "small bags of excrement" into the full cistern to accelerate fermentation (*Los Tiempos* 2000:1). In Quillacollo rumors abounded of prized recipes for chicha making—typically kept as family secrets. And one widely held conviction was that human (or, sometimes, dog) excrement embellished the absolute best local chichas. This, in part, explains why drinking jokes would often mine the linguistic potential in the similarity between *aqha* (Quechua: "chicha") and *aka* (Quechua for, you guessed it, "shit"). While Mary Douglas (1966:35) has influentially suggested that dirt and kindred filth should be understood as "matter out of place," and so as signs of that which should not be mixed, "humble" Bolivians—people counting themselves as part of the urban popular and indigenous population—are likely to retort that such impurities are right where they belong!

Even so, throughout the years of my work there were many in Quillacollo who would tell you that drinking chicha is definitely a vice. And yet a refusal to invite someone to drink is also a denial of the state of *ch'aki*, a Quechua term for "thirst," but also an invitation to social conviviality. As we have seen, such rejection was strongly associated by many Quillacolleños with the attitude of the so-called desclasado, someone who denies any public association with his or her ancestral or humble upbring-ing. This tension surfaces in felt contradictions between cultural identity and political doctrine. For example, Victor Hugo Cárdenas (1987) has decried in print the "culture blindness" of the historical Left in Bolivia. An example of what he might have had in mind is the complaints of Quillacolleños who were often critical of policies committed to supporting the "peasant," the "worker," or some other abstract category of nonperson, which neither spoke to people's actual existing concerns nor recognized everyday local cultural realities.

A bit of memorable graffiti sprayed on an adobe wall near my house, for example, read, "Chicha is poison!" It was attributed, I assume apocryphally, to one "Carlos Marx." But even longtime "intransigent" members of the Left, with well-established public careers of resistance to dictatorship in the 1960s and 1970s, as well as to neoliberalism in the 1980s and 1990s, often shared with me their disillusionment with the "demagoguery" of the Bolivian Communist Party, which forbade the consumption of chicha using such slogans as "¡Tomemos el poder y no tomemos chicha!" (Let us take power, not drink chicha). In Spanish, the verb *tomar* is used for both "to take" and "to drink." But for many in Quillacollo this "eternal song of the Left" amounted to a refusal to recognize the consanguinities of their cultural experiences as people "of humble origin." "They wanted to bring the Russian Revolution here to Bolivia," complained a former party member.

Instead of a "national Left, identified with our customs, with our tradition, with our culture," explained another, "we distanced ourselves from our own reality, we forgot our own culture. We were like foreigners in our own country." One problem with a doctrinaire politics, went these suggestions, is that it is culturally alienating. As such, many young men quit the party during these years. And many of them ended up becoming proactive militants of the UCS during the late 1980s and throughout the 1990s.

Chicha is recognized as an intimate part of popular qhochala or valluno ways of being. In a brief account of the history of the region's chicha industry, Gustavo Rodríguez and Humberto Solares (1990:142) celebrate the democratic "fraternity of the chichería" as a way to override differences of social category and political allegiance. In Quillacollo groups of political intriguers often described their nocturnal meetings to me as having been sustained purely "on the basis of chicha." Cultural activists echoed this sentiment, proclaiming chicha a "unifying brew," as well as a "drink of collective communication, despite differences in social class." As we saw in chapter 5, chicha is a basic tool for building political coalitions. Such localizing, personalistic, traditional sentiments about chicherías problematically coexisted with the frequent condemnation of them as places for drunkards and as vice ridden, where health risks bloom. As a centuries-long local tradition, imbibing chicha is one key diacritic of how to go about living a "humble life" in the region, as a potential means to restore mutual recognition. And this mixed message about chicha is one expression of the tensions built into Quillacollo's cultural politics, where indigenous ancestry—if expressed in particular ways—is at once a public source of legitimacy and a basis for stigmatization.

Quillacollo's Humble Politics

The activities of political authorities and the efforts of cultural activists in Quillacollo crosscut a consistently self-deprecatory vein of popular humor that I have equated, in Herzfeld's terms, with a kind of rueful self-definition. Along these lines we have the following joke:

> ¿En qúe se parece Superman a un argentino humilde?
> ¡En qúe ninguno de los dos existe!
> (What do Superman and a humble Argentine have in common?
> That neither exists!)

People in and around Quillacollo tell this and other jokes about Argentines as a way to differentiate between neighbors. But even after Argentina's economic collapse in 2001, such jokes carry a particular sting if we consider that thousands of undocumented Bolivians work and live in Argentina and routinely suffer poor living conditions, abuses in clandestine sweatshops and similar work environments, and even occasional racist violence. As the joke would have us understand, it is the "humble" Bolivian risking life and limb in cities like Buenos Aires. In fact, "humbleness" is an emergent cultural condition in early-twenty-first-century urban Bolivia and represents the hard to pin down, even oblique, center of political organizing, in the mode of negative solidarity, that I have been describing throughout this book. Though it remains to be seen if a "humble public" will in fact achieve sharper definition in Bolivia, the success of the MAS and of Evo Morales is in part owed to the broad-based cross-sector support the president has been able to maintain.

One well-known phenotypically indigenous-looking leader of a workers' union in Quillacollo, often criticized by rivals as an "indio bruto" or "cholo de mierda," shrugged off such comments, saying simply, "A humble worker can do many things." Statements like this one transform the stigmatization of cholos into a kind of "negative capability," to quote Keats of all people (Jackson 1989:16). But it also came as no surprise when a worker's son—college-educated journalist, local intellectual, and founder of the local cultural movement Itapallu—expansively described himself by explaining, "We're all proletarians, sons of humble folk."

These humble commitments are also used as a lens through which the town's history is locally understood. As I was told about the 1950s and 1960s, "I remember when humble folk couldn't enter the theater—only people from known families." In different ways, humble society is something to which provincial political actors in Quillacollo, historically divided in terms of ethnicity, class, and politics, can collectively (though rarely corporately) lay plausible claim. As a relatively uncontroversial euphemism or substitute for the still-pejorative term *cholo*, to be "humble" nevertheless allows public reference to different types of cholo political attitudes and behaviors in Quillacollo, including the local project of the UCS and MAS parties as well as provincial cultural projects like Itapallu.

The prevalence of public references to "humble origins"—to people considered to be de origen humilde—is also an indicator of the political efforts of popular and indigenous inclusion, particularly in border zones such as the provincial capital of Quillacollo, with its unpredictable mixtures of country and city, agriculture and industry, and Quechua, Aymara, and Spanish. In this book I have explored a variety of humble cultural registers, both personal and public, as a means to address the challenges of recognition (in contrast to the settled facts of identity) in Quillacollo. The obliqueness of people's cultural relationships to the past, as the basis of experience, self-prospecting, and potentially shared commitments, can invite skepticism and controversy. And as I have tried to make clear, this controversy greatly complicates political efforts grounded in the kind of negative solidarity described here. But all of this is also characteristic of the ways urban indigenous heritage continues to matter along this urban periphery.

One important expression of what I am calling negative solidarity has been the decade-long run in Quillacollo of the UCS party, which first appeared in 1989 and was proclaimed at the time by political analysts as a new instrument of the "cholo middle class" (*burguesía chola*) (Toranzo Roca 1991), with its founder, Max Fernandez, approvingly called an "Andean entrepreneur" (Medina 1992:185). During its long run, many people in Quillacollo typically identified the UCS as "a party for the humble folk." And even while it was the locally dominant party, the UCS generated considerable criticism from active party militants. A journalist who interviewed Max Fernandez, described him this way: "Max, who rose to wealth from humble beginnings, is not a graceful or dramatic orator, but his very awkwardness helps make him a convincing speaker for listeners who are poor and socially outcast as he once was" (Guillermoprieto 1994:182). Comments of this sort also pepper descriptions of the UCS phenomenon, couched in the terms of cholo lacks turned into political assets. In an exasperated mood one local *político* once good-naturedly dismissed Quillacollo's political arena, saying, "Well, it's a *cantinfleada!*" Referring to the famed Mexican humorist, the verb *cantinflear* sets up the piquancy of popular humor—the hybrid potpourri of the street identified with Cantinflas—as the pole opposite a desired linguistic orthodoxy. As a criticism, this aimed directly at the language gaffes committed by supposedly "semiliterate" cholos tarred for their inadequate command of Spanish. But more positively, it can also suggest an improvisational, if profane, shooting from the hip, characterized by a constant inversion of phrases, as well as intentional and unintentional destruction of verbal conventions. Vernacular expressivity is potentially satirical but may also evince negative solidarity as a cultural response to the ideological vacuum of "identity loss and identity crisis" (Ströbele-Gregor 1994:112–113), a crisis that has been aggravated during the period 1985–2005, which has corresponded to the regime of neoliberal democracy in Bolivia.

This tongue-in-cheek self-deprecatory style, akin to what Herzfeld (1997:4) has called "rueful self-recognition" in the Greek context, infected talk about the política criolla, corruption, language gaffes, and like varieties of human frailty or venality. All were good examples of the attitude often associated by Bolivians with the "humble life." That is, while part of a hardscrabble life, to be "humble" can also problematically serve as a potential avenue of negative solidarity, in a way perhaps comparable to what Victor Turner (1968:78) once called a "cult of affliction." While I stood with one local authority outside of a particularly contentious political meeting, just this attitude ruled his assessment of the goings-on inside, which was delivered with a wide smile while shaking his head: "Quillacollo is screwed." But self-recognition through affliction *and* affection is still an unreliable basis upon which to build a collective political subject.

A "humble life" is at least potentially the basis for circumstantial claims to provisional solidarity in Quillacollo among people apt to call one another "cholo" in private. A humble upbringing was offered as the foremost reason for people's decision to become politically involved in the first place. Commenting upon the "challenges" of the humble life, one político volunteered, "I come from a poor family. They always try to disrespect [*menospreciar*] humble homes. All of this led me to become involved in the Left." Or, as Santos Rojas explained to me, "I come from a peripheral barrio, a humble place. There weren't any soccer fields, lights, or any of the basic necessities. Now with my success, I haven't forgotten my people." Regional politics, despite a diversity of specific political party allegiances, was often described to me as a collective struggle "for the improvement of humble society." This commitment to humble society was explicitly contrasted with the "egoism" of normal political behavior.

And yet in a self-deprecatory spirit, even according to its own members "humble society" needs substantial improving. Despite the local dominance of the UCS, its rank and file was never shy about voicing unflattering, even brutal, assessments of the party leader, Max Fernandez. As one of the former party faithful put it, "Max wasn't charismatic.... He's of humble origins and lacks refinement, intellectual capacity. He didn't know the political game. He was a political apprentice. He has surrounded himself with castoffs [*basura*, literally, "trash"] from other parties. What they have done is to rob him of his money." Max's followers in Quillacollo—often free with their criticisms of their own leader—were nevertheless at the same time extending a self-deprecatory empathy. Their stinging barbs were as much indictments as explanations of what it means to be "humble." After all, they shared the cultural trappings, economic predicaments, and social estrangement of the party leader's humble beginnings, if not his later good fortune. In their very disillusionment about the realities of politics they counted themselves at least as vulnerable to bullying patrons and to the machinations of self-serving clients.

In 1995 the brother of then-mayor Lucho Martínez—a businessman who spent most of his time living abroad—explained the question of being humble to me in the following terms: "We are a humble family [*familia humilde*], and continue to be so. Humbleness [*la humildad*] means a lot. The more knowledgeable, the more humble one should be. But we don't forget where we come from. We shouldn't forget who we were in the past." Recognizing this humble past for him meant an ongoing, public commitment to one's own "ancestral culture," generously interpreted. Pancho Sánchez explained his political commitments to me in these terms:

> *I am a person who has a simple, humble ego and, well, this has always been my characteristic. I have never much liked to practice the word, "I, I, I, I," me-firstism.... I have a humility, alongside a simplicity [sencilléz], because that has been of great value to me because, if you like, I am a person who comes from simple families, and so I have wanted to maintain this situation.*

Note Pancho's negation of the cholo's often commented upon hyperindividualism with his emphasis upon "humility" and "simplicity."

These convictions about popular belonging were aired by a surprising diversity of people, including a great majority of those who were politically active. A migrant from Potosí, high school teacher, and town council member, explained to me:

> *My mother was of very humble extraction. This meant that my family origin permitted me to identify with this level of life, its humility more than anything. Because this is the most important part rooted in my own person. So I believe that this has meant that in my following life, I was not permitted to separate myself from a reality that I had and which sustained me. I continue it.... Deep inside, that is, in the depth of my personality, there exists this attitude that I shouldn't separate myself from what I was before. Because this would be to reject my origin, to reject my family, and to reject as well what amounted to my education in the first years of life.*

The son of a miner, this man, when I knew him, was comfortable in terms of worldly possessions. But as he made clear with this comment, the humble life is a personal alignment to the past even if it is often publicly invisible.

Diacritics of humility are found in other places than Quillacollo, or Bolivia for that matter. Rudi Colloredo-Mansfeld pointedly emphasized the importance of a comparable discourse for successful indigenous entrepreneurs from Otavalo, Ecuador:

> *The physical labor and rough implements of a rural hearth serve as an idiom of indigenous life and suffering. This idiom turns on the word yanga. Combining ideas of risk, poverty, and futility, yanga can mean*

> useless, in vain, worthless, or humble. Otavaleños use the word to con-
> trast the expectations of indigenous people with those of dominant mes-
> tizo society. Many speak of their own language (yanga simi), their core
> possessions (yanga cosas), and rural life (yanga kawsay) as being
> humble or worthless. [1999:92]

According to Colloredo-Mansfeld (1999:114), *yanga*—as an adjective con-
veying the importance of physical labor, the artifacts associated with this
work, and the fact that it is simple labor, often fruitlessly spent—is a means
to foreground the circumstances of Otavaleños' transforming "collective
obligations and identities."

The Quechua spoken around Quillacollo uses the term *wajjcha* (rather
than *yanga*), meaning "poor" or "indigent," in reference to similar preoccupations and as the nearest synonym for the frequently heard Spanish term
humilde. Interestingly—considering the pervasive discourse about cholos
and the attention throughout this book to patrimonies and their social displacement—*wajjcha* can also refer to an "orphan." I have heard people refer
approvingly to a *wajjcha runa*, someone considered at once a "peasant" and
a "poor man," because he is *noqhanchis jina* (like us). While ticking off the
several "big shots" he has managed to persuade to become his compadres,
Pancho Sánchez paused and then added to the list the name of an artisan
who was totally uninvolved in politics, simply "because of his humbleness,
his friendship,…because he is of my level." Pancho was not the only person
to reject the idea of politically expedient compadres for more "humble compadres."

The Indigenous and the Urban Periphery

"Indigenous" is a burdened category of cultural and political identity and
belonging in early-twenty-first-century Bolivia. By this I mean it is at once a
loaded term, conspicuously fraught, highly politicized, both indexing and
circumscribed by a welter of historical associations from which it can be
hard to escape. It is burdened by "five hundred years" of colonial history,
something that international and national indigenous advocates and leaders
hasten to remind us. And it has carried a more recent burden during the
years of intense social movement activism beginning in 2000, when indigenous enfranchisement became the basis of new kinds of rights and citizenship claims, in the process broadening the terms of indigenous inclusiveness
(see Albro 2006b; Canessa 2006; Postero 2007a). Recently, this burden has
been further complicated by new political contests that include attempted
reassertions of privilege in Bolivia, which have been accompanied by racist
conflicts. This was particularly on display in the lowland city of Santa Cruz,

during the ongoing standoff over regional autonomies through 2007 and 2008, where it was apparently possible to download "kill Evo" screensavers for your cell phone.

To be "indigenous" is also to be burdened by problems of chronic misrepresentation, as was apparent in a bemusing article I came across that first appeared in the *Tehran Times*, of all places, describing the events surrounding the recall vote in Bolivia in August 2008, when Evo won over 67 percent of the national vote to remain in office. For this foreign writer, "the indigenous intifada of the Americas" (Golpira 2008) had won another victory. Of course such assertions make little sense in terms of the lived experience of indigenous peoples in Bolivia (and, one assumes, elsewhere in Latin America). Much less ridiculously, to describe the spectacular multiclass protest events in Bolivia since 2000 primarily as "the latest cycle of resistance" to have originated from "the matrix of indigenous community politics" (Hylton and Thomson 2005:45) still requires that we ignore much of what is particular to the present moment of conjuncture in this country. And as Joanne Rappaport (2005) has elegantly explored for the case of Colombia, negotiating the ins and outs of the frontiers of indigenous identity in fact can add up to multiple, and at times challenging to reconcile, subject positions.

Such is the case in Bolivia as well, with its significant variety of indigenous movements. Despite the historic watershed represented by the Morales administration, multiple indigenous projects maintain an unresolved coexistence. Bolivia boasts a substantial diversity of indigenous projects and ways to assert indigenous claims. Some compete with each other for national leadership. Others reproduce persistent fault lines of Bolivian society within indigenous politics, including highland (*originario*) and lowland (*indígena*) differences (see Gustafson 2002), elite intellectual and grassroots campesino variations (see Stephenson 2002), agrarian union and ayllu-based organizational structures (Rivera 1990b), and the neighborhood-based and vocational associational life of such urban spaces as El Alto (Lazar 2008), as well as municipal and parallel forms of political participation (see Albó 2002), among other points of tension and forms of indigenous political expression. How to occupy these various categories of indigeneity is certainly not a settled question.

This landscape is further complicated by top-down and policy formulations of identity (see Paulson and Calla 2000), such as current Bolivian foreign minister David Choquehuanca's self-conscious efforts to incorporate Aymara concepts into the practice of national governance (see de Córdoba and Luhnow 2006)—less than fully representative and somewhat divorced from lived indigenous realities. Legal legibility can also be confounding, as with Bolivia's new Constitution (see Albro 2008). If in step with such international efforts as the recently approved UN Declaration on the Rights of Indigenous Peoples, say, this effort risks falling short of coming to terms with the variations of indigenous commitments in Bolivia, particularly more urban ones. If historically it has been an influential way to formulate indigenous political claims in Bolivia and Latin America, nationhood would be deeply problematic as *the only* legal and representational space within which "indigenous" were to make sense in contemporary Bolivian society. Local politics in Quillacollo, at least, makes little sense in such terms.

This diversity of indigenous movements, options, and projects continues to run up against assumptions about indigenous stakeholders in development work, efforts to formulate state policies for indigenous peoples, the representations circulated by international indigenous advocates and activists, and, in some cases, the conventional academic portrayals of indigenous realities in majority-indigenous countries such as Bolivia. As I have suggested elsewhere (Albro 2006a:422), the assumption of identity as an interpretive point of departure can become counterproductive when reduced to "interpretations of indigenous identity privileged as a function of their proximity to sources of indigenous distinctiveness." This quickly becomes a politics primarily defined by the patrolling of cultural borders of inclusion and exclusion. But at least for Quillacollo, say, qualifying such a preoccupation with authenticity as the basis for an identity politics by way of ethnographic demonstrations of cultural hybridity, while easy to do, fails to recognize the extent to which indigenous experience does matter as a basis for what I have called political self-prospecting along this urban periphery.

The challenges of representation in Bolivia include, but also go well beyond, the stereotype of indigenous peoples "as either victims or survivors of state violence" (Warren and Jackson 2002:1). This is apparent in Bolivia, which appears to be reaching a historical tipping point of sorts in the reconsideration of its own variegated indigenous legacies, at a variety of social and political levels and in different economic, legal, political, and cultural terms. Analysts of Bolivia's changing indigeneity have sought to clarify how best to talk about indigenous engagement with new urbanities (see Guss 2006), within a new "postcolonial" indigenous order (see Canessa 2007a), with a new kind of state and "postmulticultural citizenship" (see Postero 2007b), and with disparate cultural frameworks constructing a new "indigenous cosmopolitanism" (see Goodale 2006). But we also need to pay attention to ways that intimate cooperative engagement with nonindigenous political experience has moved more to the center of urban indigenous experience in Bolivia as itself a part of what it means to be indigenous—in political terms—in the first place.

In keeping with such work, this book has sought to characterize the provisionally important role that indigenous claims, heritage, but also stigma—all as registers of "humble" experience—continue to play in the provincial urban political arena of Quillacollo. This is despite the fact that Quillacollo has been conspicuous, as recently as the middle of the twentieth century, for its lack of a recognizably indigenous population. And yet through the 1970s Quillacollo was the nerve center for the province's agrarian union movement. And the 1952-era assimilationist project of mestizaje, even in its apparent stronghold of provincial Cochabamba, is being actively contested in the region through assertions of claims of traditional "uses and customs." Since the mid-1980s politics in Quillacollo has been dominated by the popular alternatives of the UCS and MAS parties, respectively. In both cases political relationships have been shaped and regularly shadowed by indigenous cultural priorities and strategies, if alongside other priorities. And these are not mutually exclusive. At the same time, people with whom I worked mobilized perceived indigenous and neoliberal realities as cultural and moral counterpoints in their political critiques and factional disputes with one another, reformulating the significance of both in the process. In this regard there is a particular contemporaneity to indigenous politics in Quillacollo.

In contemporary Quillacollo indigenous experience is a marginal but consistent fact of life, though certainly not now or perhaps ever as a collective project. In politics it is a constituent feature of people's public self-identity and of the construction of working networks among people who at once recognize and debate their indigenous patrimony while not being fully defined by it. As I have described in different ways throughout this book, contested formulations and negotiations of indigenous heritage are an important part of coalition building and of the public representational cultural politics of Quillacollo, including among people for whom "indigenous" is not necessarily their first affiliation. This heritage is produced and expressed in public arguments over questions of patrimony, sponsorship, gender, kinship (fictive and otherwise), genealogy, and clientelism, all of which compose the discourse and practice of the everyday politics of this provincial capital. If the MAS phenomenon is best understood not as an indigenous nationalist project but as an irreducibly plural, transactional, and coalitional political instrument (see Albro 2005a; Madrid 2006), Quillacollo provides an opportunity to start to understand the characteristics of these more expansive and less exclusive claims for indigenous belonging in Bolivia for at least one urban constituency at the start of the twenty-first century.

As I have given attention to it, political representation in Quillacollo confronts several challenges. On the one hand, the pervasive facts of stigma are evident reminders that continue to track a controversial provincial history of social mobility, a history that is mostly associated with the boundary-transgressing cholo. This is the arena of the política criolla, understood to be particularly at home with the behavior of local political authorities. Throughout this account we have run into the several different facets of this arena, which are particularly identified with such types as the desclasado and the llunk'u, respectively. Such regular reference to these sorts of figures makes it clear that to patrol the borders of cultural conduct—that is, commitment to a political project of identity, even if this project is never achieved—continues to be an important activity in Quillacollo.

Reference to the conduct associated with the política criolla also provides a means to point to a characteristically local experience of historical rupture, as exhibited in the generational unevenness of people's public careers and usually in critiques of the present failures or deformations wrought by neoliberal democratization, as it has been lived in Quillacollo. More often than not, condemnation is leveled at the pervasive "self-interest" of political behavior, as an overdetermined and everyday neoliberal fact but also as an identifiably cholo trait. This makes stigmatization politically and culturally productive. Even if in the context of estrangement, or in negative relief, the relevance of indigenous and popular expectations and forms of cultural practice is reasserted in the course of Quillacollo's politics.

On the other hand, the discourse of "humble origins" is also a characteristic political and cultural point of reference in Quillacollo, if in a very different way from the dynamic of stigmatization. As people of all sorts are often moved to note, "We are all from humble origins." The term cuts across class, ethnic, and political party differences and runs counter to well-defined but limiting political ideologies or doctrines. It provides a basis to claim the commonalities of indigenous and popular heritage, but also of social mobility, as one's own and in the process widens the possibilities of inclusion, and potential working relationships, in ways comparable to the "horizontal" political decision making associated with the grassroots indigenous and social movement successes since 2000 (see Dangl 2007; Gutiérrez et al. 2002). As one young town councilman exclaimed to his colleagues during a heated debate, "We have all been born from humble families. We have to forge solidarity!" This makes the register of the humble a discourse of the reconciliation of problematic "matter out of place."

Local cultural activists make this point even more strongly. If the stigmatized cholo is Bolivia's historically "forgotten actor" (Bouysse-Cassagne and Saignes 1992), politics in Quillacollo is deeply engaged with this cholo subjectivity, as a taken-for-granted state of social affairs in Bolivia's urban hinterland. And the cholo publicly occupies center stage in Quillacollo's politics, despite the embarrassment this might create both for Bolivian nationhood and for indigenous activism. In fact, by "doing politics," people attempt to transform the all too widespread experiences of social displacement, abandonment, alienation, or stigma into potential instruments of mutual political recognition, that is, the basis for political action in this place.

A longtime cultural worker in Quillacollo explained his efforts at cultural consciousness-raising in Quillacollo to me this way: "The fundamental base began with the cholo, rescuing him as an emergent social actor,...the cholo, *la cholada*,...neither campesino nor *q'ara*." The term *q'ara* is Quechua for "plucked," literally referring to white-skinned elites from the indigenous point of view. Commenting on this history of stigma, another cultural activist exasperatedly proclaimed to me, "We're cholos! We're not going to feel insulted to be cholos." Mariaca Iturri's (1998:189) celebratory call for recognition hits a comparable note when he describes the cholo as "the modern citizen who does not want to stop being Indian—an urban, monied, educated Indian."

I understand such assertions as representing a movement away from— let's call it—the traditional boundary-patrolling tendencies of Bolivia's national indigenous identity politics. To be from a "humble" background in this way directs attention to the social and cultural spaces that open up between the present and a patrimony, often as a displaced "origin." This origin is brought into the present in a variety of often contentious ways, to which people are not necessarily constantly beholden. Instead, specifically humble sensibilities can be appropriately exercised at particular times, places, and events—such as at public fiestas. To be of humble origins, therefore, is a statement about the *process* of trucking between then and now, there and here, the circumstances of ancestry and the political constitution of the self. This set of cultural commitments, then, is less about the categorical facts of identity than it is about addressing the challenges of recognition. In this way "de origen humilde" operates in Quillacollo as a nonpejorative substitute for the stigmatized cholo but with culturally connective potential. This is one of the ways that indigenous legacies are presently finding their way into Bolivia's future.

Notes

Chapter 1

1. I initially visited Quillacollo in 1991, and the bulk of fieldwork in Quillacollo was conducted over two years between 1993 and 1995, with follow-up visits and additional research in 2001 and 2003, respectively.

2. A representative example of such an approach is Brysk 2000. In what is otherwise a tour de force of activism, together with ethnography and the interpretation of contemporary indigenous movements in Latin America, Warren and Jackson's (2002) edited volume is also representative of this broad trend.

3. See Raquel Gutiérrez, Alvaro García, and Luis Tapia's (2000) discussion, "La forma multitud de la política de las necesidades vitales." See also current Bolivian vice president Álvaro García Linera's (2003) concise description of the "multitude."

4. Fieldwork was largely participant-observation ethnography. But it also included an initial thirty-five-house survey of political perceptions and dozens of structured and unstructured recorded interviews, including a modified self-understanding interview administered to twelve counterparts in the field, as well as one extended life-history project. Research also included extensive access to the archives of Quillacollo's mayor's office and its Department of Culture. In the nearby city of Cochabamba I consulted archives of the newspaper *Los Tiempos*, the National Institute of Statistics, and the Departmental Electoral Court. In addition, I enjoyed the cooperation of CARITAS-Bolivia and the Departmental Federation of Mothers' Clubs. Participant-observation was characterized by many hours in attendance at dozens of meetings of Quillacollo's town council, as well as meetings of many of its base organizations, such as the town's civic committee, the rival Comité Pro-Quillacollo, FEJUVE (the provincial federation of neighborhood committees), the Federation of Comerciantes Minoristas, and other groups. Fieldwork had me in Quillacollo on a daily basis and included participation in many choreographed, unscripted, and serendipitous events, such as political rallies, town and family fiestas, meals, and drinking

(which is central to politics). In the course of hundreds of conversations, my counterparts active in local politics were unusually frank and forthcoming about their own political careers, those of others, and the ways they understood politics in Quillacollo to work, for which I am grateful.

5. This can be boiled down still further to a hard core of thirty-four men—they were all men—with whom I worked most closely and who filled out the thirty-nine available posts of mayor or of town councilman from 1985 until 1995.

6. The work of Fernando Mayorga (1991, 2002) provides the most detailed account of the phenomenon of Max Fernandez and the neopopulism of the UCS. But see also Albro 1998a and Benavides 2004. The popularity of the UCS coincided with the emergence of another important neopopular option in Bolivia, that of CONDEPA (Conscience of the Fatherland), which is vividly described by Jeff Himpele (2008) in his recent ethnography on that subject and which has also been described by Rafael Archondo (1991).

7. The most comprehensive account of neoliberalism's various effects upon Bolivia's popular sectors since 1985 can be found in Kohl and Farthing 2006.

8. All census figures for 2001 were acquired in person from the Instituto Nacional de Estadísticas (INE), the Bolivian government office that collects census information, or downloaded from its Web site: www.ine.gov.bo. However, I have also had to calculate all proportions and percentages separately.

9. One of the centerpieces of the current Morales administration was the promise to carry through a constitutional referendum. While a draft Constitution composed of 411 distinct articles was successfully approved by a constitutional assembly in December 2007, this process was highly contentious. Nevertheless the Constitution was formally approved in January 2009.

10. While references to Bolivia's indigenous peoples are frequent and distributed throughout the new Constitution, the most important statements defining the parameters and scope of indigenous constitutional rights are found in Articles 2, 30, and 290.

11. All translations are mine unless indicated otherwise.

12. This, too, is changing. An excellent example is Daniel Goldstein's (2004) detailed analysis of the contemporary political role of collective cultural performances in Villa Pagador, a marginal barrio of the city of Cochabamba. The historian Laura Gotkowitz (2008) has also recently provided a fine-grained analysis of struggles over land, the law, citizenship, and social justice, which conspicuously departs from the assumption that "class" has been fundamental in shaping the political priorities of rural communities in Cochabamba throughout at least the republican era.

13. Mestizaje in the Andes has been explored extensively by anthropologists and historians, particularly its role in the social construction of nation building of the late nineteenth and twentieth century (for example, de la Cadena 2000; Mallón 1996; Weismantel 2001).

14. See also Sian Lazar's (2008:15–19) more recent discussion of "cholo citizenship" in El Alto, Bolivia.

15. But see Abercrombie's (1996) ethnohistorical discussion of at least one permanently enduring if interstitial colonial-era and cholo-type social identity.

16. The present argument is comparable, in this sense, to Marisol de la Cadena's (2000) innovative argument about the complex, mutually constitutive relationship between the categories of mestizo and Indian among intellectuals, politicians, and ordinary citizens in Cuzco, Peru, throughout the twentieth century.

17. The nearby city of Cochabamba also experienced unprecedented growth over the same

period. For a comparable account of the effects of in-migration upon the urban planning of Cochabamba, see Goldstein 2004:70–71.

18. For a comparison with another urban periphery in Bolivia, suffering similar problems and described in similar terms, see Lesley Gill's (2000:25–46) description of El Alto.

19. Throughout the late 1990s and into the 2000s Quillacollo has been the scene for repeated attempted, and sometimes successful, lynchings of mostly young men suspected of being gang members and thieves by residents of different barrios (see *Los Tiempos* 2001a; Ovando 2005). Daniel Goldstein (2004:214) has examined in detail the phenomenon of widespread lynching attempts in the urban periphery of the nearby city of Cochabamba. He interprets these as spectacular vehicles for the communication of demands and as instruments to attract the attention of municipal authorities and established urban dwellers to the predicaments and needs of the urban periphery.

20. According to Kohl and Farthing (2006:74), by 1991 over 60 percent of Bolivia's urban population was engaged in the informal sector, in such work as street vending, casual labor in construction, or domestics. By one estimate, nine of every ten new jobs created in Bolivia during the 1990s were informal jobs (see Bentería 2001). At present the informal sector—described as constituting a "new working class" with no social benefits except as self-generated—employs 83 percent of the working population (see Claure 2007).

21. See Dandler 1987a; Lagos 1994; Larson 1998:351; among others, for additional discussions of diversified household strategies in the provinces of Cochabamba.

22. Sian Lazar (2008:76–88) provides an extensive analysis of the role of corruption in the political discourse of local associational life in El Alto as one important way in which the expectations of the collectivity are defined against the supposed self-interested actions of its individual leaders.

23. In his long essay on choledad in Peru, for example, José Guillermo Nugent (1992:37) combines the implications of social and geographic mobility in repeating a traditional definition of cholos as "the encounter of a strongly ruralized provincial identity with modern urban culture." Writing about Bolivia, Abercrombie (1996:63) explains that cholos are "people whose cultural hybridity is manifest."

24. Unless referring to well-known public figures, such as Bolivia's current president Evo Morales, I maintain the convention of the use of ethnographic pseudonyms throughout. This is primarily to protect the confidentiality of counterparts in Quillacollo, particularly given that the book's topic—politics—is an especially contentious one.

25. A "trufi" is a bus-taxi hybrid.

26. Throughout this book I am using the concept of cultural capital in ways indebted to Bourdieu's (1984) coinage of this term to refer to the kinds of knowledge, experience, and connections people use to succeed, particularly in their acquisition of the kinds of cultural knowledge that confers power.

Chapter 2

1. Such a cultural politics, for example, has been written into the 2007 Declaration on the Rights of Indigenous Peoples, under consideration for ratification in the United Nations since 1993 and which Morales and the MAS have publicly affirmed.

2. Here I am indebted to pathbreaking approaches from anthropological linguistics emphasizing the work of dialogic co-construction in the production of culture (see Tedlock and Mannheim 1995).

3. With the cooperation of Quillacollo's Department of Culture, I was able to survey the town's municipal archives. These records were not systematically organized, and most of them had been lost in a fire several years prior. Nevertheless, surviving documents provided intermittent but valuable information about the town's municipal government during the eighteenth and early nineteenth century.

4. With few exceptions during these years only literate men actually voted. This essentially precluded women and people from a variety of popular backgrounds, most obviously the indigenous peasantry (campesinado), and ensured that the agrarian elite (also very much involved in national politics) completely controlled provincial politics. In this sense, elections were oligarchic window dressing.

5. The excellent and comprehensive work of Jorge Dandler (1971, 1983) provides the most comprehensive account of the emergence and importance of agrarian union politics in provincial Cochabamba during the 1950s and 1960s, including detailed descriptions of the factional rivalries among prominent campesino caciques in the upper and lower valleys of Cochabamba. Based in Quillacollo, Sinforoso Rivas was arguably the second most powerful campesino leader in the region throughout this period.

6. In his analysis of the politics of Cochabamba's agrarian union movement subsequent to Bolivia's 1953 Agrarian Reform, Dandler (1971:187–188) emphasized seven criteria of effective leadership, including successful exploitation of historical experience as a source of latent solidarity and effective usage of a culturally relevant repertoire of rhetoric and symbol.

7. For further discussion of Bolivia's Popular Participation Law, see Bigenho 2002:182–197; Healy and Paulson 2000; Kohl 2000; Medeiros 2001; Postero 2000.

8. For accounts of these successive protest movements, see, inter alia, Albro 2005b; Dangl 2007; García Linera 2003; Gustafson 2002; Gutiérrez et al. 2002; Olivera and Lewis 2004; Postero 2005.

9. This is a double entendre. If *mamadera* literally means "baby's bottle," the verb *mamar* is an important part of the vernacular of the política criolla and refers to acts of political deception, in this case, working without doing anything.

10. Mariaca Iturri (1998:191), for example, describes "cholo discourse" as one of "ambiguity, indecision, lack of definition, and indeterminate."

11. This distinction about cholo discourse recalls similar distinctions such as Wittgenstein's (1981) discussion of the differences between Augustine's classic propositional theory of language acquisition and his own notion of language games.

12. A misa negra is one among a variety of prepared ritual tables available for purchase in Quillacollo's market. Used for different purposes, both good and bad, people are often instructed to purchase them after having consulted with a yatiri.

Chapter 3

1. Quillacolleños' emphasis upon the strong "spiritual sentiment" imbued in compadrazgo ties is comparatively quite typical. Lola Romanucci-Ross (1986[1973]:76), in her analysis of the character of social bonds in postrevolutionary Mexico, notes the "heightened sentimental tone" of

fictive kin ties. In similar fashion, Paul Friedrich (1986:108), in his study of a Mexican strongman complex, emphasized the "emotional and to some extent sacred" nature of fictive kinship.

2. My wife and I experienced these burdens directly, as we were asked to be compadres and subsequently negotiated the ongoing expectations and obligations. The financial and other costs are not insignificant.

3. Similar examples of local perceptions of negative social change, bundled together with criticisms of neoliberalism, include local commentary on the apparent deformation of the annual fiesta of Urkupiña (see Albro 1998b).

4. When referring to indigenismo, I am referring to the backward-looking and largely pastoral corpus of organic intellectual writing about Andean culture, with its focus upon the role of the indigenous in the formation of national identity, historically associated with such figures in Peru as Mariateguí, Valcarcel, and Arguedas and in Bolivia with writers such as Medinaceli and Jesús Lara.

5. This is a rich literature in Andean studies, and what follows is an incomplete list of some of the most useful discussions for ayni in rural Bolivia and Peru: Alberti and Mayer 1974; Albó 1985; Isbell 1978; Izko 1986; Lagos 1994; Lehman 1982; Sallnow 1989; Van Vleet 2008.

6. In her vivid case study of Zumbagua, Ecuador, Mary Weismantel (1988) conveys many of the rules and meanings associated with food preparation and consumption as a central cultural practice in the definition of Andean identities.

7. José Limón (1994:123–140) offers a similar case for South Texas. He interprets *carne asadas*, the ritualistic consumption of barbecued meat, as carnivalesque events where coparticipants convivially if occasionally, reassert their Mexican American popular maleness.

Chapter 4

1. For different discussions of the importance and characteristics of cultural intimacy, consult Berlant 1998; Herzfeld 1997; and Lomnitz 1992.

2. Throughout this argument, "tradition" is treated as a provisional, contested, and politically charged cultural construction, and as a frame of reference manipulated by políticos in particular as they attempt to stake authoritative claim to regional cultural representativeness (in their view, synonymous with the political representation of tradition). As such, the various uses made of the chola's image are attempts to construct particular versions of tradition (in the sense of Hobsbawm and Ranger's [1983] pathbreaking discussion of the "invention of tradition") as a means of cultural inclusion. Since the people discussed here often themselves engaged in the process of strategic essentialization, my argument seeks to draw attention to the effects of this process.

3. Rossana Barragán (1992) provides a more detailed history of the attire of both popular and elite women and of the changing significance of the pollera.

4. The name of this group is Itapallu (Quechua for a plant thought to cure rheumatism), and it was officially founded in 1988 on the heels of unsuccessful attempts by its members to establish a cultural program associated with the political Left from within the municipality's Department of Culture. Since then Itapallu has undertaken regular activities of journalism, organizing cultural events in the region (most conspicuously the folklore festivals), and promoting Quillacollo's patrimony (typically as centered on the town's patronal fiesta to the Virgin of Urkupiña). For an in-depth account of the history of this cultural movement, see Albro 1999:chap. 9; 2000.

5. "Usos y costumbres" is the legal term of choice referring to customary law in Bolivia's 1994 Law of Popular Participation, which encourages local base organizations to advance claims upon municipal government in the terms of a collective cultural identity. For further discussion, see Albro 2006b.

6. In fact, stories of the role of womanizing in political intrigue are ubiquitous. One local political operator "sacrificed" (his word) his girlfriend—he was married and was referring to one of several women with whom he has carried on affairs—for the "good of the town." As one part of an effort to curry favor with a visiting party higher-up, he asked her to sleep with him. In the telling, it became a patriotic cause. They bought her new clothes for the rendezvous, took the VIP to an out-of-town chichería, and provided lively entertainment, after which the "couple" went off for "several hours" to a hotel.

7. Comparable relationships of women to national and international NGOs have been discussed in detail for El Alto, a city with many of the same challenges as Quillacollo (see Gill 2000:135–154; Lazar 2008:95–96; Sandoval and Sostres 1989:109–145). See also Postero's (2007b:164–188) discussion of Guaraní participation in NGO projects in suburban Santa Cruz.

8. For a comparable discussion of notions of "ideal womanhood" in prerevolutionary Bolivian identity politics, see Gill 1993, particularly her detailed characterization of the social role and reputation of the *chola paceña*. Miles's (1992:123) discussion for Ecuador of the *chola cuencana*, described as "a cultural symbol of the highest order," suggests a similar role for the chola in regional folklore.

9. In another argument (Albro 1998b), I explore some of the implications of this blurring of the gender identities of local cosmic powers, specifically the relationship between the Pachamama and the Tío, the "Devil" of the mines. Yatiris, ritual practitioners who are present in large numbers for the fiesta of Urkupiña, often refer to these two as husband and wife.

10. *Complementarity* is a term widely used by Andeanists to characterize a culturally specific relation between the genders. Referred to by Harris (1978:21) as the "complementary unity of the conjugal bond," she goes on to suggest its importance for the Laymi of Norte de Potosí: "*Chachawarmi*, man-woman, represents symbolically many of the fundamental relationships of Andean society, but it also has a direct social referent in the peasant household which is the basic unit of the traditional Andean economy" (1978:22). A key to the *chachawarmi* concept is that any predominance (of male or female) is ideally "highly relative, and to be understood in the context of overall mutuality in the relationship" (1978:27). This Andeanist notion of gender complementarity has been used as a means to understand women's particular sort of political intervention, described as "collective resistance, complementing male action" (Rivera 1990a:165). As summarized by one longtime observer of gender relations in the Bolivian Andes, "Women's participation in situations of violent confrontation conforms to the model of complementarity and hierarchical man/woman unit and reproduces *those aspects of daily life* in which this model is apparent" (Rivera 1990a:166; emphasis mine). This same assumption of complementarity, as typifying women's political interventions in terms of everyday resistance, has informed the Andean wing of Bolivia's gender technocracy in development, where "champions of Andean ethnicity" have rejected "gender concepts and methods as an imperialist imposition" (Paulson and Calla 2000:127). Instead, they hold up the chachawarmi model as an appropriate alternative. This continues to be apparent during the Morales administration, in which a detailed discussion of the chachawarmi concept has been incorporated into its current Poverty Reduction Strategy (see Ranta-Owusu 2008).

11. In Quillacollo, and elsewhere in Bolivia, there are recognized differences between "cholas" and "cholitas," which, for example, are younger and unmarried. As such, cholitas in particular are much more associated with the erotic and sexual dimensions of fiesta contexts.

12. For an insightful and comprehensive discussion of the significance of "traditional" Andean folkloric music and dance in relationship to other kinds of music in Bolivia, see Bigenho 2002:29–60. For other recent discussions of the relationship of public festivals or fiestas (as well as music and dance) to the politics of community development, see Goldstein 2004:134–178 and Lazar 2008:118–143, respectively.

13. While its etymology is unclear, wisk'atatay is a Quechua term people typically use in provincial Cochabamba to refer to a man (presumably a mestizo) romantically or sexually involved with a cholita. Wisk'ay, the verb, literally means "to close" or "to lock up." The implication might refer to the fiercely jealous or commanding reputation of cholas, who brook no competition. The paramour is thus trapped by his own love; he is a prisoner to the cholas's powers, as with the eventual fate of the protagonist in Medinaceli's La chaskañawi.

14. Strictly speaking, in provincial Bolivia the word sipas is used in Quechua to refer to a young girl. But in the Quechuañol more typical of Quillacollo and of the folkloric milieu, imilla has come to function as a synonym for the "innocence" of the cholita and, therefore, as the subject of much indigenist-type regional literature.

15. The sexual intimacy of the k'alincha is, furthermore, understood to give birth to the hybrid popular male. In her useful discussion, Berlant (1998:281) suggests that such intimacy "involves an aspiration for a narrative about something shared, a story about both oneself and others that will turn out in a particular way." Playing on the shared cognate between "intimacy" and "intimation," she also suggests that this aspiration is communicated "with the sparest of signs and gestures." In the present analysis, the k'alincha, but also the chola's various other folkloric incarnations, publicly intimates an invisible shared intimacy with a local popular culture, presumably acted out backstage and in people's private lives.

16. Space does not permit a fuller description of the many details of Quillacollo's fiesta of Urkupiña. For more on this internationally known and colossal annual event, consult Albro 1998b; Díaz-Barriga 2003; Lagos 1993; Peredo 1990; Scarborough 2005.

17. Janet Page-Reeves's (1999) research examining the relationship of a cooperative of women's knitters in nearby Tarata, Bolivia, to a global marketing network has emphasized this tendency.

18. The claim among festival organizers in Quillacollo that cholas play a special role in inviting people to such popular festivals and ferias has been ethnographically corroborated for Mizque (Paulson 1996:134).

19. A yapa is literally a "little something extra" and is used by market sellers both to attract and to maintain an exclusive relationship with permanent customers, who are called caseros.

20. This state of affairs perhaps unexpectedly returns us to a familiar anthropological problem, that of the reproduction of social relationships and political alliances by virtue of the exchange of women (compare Leach 1954; Lévi-Strauss 1963).

Chapter 5

1. Daniel Goldstein's (2004) ethnography of nearby Villa Pagador likewise deals in depth with community-based political organizing along the urban periphery among recent in-migrants

from Oruro, including the lengthy and difficult negotiations, as well as conflicts, with municipal representatives in the effort to achieve legal recognition and to extract municipal services from the city of Cochabamba.

2. There is a prodigious literature on the ubiquitous theme of drinking and rituals of drinking throughout the Andes, a sample of which includes Saignes 1993 for the colonial period, Bunker 1987 and Brass 1989 for Peru, Butler 2006 for Ecuador, as well as Heath 1995 and Rodríguez and Solares 1990 for Bolivia, among many others.

3. "Patrimony," in this sense, should be differentiated from a classificatory concern with *patrilineal descent*, which has been a signature anthropological preoccupation in the study of kinship. Patriliny usually refers to publicly recognized rights and duties specifically inherited through the male line, and usually in a context of corporate ethnic politics. There exists a large literature documenting the ways that political operators seek to extend personal networks of patrons, clients, and followers through the idiom of kinship. Much of this work rests upon residually functionalist treatments of the nuclear family as an apparently natural social unit. Innovative work on kinship in the Andes (see Paulson 1996; Van Vleet 2008; Weismantel 1995), however, has productively complicated any such story.

4. For comparative discussions of the role of national patrimonies in Bolivia, see Albro 1998b; Bigenho 2002:221–225; Goldstein 2004:134–178; Lagos 1993; Salmón 1997.

5. Pursuing the implications, as I do here for local politics in Bolivia, of the constitutive cultural discourses of self and of public discursive strategies of self-representation, I have benefited from the comparable approaches and insights in particular of Battaglia (1995), Crapanzano (1980, 1993), Gal (1991), Herzfeld (1997), Keane (1997), and Rorty (1989).

6. For ethnographic summaries of the festival of Todos Santos in Bolivia, see Izko 1986:147–150 and Rocha 1990:60.

7. Space does not permit the full elaboration of this important topic. But, beginning in 1985, provincial mayors' offices like Quillacollo's were restructured to include a Department of Culture, or Casa de Cultura. Soon after its creation, Quillacollo's was occupied by a group of cultural activists who actively promoted a unique local and regional identity and who embraced a "cholo identity" in positive terms rather than as a stigma. Even after it no longer controlled the modest cultural apparatus of the municipality, this group continued to be responsible for a wide variety of popular cultural events, including regular folklore festivals, for many years afterward.

8. Max Fernandez, founder and national head of the UCS party, was notorious for his inadequate Spanish. A journalist commented, "Max, who rose to wealth from humble beginnings, is not a graceful or dramatic orator, but his very awkwardness helps make him a convincing speaker for listeners who are poor and socially outcast as he once was" (Guillermoprieto 1994:182).

9. Rather than prioritize the one or the other as more fundamental, in comparable ways Maria Lagos (1994), Lesley Gill (1994), and Linda Seligmann (2004) have all written extensively and persuasively about the interplay and tensions of class and ethnicity (as well as gender) in the constitution of people's identities in the Andes.

10. When last recorded by INE in 2001, the province was growing at an annual rate of between 4.1 percent and 6.5 percent.

11. In another context, Katherine Ewing (1990) has explored a comparable instance of the "illusion of wholeness" with regard to self-identity among Pakistani women, who produce selective life history accounts through their multiple, inconsistent self-representations.

12. As Fernandez (1986:215) describes them, inchoate images refer to the "uncharted and imperfectly chartable hinterland to thought and feeling which nevertheless exerts its plenipotentiary attractions and repulsions upon us."

13. Such awkward, even threatening, moments were relatively rare throughout my fieldwork. Typically, I successfully negotiated a role as part of Quillacollo's political arena that allowed me to cross otherwise factionally charged boundaries between different political parties and groups of associated political actors. As such, I was very much a part of the rumor mill so central to the kinds of politics I describe here, as an interested consumer of people's stories about one another. While drinking or in private interviews people willingly, without my prompting, communicated their views of others to me. These views could rise to the level of character assassination. But I also systematically followed up such accounts, most often when they happened to straddle factional lines. As such, my own "genealogical method" of fieldwork, particularly apparent in chapters 5 and 6 and dedicated to filling in the family histories, careers, and backstories of various key political figures in Quillacollo, was inspired by the ways that people already talked about each other in political terms. The case of Buendía and his family was unique, in part because he could be described as the absent center of Quillacollo's then-dominant political machine. Nevertheless, Buendía's rejection of my modest efforts to learn about his family was illustrative of what I describe here as the culturally productive estrangement typified by the public discourse surrounding the behavior of the so-called cholo desclasado.

14. As it happened, Buendía himself was a subject of regular speculation about possible corruption. The regional press reported a variety of scandals during his several administrations, and multiple inquiries were initiated by national authorities, although with no definitive outcome. These scandals followed him to La Paz where, as a national congressman, he was subject to a highly publicized corruption probe.

15. In addition to a wide variety of interactions with Santos Rojas over a two-year period between 1993 and 1995 while engaged in ethnographic fieldwork and further extensive conversations during a six-week return to Quillacollo in 2001, the majority of Santos's life history was recorded in five intensive sessions from late June through mid-July 1994. The present fragment is taken from the first of these sessions.

16. The centrality of self-narration to political self-presentation is not unique to local politics in Bolivia. My discussion of Santos Rojas's life history is comparable, for example, to more celebrated instances by national Bolivian politicians of indigenous descent, such as Victor Hugo Cárdenas and Evo Morales, who offer regular public retellings of their early life histories and humble beginnings.

17. The expression used by Santos's father in his refusal to work, "to swallow his lungs," is especially prevalent among miners in reference to the inevitable silicosis that comes of working in the mines for an extended period.

18. In a comparable argument, Matthew Gutmann (2002:49–57) discusses the cultural constraints upon father abandonment in urban Mexico as a doorway to exploring the contemporary political agency of that country's popular classes.

19. See also Comaroff and Roberts (1981) and Keane (1997), who explore similar genealogical machinations for the cases of South Africa and Indonesia, respectively.

20. As I repeatedly emphasize throughout this chapter, in the popular cultural and provincial environment of Quillacollo politics is in large part a contest over one's relative ability to define himself in his own terms, as against others' competing definitions. An inspiration for this

argument has been Greenblatt's virtuoso discussion of "Renaissance self-fashioning." He refers to Thomas More's frequent use of the rhetorical trope litotes, "in which a thing is affirmed by stating the negative of its opposite" (1980:23). As Greenblatt (1980:58) notes about More, "His self-fashioning rests upon his perception of all that it excludes, all that lies in perpetual darkness, all that is known only as absence."

Chapter 6

1. Contemporary treatments of ch'allas in Bolivia, primarily in rural Aymara communities, include Abercrombie 1993; Arnold 1992; Orta 1999, 2004.

2. This chapter is also concerned with illustrating an approach to the contextualization of factional politics that resituates both performance-based theories of rhetoric and ethnographic treatments of life histories in a more comprehensively interpretive frame.

3. This parallelism is even more explicit during the fiesta of Urkupiña, where priests and traditional ritualists called yatiris operate almost side by side, for the benefit of the thousands of pilgrims.

4. As a sign of provincial identity, the aypurita (along with the Virgin) is a concrete incarnation of the felt need to "restore our cultural values," a stock phrase that is often on the lips of local authorities. These ceremonial vessels are miniature replicas of the large ceramic cisterns used to store fermenting chicha and figure prominently in the many political murals painted throughout the town by political parties.

5. Something comparable to the fiesta-cargo complex found in other provincial towns in Bolivia either no longer exists or never existed in Quillacollo (compare Buechler and Buechler 1971; Carter and Mamani 1982). But for a detailed account of the activities and responsibilities of pasantes on the urban periphery of nearby Cochabamba, see Goldstein 2004:134–178.

6. The term *Quechuañol* combines *Quechua* (an indigenous language spoken in Quillacollo and throughout the Andean highlands) and *Español*. See Albó 1974 for a sociolinguistic analysis of this regional vernacular. In Cochabamba's provinces Quechua and Spanish are mutually and heavily leavened with loanwords. Lucho's stumping rhetoric is a variant of this, advertising his idiomatic fluency in this popular speech style.

7. For more detailed discussions of the term *llakta*, consult Allen 1988:260; Fuenzalida 1970; and Salomon 1991:23.

8. Sian Lazar (2008:76–88) offers a comparable analysis of the role of gossip, suspicion, rumor, and other forms of accountability talk with her description of the stories told by and about neighborhood leaders in the community of Rosas Pampa in El Alto, Bolivia.

9. If seldom theorized, *plausibility* is at least a familiar issue, from Machiavelli's preoccupation with princely *virtù* to the "character issues" routinely shaping US presidential politics. With some exceptions, such as Victor Turner's (1957) trailblazing ethnography documenting a failed bid for authority among the Ndembu, the plausibility of ritual performance has received scant attention (see Bell 1992; Kelly and Kaplan 1990; Kertzer 1988).

10. Research on ch'allas in rural Bolivia has given particular emphasis to their genealogical structure, as indexical acts linking place-names, identities, and social memory (see Abercrombie 1993; Arnold 1992).

11. Hanks (1984), Gal (1991), and especially Connerton (1989) have all explored the cultural

politics of rituals of commemoration and the link between ritual and history. For an Andean case, see Rappaport (1994:152), working with the Cumbales in Colombia, who writes, "In most societies ritual is the most powerful source of historical knowledge. Commemorative ceremonies in particular serve as vehicles for historical interpretation, insofar as they not only remind participants of events but re-present them, thereby lending an instrumentality to history by shifting its focus from the past to the metaphysical present."

12. This chapter pursues a largely anthropological approach to the self that emphasizes the differences, fissures, echoes, and shadows produced through the embedding of multiple self-representations in specific contexts, which have been variously discussed in the terms of self-representation and biography (Crapanzano 1993), self-representation and self-knowledge (Herzfeld 1997), representations and their histories (Behar 1995), narrative and historical selves (Spence 1982), front stage and backstage (Goffman 1959), visibility and invisibility (Meyerhoff 1978), demonstrated and revealed signs (Keane 1997), replication and dissemination (Urban 1997), or factuals and counterfactuals (Hawthorn 1991).

13. My analysis is indebted to Kay Warren's discussion of the meaning of *costumbre* in Maya communities, which she describes as problematizing relations between the past and present. For Warren (1998:169), the prayers of Maya elders, done "because of costumbre," are "not really an affirmation of unproblematic continuities, consensus, common knowledge, integration, or the coercive powers of a closed community." Rather, they refer to ruptures, "the alienation of youths from the elders they were supposed to respect and the lack of empathy in the community for others' pain" (1998:170).

14. This conception has a comparative resonance throughout the Andes. For example, Rappaport (1994:90) explains how the Cumbales in Colombia "draw a link between themselves and their forebears, built upon a moral continuity originating in the family, which is a fundamental vehicle for historical expression."

15. As many ethnographers have documented (see Herzfeld 1997:212–226), the familial metaphor is comparatively widespread, particularly in politics, as a cover for asymmetric or hierarchical social relations, a fact characteristic of Quillacollo as well, where peasants are often patronized as "like children."

16. The Movimiento Nacionalista Revolucionario (or MNR) party was the party that came into power after the 1952 Revolution, but it was also the party that instituted neoliberal reforms beginning in 1985.

17. Andy Orta's (1999) work on ch'allas conducted in Aymara-speaking Jesus de Machaqa, Bolivia, draws interesting relations comparable to those discussed here between libations, memory, and personhood. Orta has argued that ch'allas are ritual acts of memory that help to align a "remembered subject" (in this case, a person's *chuyma* [Aymara: "heart"]) with the shifting social and material world.

18. He now has at least one child.

19. As a firebrand civic leader, Lucho found himself in a potential quandary. Though his political activism legitimated him, as an intransigent member of the "opposition," it also ensured that, as a critic of representatives of the state, he was effectively barred from access to municipal resources. He was largely unable, therefore, to translate national patronage ties into concrete resources for Quillacollo.

20. This assertion, however, turned a blind eye to the wholesale shift in ideological platforms of the MNR party during these years. In the revolutionary era of the 1950s, the MNR was

moderately socialist, as exhibited in its various doctrines of governmental centralization, pro-labor stance, Indian rights, and agrarian reforms. The post-1985 MNR, however, has done a literal about-face, adopting neoliberal economic principles, with policies of governmental decentralization, privatization, and a trickle-down theory of benefits for the popular sectors. For more on this comparison, see Klein 1992:227–245 and Gamarra 1994. To collapse these gross distinctions by reference to the "historic MNR," as is often done, is thus itself political gamesmanship.

21. Regardless of different approaches to cultural research in the Andes—if exemplified by disguised class confrontations (Lagos 1994), via fetishized expressions of material inequalities (Taussig 1980), the symbolic hegemony of a national society (Crain 1990), reciprocal relations between encompassing and encompassed polities (Platt 1982), or appeals to pluralism (Crandon-Malamud 1991)—the colonial frame remains fundamental.

22. This encourages a rethinking of the value of starting with the hegemonic status of colonial/ethnic categorization of belonging in Latin American ethnography (compare Urban and Sherzer 1991). For a similar critique of the mistake of beginning with established racial categories in the United States, see Goldschmidt 2006.

Chapter 7

1. See Colloredo-Mansfeld 1999:57–86; de la Cadena 2000:44–85; Goldstein 2004:70–79; and Weismantel 2001:22–26 for comparable discussions of hygiene-based fears of the indigenous presence in the context of urban modernization across the Andes.

2. For a history of these periodic urban hygiene programs directed at eliminating chicherías, consult Rodriguez and Solares 1990.

Glossary

A = Aymara
Q = Quechua
Sp = Spanish

abarcas (Sp). Sandals typically worn by "peasants" and made from tire rubber.

a dedo (Sp). The arbitrary naming of people to political office by a political boss.

ahijado/a (Sp). Ritual godchild.

alasitas (A). Literally "buy me" and referring to the diverse miniatures that are transacted during patronal fiestas as well as at other festive venues.

alcalde (Sp). Mayor.

alcaldía (Sp). The mayoralty or the bureaucracy of the municipality.

aqha (Q). A fermented beer widespread in the Andes and fabricated from corn. See also *chicha.*

aventura amorosa (Sp). An illicit sexual or romantic relationship.

ayllu (Q, A). Traditional pre-Hispanic and colonial Andean kingdom or ethnic federation and also prominent in the discourse of contemporary indigenous movements in Bolivia.

ayni (Q, A). The strict exchange of equivalents.

cacique (Sp). A political strongman.

calvario (Sp). The hill upon which an image of a Virgin has appeared and where her shrine is located.

camarilla (Sp). An informal political friendship circle.

camba (Sp). People from Bolivia's lowlands, in contrast to *colla*.

campesino (Sp). Adopted by the government after 1952 as a substitute for the pejorative Indian, often also a beneficiary of the 1953 Agrarian Reform and referring to a "peasant" agriculturalist or rural smallholder.

cariño (Sp). Personal affection.

casco (Sp). A drinking vessel typically for *chicha*. See also *tutuma*.

casero/a (Sp). A customer with whom a market vender maintains an ongoing relationship of buyer-seller. See also *yapa*.

castigo (Sp). Punishment or retribution by a saint for the breaking of a promise to that saint and often associated with bad luck.

chacra (Sp). An agricultural field, usually for growing corn.

ch'ajchu (Q). Literally, "a sprinkling," and the name of a regional dish that uses a little of everything, primarily beef, potatoes, carrots, onions, and freeze-dried potatoes.

ch'aki (Q). Literally, "thirst," and used as an invitation to drink.

ch'alla (Sp, Q, A). A traditional ritual libation that is performed on many occasions, typically with *chicha*, and the Hispanicized version of ch'allaku (Q).

Ch'ampa Guerra (Sp, Q). A war between rival peasant strongmen in Ucureña and Cliza in Cochabamba's upper valley between 1959 and 1963.

chicha (Sp). Andean maize beer. See also *aqha*.

chichería (Sp). A popular drinking establishment where food and *chicha* are served and which is used for informal political meetings.

chola (Sp). A woman of indigenous descent who wears the gathered skirt, or *pollera*, and is typically assumed to be a market woman.

cholaje (Sp). Refers to an indigenous remainder in circumstances of cultural mixing (in contrast to *mestizaje*).

cholita (Sp). Diminutive of *chola*, referring to an unmarried young woman but also the subject of regional folkloric literature, music, and dance. See also *imilla*.

cholo (Sp). Historically an insulting term used to describe someone who is at once upwardly mobile and of indigenous descent. See also *de origen humilde* and *wajjcha*.

cholo desclasado (Sp). A case of someone of indigenous descent who has opted to turn his back on, or to conceal, his ancestral heritage.

chota (Sp). A woman who dresses *de vestido*, that is, wears Western-style clothes rather than the traditional gathered skirts.

chuño (Sp). Freeze-dried potatoes.

chupa (Sp). A long drinking bout. See also *farra*.

club de madres (Sp). Literally, "mothers' club," as an organization of women usually of the same neighborhood or community.

Cochabambino/a (Sp). Someone born in the department or city of Cochabamba. See also *Qhochala*.

colla (Q, A). People from Bolivia's highlands, in contrast to *camba*.

comerciante minorista (Sp). Small-scale vendor or street merchant.

comité cívico (Sp). A provincial or departmental civic committee that typically occupies the role of holding the local government to public accountability.

compadrazgo (Sp). The traditional godparenthood complex that is widespread in Latin America and defined by ritualized and typically church-sanctioned obligations and responsibilities.

compadre/comadre (Sp). Ritual co-parent.

compadre de interés (Sp). A manufactured opportunity to generate a ritual co-parent for self-interested or political purposes.

compadrerío (Sp). A local conception of organizations as run by nepotism (that is, based upon favors between *compadres*).

compañero (Sp). Literally, "comrade," and used as a term of address among people in the same base organization or who share political commitments.

conciencia (Sp). Self-awareness of political, cultural, or class standing.

confianza (Sp). Trust as the basis of ongoing working relationships of all sorts.

convocatoria (Sp). The ability to command a political following.

criollo/a (Sp). A native of South America but of Spanish descent and often elite.

cueca (Sp). A traditional creole dance dramatizing an amorous flirtation.

curandero (Sp). A traditional healer. See also *sahumero* and *yatiri*.

de nañas (Sp, Q). Intimate or inseparable friendship, derived from *ñaña*, the Quechua term for "sister" to another sister.

de origen humilde (Sp). Literally, "of humble origin," used as a way to refer to a wide cross section of people from within the popular and indigenous sectors and as a way to summarize one's typically provincial, and often poor, social background. See also *cholo* and *wajjcha*.

de promoción (Sp). A fiesta or ritual godparent of advancement established in ways other than traditional.

de vestido (Sp). A woman dressed in "Western" skirts. See also *chota*.

dirigente (Sp). A leader associated with the popular and indigenous sectors and usually representing a local base organization.

doctrina (Sp). An official party line, Marxist dogma, or other kind of explicitly ideological position.

el pan del día (Sp). Literally, "the daily bread," in popular parlance referring to the need or right to make a living.

entrada (Sp). A choreographed parade of folkloric dancers and a traditional part of most municipal and national fiestas.

faena (Sp). Communal work project.

farra (Sp). Heavy drinking bout. See also *chupa*.

feria (Sp). Both a weekly agricultural market and a calendric folklore festival.

figurón (Sp). Someone who publicly presents himself as something he is not or a self-promoter without a political following.

formación (Sp). Social status derived from tradition, family, or political ideology.

gente decente (Sp). Reference to traditional and *mestizo* provincial elites prior to 1952. See also *vecino/a*.

hacerse sombra (Sp). Literally, "to shadow another," referring to the case of a political rival upstaging another or seeking to replace him in his role.

hacienda (Sp). Large-scale feudal landed estate owned by creole elites and making use of indigenous indentured labor.

hijo/a del pueblo (Sp). A native son or daughter, as someone born and raised in the town or province of Quillacollo.

hijo predilecto (Sp). An officially recognized "favorite son" of the town or province.

imilla (Q). Literally, "servant girl," but also "young girl." See also *cholita*.

indigenismo (Sp). Primarily a tradition of arts and letters, and political position, which celebrates the past greatness of indigenous Andean civilizations as the basis of modern nation building but separates the past from the present.

indio/a (Sp). A pejorative term used by nonindigenous people to refer to native Andean peoples especially prior to 1952, which, in Cochabamba, has been replaced by the term *campesino*.

indio bruto (Sp). Derogatory reference to an indigenous person as uneducated.

inquieto/a (Sp). Someone well known for agitating for public change and seeking to advance in class position.

Itapallu (Q). Literally, "nettle," and the name of a group of cultural activists in Quillacollo.

junta vecinal (Sp). A neighborhood club, often as a replacement for agrarian unions in more urban provincial zones.

k'alinchear (Sp). Hispanicized verb form of *k'alinchay* (Q) and used to refer to male womanizing.

k'araku (Q, A). Any organized political meeting, rally, or fiesta where food and drink are provided by the organizers.

k'aska (Q). Literally, "not to separate from another," referring to a close friend or constant companion.

katarismo (Sp). An Indianist movement in Bolivia, which began in the early 1970s.

k'ukeada (Q). The tradition of stealing unripe fruit from others' orchards.

lari (Q). Derogatory reference among valley dwellers to "more indigenous" and monolingual highlanders of the nearby sierra.

llakta (Q). Variously, a people, a town, a region, or a nation, depending upon context and scale.

llaktamasi (Q). Literally, "fellow townsperson," as an indication of membership in the same cultural community.

lloqhalla (Sp, Q). Dismissive term for a "youngster" or "whelp," as someone lacking in experience.

llunk'u (Q, A). A flatterer, brown noser, or enterprising or ambitious individual of indigenous descent, often upwardly mobile and in a political relationship of clientage.

mañudo (Sp). A rogue or a brute.

maquinita (Sp). A local or provincial political machine.

masi (Q). A suffix attached to a word to indicate neighborly intimacy or kinship.

mestizaje (Sp). Racial or cultural mixture, also used when referring to status in the middle class.

mestizo (Sp). A person of mixed Andean and Spanish racial or cultural heritage.

militante (Sp). An official and active member of a political party.

mink'a (Q, A). Service or labor not repaid in kind, but usually in cash.

misa (Sp). A church service, but also referring to the activities of traditional ritual practitioners, especially their "ritual tables."

misachiku (Q). A family fiesta or procession usually held to commemorate recently deceased relatives.

moreno/a (Sp). Dark or swarthy complexion, referring to gradations of difference between *campesinos*, *cholos*, and *mestizos*.

mukeo (Sp, Q). The traditional mode of fermenting *chicha* by masticating the cornmeal.

muñeca (Sp). Political influence.

ñato (Sp). An insulting term with racist connotations and referring to one's oversized proboscis.

negra (Sp). The girlfriend or lover of a married man.

Nueva Política Económica (Sp). The package of neoliberal policies, or structural adjustment, applied by the Bolivian government in 1985 and again in 1993.

obrero (Sp). Factory worker.

pacha (Q). Literally, "the world," "the earth," or "time."

Pachamama (Sp, Q, A). The Earth Mother, a female cosmic, telluric, and space/time concept that is also associated with agricultural production.

padrino (Sp). A ritual godfather and the sponsor of a festival event.

pandilla (Sp). Street gang.

pasante (Sp). A donor of money or other resources, as a sponsor of a fiesta, saint's day festival, or dance fraternity.

pasa-pasa (Sp). Someone who jumps from one political party to another.

patrimonio (Sp). Specifically jural or economic inheritance, but also extended as a way to refer to pervasive facts of cultural heritage.

patrón/a (Sp). Literally, "patron," referring both to feudal-era landowners and also to patron saints. See also *peón*.

pedir la palabra (Sp). To ask to speak at a meeting of one or another expression of local associational life.

pega (Sp). A job in the public sector, often given as a reward for political support or help in electing a candidate to office.

pendejada (Sp). A tricky or deceptive story.

peón (Sp). An indentured servant on a feudal landed estate in pre-1952 Cochabamba, usually of indigenous descent. See also *patrón*.

personalidad (Sp). Literally, "personality," but also a politically loaded term referring to the integrity of self-identity of a political actor.

picardía (Sp). Literally, "mischievousness" or "trickiness," and often associated with the behavior of *cholos*.

pichikhatero (Sp). An illegal bulk transporter of coca leaf.

pinche (Sp). A passive political client or political stooge.

piquero (Sp). Small independent provincial landholder.

p'ischar (Sp, Q, A). The meditative chewing of coca leaf.

plato típico (Sp). Traditional regional cuisine.

polilla (Sp). Homeless street urchin and caller for buses.

política criolla (Sp). Literally, "creole politics," often used to describe political activities condemned by journalists as corrupt.

político (Sp). A person, usually male, involved in specifically provincial politics and as distinct from a national or professional "politician."

pollera (Sp). Traditional and colorful gathered skirts worn by *cholas* throughout the Andes.

pongueaje (Sp). The colonial-era institution of indentured servitude by Indians on landed estates or *haciendas*.

prebenda (Sp). A political gift or bribe, in popular political transactions routinely also associated with traditional Andean forms of reciprocity and exchange.

pulpería (Sp). The company store in an isolated mining camp.

puño (Sp, Q). In Spanish literally "fist," but derived from *puñu* (Q), "leftover food," referring to large earthenware vats used to store fermenting *chicha*.

q'allu (Q). A rural dish of sliced tomatoes and onions in an oil and spicy pepper sauce.

q'ara (Q). Literally, "plucked," referring to white people from the Indian point of view.

Qhochala (Q). A person born and raised in provincial Cochabamba. See also *Cochabambino/a*.

q'oa (Q). An aromatic burnt offering.

q'otu (Q). A traditional moniker of people from Quillacollo, referring to the goiter associated with locals.

Quechuañol (Sp, Q). The unique regional dialect characterized by the heavy admixture of Quechua terms into grammatical Spanish.

Quillacolleño/a (Sp). A son or daughter of the town or province of Quillacollo.

relocalizado (Sp). Highland migrants to the Cochabamba valleys, particularly referring to the arrival of ex-miners in the wake of structural adjustment.

renegón (Q). Someone who complains or takes issue or who is resentful of his or her social standing.

rescatista (Sp). A rural trader in agricultural goods, in the valleys usually corn. See also *trueque*.

resentido (Sp). Someone spiteful of society, having fallen short of his or her personal ambitions.

revolucionismo (Sp). The historical platform of the MNR party, generally associated with interclass alliances, suffrage for the peasantry, agrarian reform, and centralized government.

rosca (Sp). Literally, "screw," referring to the traditional creole national elite.

runa (Q). Literally, "person," but also used by Spanish speakers to refer to rural indigenous people of all sorts.

sahumero (Sp). A ritual practitioner also often for large-scale fiesta events such as Urkupiña. See also *curandero*, *yatiri*, and *q'oa*.

saqrahora (Sp). The traditional meal break provided by the *patrón* for workers during planting or harvesting.

sindicato (Sp). A local union.

sin preparación (Sp). Without proper schooling, crude, ignorant, or unrefined.

suplente (Sp). An unelected substitute or alternate for an elected political post.

tata-abuelos (Sp). Great-grandparents and, by extension, generically used to refer to distant ancestors.

tatay (Q). Literally, "father," and historically used by indigenous clients when addressing political authorities and their elite patrons.

testimonio (Sp). A transcribed oral history of an account of community struggle.

t'ika (Q). Flower.

t'inka (Q). A small gift.

t'inku (Q). A traditional ritual battle between structural opposites within or between *ayllus*.

Tío (Sp). Male cosmic force associated with the inner recesses of the earth, especially applicable to miners and associated with the Devil.

Todos Santos (Sp). The celebration of All Saints.

trueque (Sp). Rural barter and exchange among market sellers. See also *rescatista*.

tutuma (Q). A gourdlike vessel for the drinking of *chicha*. See also *casco*.

Urkupiña (Sp, Q, A). Hispanicization of the term *orqopiña*, literally, "there she is, on the hilltop," and referring to the appearance of Quillacollo's patron saint, now the basis of a national-level annual fiesta.

usos y costumbres (Sp). A legal term corresponding to "customary law" and used in making cultural claims upon the state or the municipality.

valluno (Sp). Literally, "valley dweller," and referring to people living in more rural provincial towns in Cochabamba.

vecino/a (Sp). Literally, "neighbors," traditionally referring to people considered mestizos who live in provincial towns. See also gente decente.

villa miseria (Sp). A peripheral shantytown that lacks basic amenities.

vivandera (Sp). Female street vendor.

vivo (Sp). An adjective describing someone who is particularly clever or savvy, especially in politics.

wajjcha (Q). Literally, "poor" or "indigent," but also a synonym for "humble." See also *cholo* and *de origen humilde*.

wallunk'a (Q). Literally, "swing," referring to a festival that accompanies the time of All Saints.

wilkaparu (Q). A regional variety of ground maize particularly favored for the fabrication of *chicha*.

yanapa (Q). An informal favor between friends or family, which does not entail any reciprocal response.

yapa (Sp, Q). Something extra added to one's purchase by someone from whom one routinely buys. See also *casero*.

yatiri (Q, A). Literally, "one who knows," referring to indigenous ritual practitioners. See also *curandero* and *sahumero*.

References

Abercrombie, Thomas

1992   La fiesta del carnaval postcolonial en Oruro: Clase, etnicidad y nacionalismo en la danza folklórica. Revista Andina 10(2):279–326.

1993   Caminos de la memoria en un cosmos colonizado: Poética de la bebida y la conciencia histórica en K'ulta. *In* Borrachera y memoria. Thierry Saignes, ed. Pp. 139–170. La Paz: Instituto de Historia Social Boliviana (HISBOL).

1996   Q'aqchas and la Plebe in "Rebellion": Carnival vs. Lent in 18th Century Potosí. Journal of Latin American Anthropology 2(1):62–111.

1998   Pathways of Memory and Power: Ethnography and History among an Andean People. Madison: University of Wisconsin Press.

Alberti, Giorgio, and Enrique Mayer

1974   Reciprocidad y cambio en los Andes peruanos. Lima: Instituto de Estudios Peruanos.

Albó, Xavier

1974   Los mil rostros del Quechua. Lima: Instituto de Estudios Peruanos.

1985   Desafíos de la solidaridad Aymara. Cuaderno de Investigación 25. La Paz: Centro de Investigación y Promoción del Campesinado (CIPCA).

1987a   From MNRista to Katarista to Katari. *In* Resistance, Rebellion, and Consciousness in the Andean Peasant World, 18th to 20th Centuries. Steve J. Stern, ed. Pp. 379–419. Madison: University of Wisconsin Press.

1987b   Por qúe el campesino qhochala es diferente? Cuarto Intermedio 2:43–59.

1990   Lo andino en Bolivia: Balance y prioridades. Revista Andina 8(2):411–463.

1994   And from Kataristas to MNRistas? The Surprising and Bold Alliance between Aymaras and Neoliberals in Bolivia. *In* Indigenous Peoples and Democracy in Latin America. Donna Lee Van Cott, ed. Pp. 55–79. New York: St. Martin's Press.

1997   La Paz/Chukiyawu: The Two Faces of a City. *In* Migrants, Regional Identities and Latin
         American Cities. Teófilo Altamirano and Lane Ryo Hirabayashi, eds. Pp. 113–150.
         Arlington, VA: American Anthropological Association.

2002   Bolivia: From Indian and Campesino Leaders to Councillors and Parliamentary
         Deputies. *In* Multiculturalism in Latin America: Indigenous Rights, Diversity and
         Democracy. Rachel Sieder, ed. Pp. 74–102. New York: Palgrave.

Albó, Xavier, and M. Preiswerk
1986   Los señores del Gran Poder. La Paz: Centro de Teología Popular.

Albro, Robert
1998a   Introduction: A New Time and Place for Bolivian Popular Politics. Ethnology
         37(2):99–115.

1998b   Neoliberal Ritualists of Urkupiña: Bedeviling Patrimonial Identity in a Bolivian Patronal
         Fiesta. Ethnology 37(2):133–164.

1999   Hazarding Popular Spirits: Metaforces of Political Culture and Cultural Politicking in
         Quillacollo, Bolivia. PhD dissertation, University of Chicago.

2000   As Witness to Literary Spectacle: The Personality of Folklore in Provincial Bolivian
         Politics. Journal of Latin American Cultural Studies 9(3):305–332.

2004   Populism (Latin America). *In* New Dictionary of the History of Ideas. Maryanne Cline
         Horowitz, ed. New York: Charles Scribner's Sons.

2005a   The Indigenous in the Plural in Bolivian Oppositional Politics. Bulletin of Latin
         American Research 24(4):433–454.

2005b   "The Water Is Ours Carajo!" Deep Citizenship in Bolivia's Water War. *In* Social
         Movements: An Anthropological Reader. June Nash, ed. Pp. 249–271. London: Basil
         Blackwell.

2006a   Bolivia's "Evo Phenomenon": From Identity to What? Journal of Latin American
         Anthropology 11(2):408–428.

2006b   The Culture of Democracy and Bolivia's Indigenous Movements. Critique of
         Anthropology 24(6):387–410.

2008   MAScalculations and the Constitutional Assembly: The New Legislative Terms of
         Indigenous Representation vis-à-vis the Bolivian State. Paper presented at the invited
         conference "Decolonizing the Nation, (Re) Imagining the City: Indigenous Peoples
         Mapping New Political Terrain," Northwestern University, May 8–9.

Allen, Catherine
2002   The Hold Life Has: Coca and Cultural Identity in an Andean Community. 2nd edition.
         Washington, DC: Smithsonian Institution Press.

Alonso, Ana María
1988   The Effects of Truth: Re-Presentations of the Past and the Imagining of Community.
         Journal of Historical Sociology 1(1):33–57.

Alvarez, Sonia, Evelina Dagnino, and Arturo Escobar
1998   Introduction: The Cultural and the Political in Latin American Social Movements. *In*
         Cultures of Politics and Politics of Cultures: Re-Visioning Latin American Social
         Movements. Sonia Alvarez, Evelina Dagnino, and Arturo Escobar, eds. Pp. 1–29.
         Boulder, CO: Westview Press.

Arbona, Juan
2007   Neo-liberal Ruptures: Local Political Entities and Neighborhood Networks in El Alto, Bolivia. Geoforum 38(1):127–137.

Archondo, Rafael
1991   Compadres al micrófono: La resurrección metropolitana del ayllu. La Paz: HISBOL.

Arguedas, Alcides
1937   Pueblo enfermo. Santiago de Chile: Ediciones Ercilla.

Arias, Arturo, ed.
2001   The Rigoberta Menchú Controversy. Minneapolis: University of Minnesota Press.

Arnold, Denise
1992   La casa de adobes y piedras del Inka: Género, memoria y cosmos en Qaqachaka. *In* Hacia un orden andino de las cosas. D. Arnold, D. Jeménez, and J. de Dios Yapita, eds. Pp. 31–108. La Paz: HISBOL.

Auyero, Javier
2000   Poor People's Politics: Peronist Survival Networks and the Legacy of Evita. Durham, NC: Duke University Press.
2003   Contentious Lives: Two Argentine Women, Two Protests, and the Quest for Recognition. Durham, NC: Duke University Press.

Babb, Florence E.
1985   Middlemen and "Marginal" Women: Marketers and Dependency in Peru's Informal Sector. *In* Markets and Marketing. Stuart Plattner, ed. Pp. 287–308. Monographs in Economic Anthropology, 4. New York: University Press of America.
1989   Between Field and Cooking Pot: The Political Economy of Marketwomen in Peru. Austin: University of Texas Press.

Bailey, F. G.
1988   Humbuggery and Manipulation: The Art of Leadership. Ithaca, NY: Cornell University Press.
1991   The Prevalence of Deceit. Ithaca, NY: Cornell University Press.

Bakhtin, Mikhail
1984   Rabelais and His World. Bloomington: Indiana University Press.

Barnes de Marschall, Katherine, and Juan Torrico
1971   Cambios socio-económicos en el valle alto de Cochabamba desde 1952: Los pueblos provinciales de Cliza, Punata, Tiraque, Arani, Sacaba, y Tarata. Estudios Andinos 2(1):141–171.

Barragán, Rossana
1992   Entre polleras, lliqllas y ñañacas: Los mestizos y la emergencia de la Tercera República. *In* Etnicidad, economía y simbolismo en los Andes. S. Arze, R. Barragán, L. Escobari, and X. Medinacelli, eds. Pp. 85–127. La Paz: HISBOL.

Bastien, Joseph
1978   Mountain of the Condor: Metaphor and Ritual in an Andean Ayllu. New York: West.

Battaglia, Debbora
1995   On Practical Nostalgia: Self-Prospecting among Urban Trobrianders. *In* Rhetorics of Self-Making. Debbora Battaglia, ed. Pp. 77–96. Berkeley: University of California Press.

Bauman, Zygmunt
1999   In Search of Politics. Stanford, CA: Stanford University Press.

Behar, Ruth
1993   Translated Woman. Boston: Beacon Press.
1995   Rage and Redemption: Reading the Life of a Mexican Marketing Woman. *In* The Dialogic Emergence of Culture. Dennis Tedlock and Bruce Mannheim, eds. Pp. 148–178. Urbana: University of Illinois Press.

Bell, Catherine
1992   Ritual Theory, Ritual Practice. Oxford: Oxford University Press.

Benavides, Jimena Costa
2004   Los partidos neopopulistas en Bolivian (1989–2004). Diálogo Político 3:63–87.

Benería, Lourdes
2001   Shifting the Risk: New Employment Patterns, Informalization, and Women's Work. International Journal of Politics, Culture and Society 15(1):27–53.

Berlant, Lauren
1998   Intimacy: A Special Issue. Cultural Inquiry 24(2):281–288.

Bigenho, Michelle
2002   Sounding Indigenous: Authenticity in Bolivian Musical Performance. New York: Palgrave Macmillan.

Blanes, José
1992   Descentralización político-administrativa y gobernabilidad. *In* Democracia y gobernabilidad en América Latína. F. Mayorga, ed. Pp. 111–128. La Paz: Editorial Nueva Sociedad.

Bourdieu, Pierre
1984   Distinction: A Social Critique of the Judgement of Taste. Cambridge, MA: Harvard University Press.

Bouysse-Cassagne, Thérèse, and Tierry Saignes
1992   El cholo: Actor olvidado de la historia. *In* Etnicidad, economía y simbolismo en los Andes. S. Arze, R. Barragán, L. Escobari, and X. Medinacelli, eds. Pp. 129–143. La Paz: HISBOL.

Brass, Tom
1989   Beer Drinking Groups in a Peruvian Agrarian Cooperative. Bulletin of Latin American Research 8(2):235–256.

Brysk, Alison
2000   From Tribal Village to Global Village: Indian Rights and International Relations in Latin America. Palo Alto, CA: Stanford University Press.

Buechler, Hans
1980   The Masked Media: Fiestas and Social Interaction in the Bolivian Highlands. The Hague: Mouton.

Buechler, Hans, and Judith-Maria Buechler
1971   The Bolivian Aymara. New York: Holt, Rinehart and Winston.
1996   The World of Sofía Velasquez: The Autobiography of a Bolivian Market Vendor. New York: Columbia University Press.

Buenavides, Jimena Costa
2004   Los partidos neopopulistas en Bolivia (1989–2004). Diálogo Político 3:63–87.

Bunker, S. G.
1987   Ritual, Respect and Refusal: Drinking Behavior in an Andean Village. Human Organization 46(4):334–342.

Burkett, Elinor C.
1978   Indian Women and White Society: The Case of Sixteenth-Century Peru. In Latin American Women: Historical Perspectives. Asunción Lavrin, ed. Contributions in Women's Studies 3. Pp. 101–128. Westport, CT: Greenwood Press.

Bustamante, Rocio, John Buttorworth, and Nicolas Faysse
2004   Is There a Future for Locally Managed Domestic Water Supply Systems in Peri-Urban Cochabamba, Bolivia? Analysis of Performance and Some Possible Scenarios. Unpublished working paper for NEGOWAT project workshop, São Paolo, Brazil, August 16–21.

Butler, Barbara
2006   Holy Intoxication to Drunken Dissipation: Alcohol among Quechua Speakers in Otavalo, Ecuador. Albuquerque: University of New Mexico Press.

Caero, María Isabel
1997   Espacios de género en el municipio de Cochabamba: Desencantos y esperanzas. In Teorías y prácticas de género: Una conversación dialéctica. S. Paulson and M. Crespo, eds. Pp. 71–81. Cochabamba: Embajada Real de los Países Bajos.

Calderón, Fernando, and Roberto Laserna
1983   El poder de las regions. Cochabamba: CERES.

Calzavarini, Lorenzo, Roberto Laserna, and Roberto Valdivieso
1979   Quillacollo: Barrio o pueblo? Cochabamba: IESE.

Canedo Olguin, Mery
1994   El rol del municipio en el desarollo urbano en ciudades intermedias. Quillacollo: Honorable Gobierno Municipal de Quillacollo.

Canessa, Andrew
2006   Todos somos indígenas: Towards a New Language of National Political Identity. Bulletin of Latin American Research 25(2):241–263.
2007a   A Postcolonial Turn: Social and Political Change in the New Indigenous Order in Bolivia. Urban Anthropology 36(3):145–160.

2007b   Who Is Indigenous? Self-Identification, Indigeneity, and Claims to Justice in
         Contemporary Bolivia. Urban Anthropology 36(3):195–238.

Cárdenas, Victor Hugo
1987   La CSUTCB: Elementos para entender su crisis de crecimiento. *In* Crisis del sindical-
         ismo en Bolivia. Carlos Toranzo, ed. Pp. 223–233. La Paz: ILDIS.

Carpio San Miguel, Edwin
2001a   Cochabamba vive el "boom" de las ferias. Los Tiempos (de Cochabamba), July 29.
2001b   Contaminación, un drama en Quillacollo. Los Tiempos (de Cochabamba), October 21.

Carrillo, Marco
2003   Danza, la chispa picante de las copleras del valle. Los Tiempos (de Cochabamba),
         March 2.

Carter, William, and Mauricio Mamani
1982   Irpa Chico: Individuo y comunidad en la cultural Aymara. La Paz: Editorial Juventud.

Cevallos Tovar, W.
1971   Quillacollo y su porvenir. La Provincia: Órgano del Comité Pro-Quillacollo. September:
         25.

Claure, Bernarda
2007   Bolivia's New Style Work Force. Inter Press Service, April 30.

Clifford, James
1986   Introduction: Partial Truths. In Writing Culture: The Poetics and Politics of
         Ethnography. James Clifford and George Marcus, eds. Pp. 1–26. Berkeley: University of
         California Press.
1988   The Predicament of Culture: Twentieth-Century Ethnography, Literature, and Art.
         Cambridge, MA: Harvard University Press.

Cohen, A. P., and John Comaroff
1976   The Management of Meaning: On the Phenomenology of Political Transactions. *In*
         Transaction and Meaning: Directions in the Anthropology of Exchange and Symbolic
         Behavior. Bruce Kapferer, ed. Pp. 87–107. Philadelphia: Institute for the Study of
         Human Issues.

Colloredo-Mansfeld, Rudi
1999   The Native Leisure Class: Consumption and Cultural Creativity in the Andes. Chicago:
         University of Chicago Press.

Colque, Sabino
1993   Fiestas y ferias rurales al acecho de los partidos. Los Tiempos (de Cochabamba), April
         10.

Comaroff, John, and Simon Roberts
1981   Rules and Processes: The Cultural Logic of Dispute in an African Context. Chicago:
         University of Chicago Press.

Connerton, Paul
1989   How Societies Remember. Cambridge: Cambridge University Press.

Conniff, Michael L.
1999   Introduction. *In* Latin American Populism in Comparative Perspective. 2nd edition. Michael L. Conniff, ed. Pp. 1–21. Albuquerque: University of New Mexico Press.

Contreras Baspineiro, Alex
2000   Algunos locales nocturnos venden tragos adulterados. Los Tiempos (de Cochabamba), November 5.
2001   Quillacollo crece más rápido que Santa Cruz. Los Tiempos (de Cochabamba) January 15.

Crain, Mary
1990   The Social Construction of National Identity in Highland Ecuador. Anthropological Quarterly 63(1):43–59.

Crandon-Malamud, Libbet
1991   From the Fat of Our Souls: Social Change, Political Process, and Medical Pluralism in Bolivia. Berkeley: University of California Press.
1993   Blessings of the Virgin in Capitalist Society: The Transformation of a Rural Bolivian Fiesta. American Anthropologist 95(3):574–596.

Crapanzano, Vincent
1980   Tuhami: Portrait of a Moroccan. Chicago: University of Chicago Press.
1993   Self-Characterization: Text, Transference, and Indexicality. *In* Hermes' Dilemma and Hamlet's Desire: On the Epistemology of Interpretation. Pp. 115–135. Cambridge, MA: Harvard University Press.
1996   "Self-" Centering Narratives. *In* Natural Histories of Discourse. Michael Silverstein and Greg Urban, eds. Pp. 106–127. Chicago: University of Chicago Press.

Dandler, Jorge
1971   Politics of Leadership, Brokerage and Patronage in the Campesino Movement of Cochabamba. PhD dissertation, Department of Anthropology, University of Wisconsin–Madison.
1976   Peasant Sindicatos and the Process of Cooptation in Bolivian Politics. *In* Popular Participation in Social Change: Cooperatives, Collectives and Nationalized Industry. Jorge Dandler, June Nash, and Nicholas Hopkins, eds. Pp. 341–352. The Hague: Mouton.
1983   El sindicalismo campesino en Bolivia. La Paz: CERES.
1984   Campesinado y reforma agraria en Cochabamba (1952–53): Dinámica de un movimiento campesino en Bolivia. *In* Bolivia: La fuerza histórica del campesinado. Fernando Calderón and Jorge Dandler, eds. Pp. 203–239. Cochabamba: CERES.
1987a   Diversificación, procesos de trabajo y movilidad espacial en los valles y serranías de Cochabamba. *In* La participación indígena en los mercados surandinos. Olivia Harris, Brooke Larson, and Enrique Tandeter, eds. Pp. 639–682. La Paz: CERES.
1987b   From the National Indigenous Congress to the Ayopaya Rebellion: Bolivia, 1945–1947. *In* Resistance, Rebellion, and Consciousness in the Andean Peasant World, 18th to 20th Centuries. Steve J. Stern, ed. Pp. 334–378. Madison: University of Wisconsin Press.

Dangl, Benjamin
2007   The Price of Fire: Resource Wars and Social Movements in Bolivia. Edinburgh: AK Press.

de Córdoba, José, and David Luhnow
2006   A Dash of Mysticism: Governing Bolivia the Aymara Way. Wall Street Journal, July 6.

de la Cadena, Marisol
2000   Indigenous Mestizos: The Politics of Race and Culture in Cuzco, Peru, 1919–1991. Durham, NC: Duke University Press.

de la Torre, Carlos
2000   Populist Seduction in Latin America: The Ecuadorian Experience. Research in International Studies. Latin American Series, 32. Athens: Ohio University Center for International Studies.

Delgado, Freddy, Juan San Martín, and Domingo Torrico
1998   Reciprocity for Life Security. ILEIA Newsletter. December: 28–29.

De Vries, Peter
2002   Vanishing Mediators: Enjoyment as a Political Factor in Western Mexico. American Ethnologist 29(4):901–927.

Díaz-Barriga, Miguel
2003   Materialism and Sensuality: Visualizing the Devil in the Festival of Our Lady of Urkupiña. Visual Anthropology 16:245–261.

Douglas, Mary
1966   Purity and Danger: An Analysis of Concepts of Pollution and Taboo. London: Routledge and Kegan Paul.

Dunkerley, James
1987   Rebelión en las venas: La lucha política en Bolivia, 1952–1982. La Paz: Editorial Quipus.

Encinas, Enrique
1989   Jinapuni: Testimonio de un dirigente campesino. La Paz: HISBOL.

Ewing, Katherine
1990   The Illusion of Wholeness: Culture, Self, and the Experience of Inconsistency. Ethos 18(3):251–278.

Fernandez, James
1986   Persuasions and Performances: The Play of Tropes in Culture. Bloomington: Indiana University Press.
1998   Genealogical Fictions and Their Uses. Unpublished MS. Author's files.

Flores, Mario
1977   Esclavitud—Matrimonio. In El país machista: La condición social de la mujer en Bolivia. M. Baptista Gumucio, ed. Pp. 54–60. La Paz: Ediciones Los Amigos del Libro.

Forero, Juan
2004   Even the Upscale Wear Indian Dress, but Not in the Office. New York Times, October 14.

Foucault, Michel

1972   The Archaeology of Knowledge. A. M. Sheridan Smith, trans. New York: Pantheon Books.

1984a   Nietzsche, Genealogy, History. *In* The Foucault Reader. Paul Rabinow, ed. Pp. 76–100. Harmondsworth: Penguin.

1984b   On the Genealogy of Ethics. *In* The Foucault Reader. Paul Rabinow, ed. Pp. 340–372. Harmondsworth: Penguin.

1988   Technologies of the Self. *In* Technologies of the Self: A Seminar with Michel Foucault. Luther H. Martin, Huck Gutman, and Patrick H. Hutton, eds. Pp. 16–49. Amherst: University of Massachusetts Press.

Fraser, Nancy

1989   Unruly Practices: Power, Discourse, and Gender in Contemporary Social Thought. Minneapolis: University of Minnesota Press.

Fried, Jacob

1961   The Indian and Mestizaje in Peru. Human Organization 20(1):23–26.

Friedrich, Paul

1977   Agrarian Revolt in a Mexican Village. 2nd edition. Chicago: University of Chicago Press.

1986   The Princes of Naranja. Austin: University of Texas Press.

Fuenzalida, Fernando

1970   La matríz colonial. Revista del Museo Nacional (Lima) 35:92–123.

Gal, Susan

1991   Bartók's Funeral: Representations of Europe in Hungarian Political Rhetoric. American Ethnologist 18(3):440–458.

Gamarra, Eduardo

1994   Market-Oriented Reforms and Democratization in Latin America: Challenges of the 1990's. *In* Latin American Political Economy in the Age of Neoliberal Reform: Theoretical and Comparative Perspectives for the 1990s. William C. Smith, Carlos H. Acuña, and Eduardo A. Gamarra, eds. Pp. 1–16. Miami: Transaction.

García, Edgar

2005   Pandillas y "chicos de la clefa" toman Quillacollo. Los Tiempos (de Cochabamba), August 7.

García Canclini, Nestor

1995   Hybrid Identities: Strategies for Entering and Leaving Modernity. Minneapolis: University of Minnesota Press.

2001   Consumers and Citizens: Globalization and Multicultural Conflicts. Minneapolis: University of Minnesota Press.

García Canedo, Caesar Eduardo

1995   Florinda. *In* En el ala del horizonte: Relatos. Pp. 45–49. Cochabamba: Editorial Arol Srl.

García Linera, Álvaro

2003   La muchedumbre. Pulso Boliviano, February 27.

2004   The Multitude. In ¡Cochabamba! Water War in Bolivia. Tom Lewis, ed. Pp. 65–86. Cambridge, MA: South End Press.

Gay, Robert

1998   Rethinking Clientelism: Demands, Discourses and Practices in Contemporary Brazil. European Review of Latin American and Caribbean Studies 65:7–24.

Geertz, Clifford

1973   Ritual and Social Change: A Javanese Example. In The Interpretation of Cultures. Pp. 142–169. New York: Basic Books.

1980   Negara: The Theatre State in Nineteenth-Century Bali. Princeton, NJ: Princeton University Press.

Gill, Lesley

1993   "Proper Women" and City Pleasures: Gender, Class, and Contested Meanings in La Paz. American Ethnologist 20(1):72–88.

1994   Precarious Dependencies: Gender, Class and Domestic Service in Bolivia. New York: Columbia University Press.

2000   Teetering on the Rim: Global Restructuring, Daily Life, and the Armed Retreat of the Bolivian State. New York: Columbia University Press.

Gilroy, Paul

1991   There Ain't No Black in the Union Jack: The Cultural Politics of Race and Nation. Chicago: University of Chicago Press.

Ginzburg, Carlo

1980   The Cheese and the Worms: The Cosmology of a Sixteenth-Century Miller. Baltimore: Johns Hopkins University Press.

Girault, Louis

1988   Rituales en las regiones andinas de Bolivia y Peru. La Paz: CERES.

Goffman, Erving

1959   The Presentation of Self in Everyday Life. Woodstock, NY: Overlook Press.

1963   Stigma: Notes on the Management of Spoiled Identity. Englewood Cliffs, NJ: Prentice-Hall.

Goldschmidt, Henry

2006   The Voices of Jacob on the Streets of Brooklyn: Black and Jewish Israelites in and around Crown Heights. American Ethnologist 33(3):378–396.

Goldstein, Daniel

2004   The Spectacular City: Violence and Performance in Urban Bolivia. Durham, NC: Duke University Press.

Golpira, Hamid

2008   The Trigger of South America: The Indigenous Intifada of the Americas Has Won Another Victory. Electronic document, http://boliviarising.blogspot.com/2008/08/trigger-of-south-america.html, accessed September 3, 2008.

Gonzales, Walter
1991   Balance de ferias culturales en provincias de Cochabamba. Los Tiempos (de Cochabamba), May 13.

Goodale, Mark
2006   Reclaiming Modernity: Indigenous Cosmopolitanism and the Coming of the Second Revolution in Bolivia. American Ethnologist 33(4):634–649.

Gordillo, Gastón
2002   The Dialectic of Estrangement: Memory and the Production of Places of Wealth and Poverty in the Argentinean Chaco. Cultural Anthropology 17(1):3–31.

Gordillo, José
2000   Campesinos revolucionarios en Bolivia: Identidad, territorio y sexualidad en el Valle Alto de Cochabamba, 1952–1964. La Paz: Plural.

Gordillo, José, Víctor H. Blanco, and Patricia Richmond
1995   Diagnóstico de la vivienda de la conurbación de Cochabamba. Cochabamba: CERES.

Gotkowitz, Laura
2008   A Revolution for Our Rights: Indigenous Struggles for Land and Justice in Bolivia, 1880–1952. Durham, NC: Duke University Press.

Greaves, Thomas
1972   The Andean Rural Proletarians. Anthropological Quarterly 45(2):65–83.

Greenblatt, Stephen
1980   Renaissance Self-Fashioning: From More to Shakespeare. Chicago: University of Chicago Press.

Guamán Pomo de Ayala, Felipe
1980[1615] El primer nueva corónica y buen gobierno. Mexico City: Colección America Nuestra.

Guillermoprieto, Alma
1994   The Heart That Bleeds: Latin America Now. New York: Vintage.

Guss, David
2006   Introduction: Indigenous Peoples and New Urbanisms. Journal of Latin American Anthropology 11(2):259–266.

Gustafson, Bret
2002   Paradoxes of Liberal Indigenism: Indigenous Movements, State Process, and Intercultural Reform in Bolivia. In Identities and Conflict: Indigenous Peoples in Latin American States. David Maybury-Lewis, ed. Pp. 267–306. Cambridge, MA: Harvard University Press.

Gutiérrez, Raquel, Alvaro García, and Luis Tapia
2000   La forma multitud de la política de las necesidades vitales. In El retorno de la Bolivia plebeya. Alvaro García, Raquel Gutiérrez, Raúl Prada, and Luis Tapia, eds. Pp. 133–184. La Paz: Muela del Diablo.

Gutiérrez, Raquel, Alvaro García, Raúl Prada, and Luis Tapia, eds.
2002 Democratizaciones plebeyas. La Paz: Muela del Diablo.

Guttman, Matthew
1996 The Meaning of Macho: Being a Man in Mexico City. Berkeley: University of California Press.
2002 The Romance of Democracy: Compliant Defiance in Contemporary Mexico. Berkeley: University of California Press.

Guzmán, Jaime
2000 Llunk'ometro. Los Tiempos (de Cochabamba), July 6.

Hale, Charles
1994 Between Che Guevara and the Pachamama: Mestizos, Indians, and Identity Politics in the Anti-Quincentenary Campaign. Critique of Anthropology 14(1):9–40.
1997 Cultural Politics of Identity in Latin America. Annual Review of Anthropology 26:567–590.
2002 Does Multiculturalism Menace? Governance, Cultural Rights, and the Politics of Identity in Guatemala. Journal of Latin American Studies 34(3):485–524.
2006 Más Que un Indio (More than an Indian): Racial Ambivalence and the Paradox of Neoliberalism in Guatemala. Santa Fe, NM: School of American Research Press.

Hanks, William
1984 Sanctification, Structure and Experience in a Yucatec Ritual Event. Journal of American Folklore 97:131–166.

Harris, Olivia
1978 Complementarity and Conflict: An Andean View of Women and Men. In Sex and Age as Principles of Social Differentiation. J. S. La Fontaine, ed. Pp. 21–40. ASA Monograph 17. London: Academic Press.
1995 Ethnic Identity and Market Relations: Indians and Mestizos in the Andes. In Ethnicity, Markets, and Migration in the Andes. Brooke Larson and Olivia Harris, eds. Pp. 351–390. Durham, NC: Duke University Press.
2000 To Make the Earth Bear Fruit: Ethnographic Essays on Fertility, Work and Gender in Highland Bolivia. London: Institute of Latin American Studies.

Hawthorn, Geoffrey
1991 Plausible Worlds: Possibility and Understanding in History and the Social Sciences. Cambridge: Cambridge University Press.

Healy, Kevin
2001 Llamas, Weavings, and Organic Chocolate: Multicultural Grassroots Development in the Andes and Amazon of Bolivia. South Bend, IN: University of Notre Dame Press.

Healy, Kevin, and Susan Paulson
2000 Introduction: Political Economies of Identity in Bolivia, 1952–1998. Journal of Latin American Anthropology 5(2):2–29.

Heath, Dwight
1995 Changes in Drinking Patterns in Bolivian Cultures. Addiction Research and Theory 2(3):307–318.

Herzfeld, Michael
1997   Cultural Intimacy: Social Poetics in the Nation-State. New York: Routledge.

Himpele, Jeffrey D.
2008   Circuits of Culture: Media, Politics, and Indigenous Identity in the Andes. Minneapolis: University of Minnesota Press.

Hobsbawm, Eric, and Terence Ranger
1983   The Invention of Tradition. Cambridge: Cambridge University Press.

Hylton, Forrest, and Sinclair Thomson
2005   The Chequered Rainbow. New Left Review 35:41–64.

INE. See Instituto Nacional de Estadísticas.

Instituto Nacional de Estadísticas (INE)
1994   Censo92, Provincia: Quillacollo. Volumen 9. Cochabamba: INE

ILDIS. See Instituto Latinoamericano de Investigaciones Sociales.

Instituto Latinoamericano de Investigaciones Sociales (ILDIS)
1990   El regimen municipal: Aportes y debate. La Paz: Publicidad Arte Producciones.
1993   Lo pluri-multi o el reino de la diversidad. La Paz: Publicidad Arte Producciones.

Irurozqui Victoriano, Marta
1995   La amenaza chola: La participación popular en las elecciones bolivianas, 1900–1930. Revista Andina 13(2):357–388.

Irvine, Judith
1996   Shadow Conversations: The Indeterminacy of Participant Roles. *In* Natural Histories of Discourse. Michael Silverstein and Greg Urban, eds. Pp. 131–159. Chicago: University of Chicago Press.

Isbell, Billie Jean
1978   To Defend Ourselves: Ecology and Ritual in an Andean Village. Boulder, CO: Westview Press.

Ivy, Marilyn
1995   Discourses of the Vanishing: Modernity, Phantasm, Japan. Chicago: University of Chicago Press.

Izko, Xavier
1986   Comunidad andina: Persistencia y cambio. Revista Andina 4(1):59–99.

Jackson, Jean
1991   Being and Becoming an Indian in the Vaupés. *In* Nation-State and Indian in Latin America. Greg Urban and Joel Sherzer, eds. Pp. 131–155. Austin: University of Texas Press.
1995   Culture, Genuine and Spurious: The Politics of Indianness in Vaupés, Colombia. American Ethnologist 22(1):3–27.

Jackson, Michael
1989   Paths toward a Clearing: Radical Empiricism and Ethnographic Inquiry. Bloomington: Indiana University Press.

James, William
1976   Essays in Radical Empiricism. Cambridge, MA: Harvard University Press.

Keane, Webb
1997   Signs of Recognition: Powers and Hazards of Representation in an Indonesian Society. Berkeley: University of California Press.
2002   Sincerity, "Modernity," and the Protestants. Cultural Anthropology 17(1):65–92.

Kearney, Michael
1996   Reconceptualizing the Peasantry: Anthropology in Global Perspective. Boulder, CO: Westview Press.

Kelly, John, and Martha Kaplan
1990   History, Structure, and Ritual. Annual Review of Anthropology 19:119–150.

Kertzer, David
1988   Ritual, Politics, and Power. New Haven, CT: Yale University Press.

Klein, Herbert
1992   Bolivia: The Evolution of a Multi-Ethnic Society. 2nd edition. New York: Oxford University Press.

Kohl, Benjamin
2000   Restructuring Citizenship in Bolivia at the End of the Twentieth Century. Paper presented at the meeting of the Latin American Studies Association, Miami, March 16–18.

Kohl, Benjamin, and Linda Farthing
2006   Impasse in Bolivia: Neoliberal Hegemony and Popular Resistance. London: Zed Books.

Kohl, James
1982   The Cliza and Ucureña War: Syndical Violence and National Revolution in Bolivia. Hispanic American Historical Review 62:607–628.

Kruse, Thomas
2001   Transición política y recomposición sindical: Reflexiones desde Bolivia. In Los sindicatos frente a los procesos de transición. Enrique de la Garza Toledo, ed. Pp. 153–191. Buenos Aires: CLACSO.
2003   The IMF and the Bolivian Crisis. Electronic document, www.americas.org, accessed October 24, 2005.

Laclau, Ernesto
1977   Politics and Ideology in Marxist Theory: Capitalism, Fascism, Populism. London: NLB.

Lagos, María
1993   "We Have to Learn to Ask": Hegemony, Diverse Experiences and Antagonistic Meanings in Bolivia. American Ethnologist 20(1):52–71.
1994   Autonomy and Power: The Dynamics of Class and Culture in Rural Bolivia. Philadelphia: University of Pennsylvania Press.

1997   "Bolivia La Nueva": Constructing New Citizens. Paper presented at the meeting of the Latin American Studies Association, Guadalajara, April 17–20.

Langer, Suzanne
1979[1942] Philosophy in a New Key. Cambridge, MA: Harvard University Press.

Lara, Jesús
1971   Diccionario Qheshwa-Castellano, Castellano-Qheshwa. Cochabamba: Editorial Amigos del Libro.

Larson, Brooke
1998   Colonialism and Agrarian Transformation in Bolivia. 2nd edition. Princeton, NJ: Princeton University Press.

Laserna, Roberto
1994   El massacre del valle: El desencuentro militar campesino. Cochabamba: CERES.

Lasswell, Harold
1930   Psychopathology and Politics. Chicago: University of Chicago Press.

Laurie, Nina, Robert Andolina, and Sarah Radcliffe
2002   The Excluded "Indigenous"? The Implications of Multi-Ethnic Politics for Water Reform in Bolivia. *In* Multiculturalism in Latin America: Indigenous Rights, Diversity and Democracy. Rachel Sieder, ed. Pp. 252–276. New York: Palgrave.

Lazar, Sian
2008   El Alto, Rebel City: Self and Citizenship in Andean Bolivia. Durham, NC: Duke University Press.

Lazarte, Jorge
1998   Partidos políticos e informalización de la política. *In* Populismo y neopopulismo en América Latina. María Moira Mackinnon and Mario Alberto Petrone, eds. Pp. 409–433. Buenos Aires: Eudeba.

Leach, Edmund R.
1954   Political Systems of Highland Burma. London: Athlone.

Lehman, David, ed.
1982   Ecology and Exchange in the Andes. Cambridge: Cambridge University Press.

León, Rosario
1990   Bartolina Sisa: The Peasant Women's Organization in Bolivia. *In* Women and Social Change in Latin America. Elizabeth Jelin, ed. Pp. 135–150. Geneva: United Nations Research Institute for Social Development.

Lévi-Strauss, Claude
1963   Structural Anthropology. New York: Basic Books.

Limón, José
1994   Dancing with the Devil: Society and Cultural Poetics in Mexican-American South Texas. Madison: University of Wisconsin Press.

Lomnitz, Claudio
1992   Exits from the Labyrinth: Culture and Ideology in the Mexican National Space. Berkeley: University of California Press.

Los Tiempos (de Cochabamba)
1992   Niños "grillos polillas" son ignorados por instituciones y la propia sociedad. December 22.
1994   Festival de la wallunk'a y coplas permitirán fortalecer tradiciones. April 10.
2000   No hay normas para la elaboración de la chicha. November 7.
2001a   El pueblo tomó justicia "por manos propias." April 11.
2001b   Quillacollo: Agua barata, ciudad sucia. May 8.
2002   Más de 10 mil comerciantes ocupan calles de Quillacollo. December 27.
2004   Crece la presencia de los pandilleros en Quillacollo. January 4.

Lowenthal, David
2006   Heritage Wars. Spiked Online. Electronic document, www.spiked-online.com/Articles/0000000CAFCC.htm, accessed March 16, 2007.

Luykx, Aurolyn
2000   Gender Equity and Interculturalidad: The Dilemma in Bolivian Education. Journal of Latin American Anthropology 5(2):150–178.

Madrid, Raúl
2006   The Rise of Ethno-Populism in Latin America: The Bolivian Case. Paper presented at the Annual Meeting of the American Political Science Association, Philadelphia, August 31–September 3.

Mallón, Florencia
1996   Constructing Mestizaje in Latin America: Authenticity, Marginality and Gender in the Claiming of Ethnic Identities. Journal of Latin American Anthropology 2(1):170–181.

Mariaca Iturri, Guillermo
1998   Nosotros los cholos: Las políticas de la representación. Universidad Católica Boliviana Revista 4:90–97.

Mayorga, Fernando
1991   Max Fernandez: La política del silencio. La Paz: Instituto Latinoamericanos de Investigaciones Sociales.
1994   Los desafíos de la participación popular. Los Tiempos (de Cochabamba), August 31.
2002   Neopopulismo y democracia: Compadres y padrinos en la política boliviana (1988–1999). Cochabamba: Plural.

Medeiros, Carmen
2001   Civilizing the Popular? The Law of Popular Participation and the Design of a New Civil Society in 1990s Bolivia. Critique of Anthropology 21(4):401–425.

Medina, Javier
1992   Repensar Bolivia. La Paz: HISBOL.

Medinaceli, Carlos
1981[1929] La chaskañawi. Sucre: Editorial Tupac Katari.

Medrano, Alfredo
2002   Teoría y práctica de la chicha: Bebida y cultural popular. Los Tiempos (de Cochabamba), March 24.

Menchú, Rigoberta
1984   I, Rigoberta Menchú: An Indian Woman in Guatemala. Elisabeth Burgos-Debray, ed. Ann Wright, trans. London: Verso.

Méndez, Cecilia
1996   Incas Sí, Indios No: Notes on Peruvian Creole Nationalism and Its Contemporary Crisis. Journal of Latin American Studies 28:197–225.

Miles, Ann
1992   Pride and Prejudice: The Urban Chola and the Transmission of Class and Gender Ideologies in Cuenca, Ecuador. In Balancing Acts. Patricia Lyons Johnson, ed. Pp. 120–139. Boulder, CO: Westview Press.

Mintz, Sidney, and Eric Wolf
1977[1950] An Analysis of Ritual Co-Parenthood (Compadrazgo). Southwestern Journal of Anthropology 6(4):341–368.

Monasterios, Karin
2007   Bolivian Women's Organizations in the MAS era. NACLA Report on the Americas 40(2):34–43.

Montaño Aragón, Mario
1977   Patriarcado y matriarcado en la sociedad chola. In El país machista: La condición social de la mujer en Bolivia. M. Baptista Gumucio, ed. Pp. 194–200. Cochabamba: Los Amigos del Libro.

Murra, John
1975   La función del tejido en varios contextos sociales y políticos. In Formaciones económicas y políticas del mundo andino. J. Murra, ed. Pp. 145–170. Lima: Instituto de Estudios Peruanos.

Myerhoff, Barbara
1978   Number Our Days. New York: Dutton.

Nash, June
1979   We Eat the Mines and the Mines Eat Us. New York: Columbia University Press.
1993   We Eat the Mines and the Mines Eat Us. 2nd edition. New York: Columbia University Press.

Nietzsche, Friedrich
1967   On the Genealogy of Morals. New York: Vintage Books.

Nugent, José Guillermo
1992   El laberinto de la choledad. Lima: Fundación Friedrich Ebert.

Nutini, Hugo G., and Betty Bell
1980   Ritual Kinship: The Structure and Historical Development of the Compadrazgo System

in Rural Tlaxcala. Princeton, NJ: Princeton University Press.

Olivera, Oscar, and Tom Lewis
2004   ¡Cochabamba! Water War in Bolivia. Cambridge, MA: South End Press.

Orta, Andrew
1999   Syncretic Subjects and Body Politics: Doubleness, Personhood, and Aymara Catechists. American Ethnologist 26(4):864–889.
2002   Burying the Past: Locality, Lived History and Death in an Aymara Ritual of Remembrance. Cultural Anthropology 17(4):471–511.
2004   Catechizing Culture: Missionaries, Aymara, and the "New Evangelization." New York: Columbia University Press.

Osorio, María Julia
2005   Hallan videos "porno" con probables cholitas menores. Los Tiempos (de Cochabamba), September 20.

Ovando, David
2005   Linchamiento en Quillacollo: 1 muerto 2 heridos. Los Tiempos (de Cochabamba), November 23.

Pacheco Balanza, Máximo
2001   Desde la profunda choledad. Correo del Sur, October 25.

Page-Reeves, Janet
1999   Challenging Boundaries, Redefining Limits: The Experience of Bolivian Handknitters in the Global Market. PhD dissertation, City University of New York.

Painter, Michael
1991   Re-creating Peasant Economy in Southern Peru. In Golden Ages, Dark Ages: Imagining the Past in Anthropology and History. Jay O'Brien and William Roseberry, eds. Pp. 302–345. Berkeley: University of California Press.

Paulovich
1978   Diccionario del cholo ilustrado. La Paz: Ojo Publicaciones.

Paulson, Susan
1992   Gender and Ethnicity in Motion: Identity and Integration in Andean Households. PhD dissertation, Department of Anthropology, University of Chicago.
1996   Familias que no "conyugan" e identidades que no conjugan: La vida en Mizque disafía nuestras categorías. In Ser mujer indígena, chola o birlocha en la Bolivia postcolonial de los años 90. S. Rivera, ed. Pp. 85–161. La Paz: Plural.
2007   Model Families of Modern Development Cede to Alternative Bonds in Bolivia's Social Movements. Urban Anthropology 36(3):239–280.

Paulson, Susan, and Pamela Calla
2000   Gender and Ethnicity in Bolivian Politics: Transformation or Paternalism? Journal of Latin American Anthropology 5(2):112–149.

Paz, Octavio
1961   The Labyrinth of Solitude: Life and Thought in Mexico. New York: Grove Press.

Peredo Antezana, Rafael
1963   La provincia de Quillacollo. Cochabamba: Editorial Canelas.
1990   El milagro de Urkupiña. 3rd edition. Cochabamba: Editora Offset "Cueto."

Peredo Beltrán, Elizabeth
1992   Recoveras de los Andes: La identidad de la chola del mercado. La Paz: ILDIS.

Platt, Tristan
1982   Estado boliviano y ayllu andino: Tierra y tributo en el Norte de Potosí. Lima: Instituto de Estudios Peruanos.

Polanyi, Michael
1969   The Logic of Tacit Inference. *In* Knowing and Being. Marjorie Greene, ed. Pp. 138–158. Chicago: University of Chicago Press.

Polo Nájera, Teresa
1991   Aspectos demográficos y ocupacionales de la población de Quillacollo. Cochabamba: Universidad Mayor de San Simón.

Postero, Nancy
2000   Bolivia's Indigena Citizen: Multiculturalism in a Neoliberal Age. Paper presented at the meeting of the Latin American Studies Association, Miami, March 16–18.
2005   Indigenous Responses to Neoliberalism: A Look at the Bolivian Uprising of 2003. Political and Legal Anthropology Review 28(1):73–92.
2007a   Andean Utopias in Evo Morales's Bolivia. Latin American and Caribbean Ethnic Studies 2(1):1–28.
2007b   Now We Are Citizens: Indigenous Politics in Postmulticultural Bolivia. Stanford, CA: Stanford University Press.

Ranta-Owusu, Eija
2008   From Post–Washington Consensus to Indigenous Worldview: Policy and Ideology in Contemporary Bolivia. El Norte: Finnish Journal of Latin American Studies 1:1–20.

Rappaport, Joanne
1994   Cumbe Reborn: An Andean Ethnography of History. Chicago: University of Chicago Press.
2005   Intercultural Utopias: Public Intellectuals, Cultural Experimentation, and Ethnic Pluralism in Colombia. Durham, NC: Duke University Press.

Reinaga, Fausto
1964   El indio y el cholaje boliviano. La Paz: Ediciones PIAKK.

Rejas, Damián Z.
1950   Monografía de Quillacollo. Cochabamba: Editorial Universo.

Rivas, Sinforoso
2000   Los hombres de la revolución. J. M. Gordillo, ed. Cochabamba: CERES.

Rivera, Silvia
1984   Oprimidos pero no vencidos: Luchas del campesinado aymara y quechua. La Paz: HISBOL.

1990a   Indigenous Women and Community Resistance: History and Memory. *In* Women and Social Change in Latin America. Elizabeth Jelin, ed. Pp. 151–183. Geneva: United Nations Research Institute for Social Development.

1990b   Liberal Democracy and Ayllu Democracy in Bolivia: The Case of Norte de Potosí. Journal of Development Studies 26(4):97–121.

1993a   Anthropology and Society in the Andes. Critique of Anthropology 13(1):77–96.

1993b   La raíz: Colonizadores y colonizados. *In* Violencias encubiertas en Bolivia. Silvia Rivera and Raul Barrios, eds. Pp. 27–139. La Paz: CIPCA.

1996   Los desafíos para una democracia étnica y genérica en los albores del tercer milenio. *In* Ser mujer indígena, chola o birlocha en la Bolivia postcolonial de los años 90. Silvia Rivera, ed. Pp. 17–84. La Paz: Plural.

Rocha, José Antonio
1990   Sociedad agraria y religión: Cambio social e identidad en los valles de Cochabamba. La Paz: HISBOL.

Rocha Monroy, Ramón
1979   El padrino. Cochabamba: Editorial Los Amigos del Libro.

Rodríguez Ostria, Gustavo, and Humberto Solares Serrano
1990   Sociedad oligárquica, chicha y cultura popular. Cochabamba: Editorial Serrano.

Rojas Delboy, Daniel
1996   Semblanzas anécdotas y cuentos de un pueblo. Cochabamba: Imprenta Cueto.

Romanucci-Ross, Lola
1986[1973] Conflict, Violence, and Morality in a Mexican Village. Chicago: University of Chicago Press.

Rorty, Richard
1989   Contingency, Irony and Solidarity. Cambridge: Cambridge University Press.

Rojas Rosales, Julián M., and Mario R. Galarza Garamendi
1975   Quillacollo: Estudio socio-habitacional. La Paz: Ministerio de Urbanismo y Vivienda.

Rowe, William, and Vivian Schelling
1991   Memory and Modernity: Popular Culture in Latin America. London: Verso Books.

Saignes, Tierry, ed.
1993   Borrachera y memoria: La experiencia de lo sagrado en los Andes. La Paz: HISBOL.

Salamanca, Octavio
1931   El socialismo en Bolivia. Cochabamba: Editorial Bolívar.

Sallnow, Michael
1989   Cooperation and Contradiction: The Dialectics of Everyday Practice. Dialectical Anthropology 14:241–257.

Salmón, Josefa
1997   El espejo indígena: El discurso indigenista en Bolivia, 1900–1956. La Paz: Ediciones Plural.

Salomon, Frank
1991   Introduction. *In* The Huarochirí Manuscript: A Testament of Ancient and Colonial Andean Religion. Frank Salomon and George Urioste, trans. Pp. 1–38. Austin: University of Texas Press.

Sánchez-Albornóz, Nicolás
1978   Indios y tributas en el Alto Perú. Lima: Instituto de Estudios Peruanos.

Sandoval, Angel Herbas
1998   Diccionario Quichua a Castellano. N.p.: Tunturi Qañiywa.

Sandoval, Godofredo, and M. Fernanda Sostres
1989   La ciudad prometida: Pobladores y organizaciones sociales en El Alto. La Paz: ILDIS.

Sanjinés, Javier
2004   Mestizaje Upside-Down: Aesthetic Politics in Modern Bolivia. Pittsburgh: University of Pittsburgh Press.

Sapir, Edward
1949[1924]   Culture, Genuine and Spurious. *In* Selected Writings in Language, Culture, and Personality. David Mandelbaum, ed. Pp. 308–331. Berkeley: University of California Press.

Scarborough, Isabel
2005   Construyendo identidad cultural y patrimonio en la festividad de la Virgin de Ukupiña de Quillacollo. *In* Cambio y continuidad en Bolivia: Etnicidad, cultura e identidad. Nicholas Robins, ed. Pp. 119–132. La Paz: Plural.

Seligmann, Linda
1993   Between Worlds of Exchange: Ethnicity among Peruvian Market Women. Cultural Anthropology 8(2):187–213.

2004   Peruvian Street Lives: Culture, Power, and Economy among Market Women in Cuzco. Urbana: University of Illinois Press.

Silverblatt, Irene
1987   Moon, Sun, and Witches: Gender Ideologies and Class in Inca and Colonial Peru. Princeton, NJ: Princeton University Press.

Simmons, R. A.
1974   Palca and Pucara: A Study of Two Bolivian Haciendas. Berkeley: University of California Press.

Skar, Sandra L.
1995   Appropriating Pawns: Andean Dominance and the Manipulation of Things. Journal of the Royal Anthropological Institute 1:787–803.

Soruco Sologuren, Ximena
2006   The Unintelligibility of the Cholo in Bolivia. T'inkazos 21:77–96.

Soto, César
1994   Historia del pacto militar-campesino: Entre la subordinación y la reciprocidad. Cochabamba: CERES.

Spence, Donald P.
1982   Narrative Truth and Historical Truth: Meaning and Interpretation in Psychoanalysis. New York: W. W. Norton.

Stephenson, Marcia
1999   Gender and Modernity in Andean Bolivia. Austin: University of Texas Press.
2002   Forging an Indigenous Counterpublic Sphere: The Taller de Historia Oral Andina in Bolivia. Latin American Research Review 37(2):99–118.

Stoll, David
1999   Rigoberta Menchú and the Story of All Poor Guatemalans. Boulder, CO: Westview Press.

Ströbele-Gregor, Juliana
1994   From Indio to Mestizo to Indio: New Indianist Movements in Bolivia. Latin American Perspectives 21(2):106–123.

Suárez Ávila, Manuel
2002   He dicho que el Mallku es un cholo pendejo. Los Tiempos (de Cochabamba), March 24.

Tamayo, Franz
1910[1944] Creación de la pedagogía nacional. La Paz: Editoriales de "El Diario."

Taussig, Michael
1980   The Devil and Commodity Fetishism in South America. Chapel Hill: University of North Carolina Press.
1987   Shamanism, Colonialism, and the Wild Man: A Study of Terror and Healing. Chicago: University of Chicago Press.

Taylor, Charles
1994   Multiculturalism and the Politics of Recognition: An Essay. Princeton, NJ: Princeton University Press.

Tedlock, Dennis, and Bruce Mannheim
1995   Introduction. In The Dialogic Emergence of Culture. Dennis Tedlock and Bruce Mannheim, eds. Pp. 1–32. Urbana: University of Illinois Press.

Ticona, Eseban, Gonzalo Rojas, and Xavier Albó
1995   Votos y whiphalas: Campesinos y pueblos originarios en democracia. La Paz: CIPCA.

Toranzo Roca, Carlos
1989   Desproletarización e "informalización" de la sociedad boliviana. In Bolivia hacia el 2000: Desafios y opciones. Carlos Toranzo, ed. Pp. 219–247. La Paz: Nueva Sociedad.
1991   Burgesía chola y señorialismo conflictuado. In La política del silencio. Fernando Mayorga and Max Fernandez, eds. Pp. 13–29. La Paz: Instituto Latinoamericano de Investigaciones Sociales.

Turner, Victor
1957   Schism and Continuity in an African Society: A Study of Ndembu Village Life. Manchester: Manchester University Press.

1968   The Drums of Affliction: A Study of Religious Processes among the Ndembu of
        Zambia. London: Clarendon Press.

Urban, Greg
1997   Modern Cultural Replication and Its Semiotic Properties. Paper presented at the
        Annual Meeting of the American Anthropological Association, Washington DC,
        November 21.

Urban, Greg, and Joel Sherzer, eds.
1991   Nation-States and Indians in Latin America. Austin: University of Texas Press.

Urbano Campos
1995   Feria de la manzana. Los Tiempos (de Cochabamba), April 16.
2000   La porquería que respiramos. Los Tiempos (de Cochabamba), July 29.

Van Cott, Donna Lee
2007   From Movements to Parties in Latin America: The Evolution of Ethnic Politics.
        Cambridge: Cambridge University Press.

Van den Berg, Hans
1989   La tierra no da así no más: Los ritos agrícolas en la religión de los Aymara-Cristianos.
        Amsterdam: CEDLA.

Van Vleet, Krista
2008   Performing Kinship: Narrative, Gender, and the Intimacies of Power in the Andes.
        Austin: University of Texas Press.

Wachtel, Nathan
1982   The Mitimas of the Cochabamba Valley: The Colonization Policy of Huayna Capac. *In*
        The Inca and Aztec States, 1400–1800: Anthropology and History. George Collier,
        Renato Rosaldo, and John Wirth, eds. Pp. 199–235. New York: Academic Press.

Warren, Kay
1998   Indigenous Movements and Their Critics: Pan-Maya Activism in Guatemala. Princeton,
        NJ: Princeton University Press.

Warren, Kay, and Jean Jackson, eds.
2002   Indigenous Movements, Self-Representation, and the State in Latin America. Austin:
        University of Texas Press.

Weismantel, Mary
1988   Food, Gender, and Poverty in the Ecuadorian Andes. Prospect Heights, IL: Waveland
        Press.
1995   Making Kin: Kinship Theory and Zumbagua Adoptions. American Ethnologist
        22(4):685–709.
2001   Cholas and Pishtacos: Stories of Race and Sex in the Andes. Chicago: University of
        Chicago Press.

Williams, Gareth
2002   The Other Side of the Popular: Neoliberalism and Subalternity in Latin America.
        Durham, NC: Duke University Press.

Wittgenstein, Ludwig
1981   Philosophical Investigations. New York: Prentice-Hall.

Yashar, Deborah
2005   Contesting Citizenship in Latin America: The Rise of Indigenous Movements and the Postliberal Challenge. Cambridge: Cambridge University Press.

Yúdice, George
2003   The Expediency of Culture: Uses of Culture in the Global Era. Durham, NC: Duke University Press.

Zelada, Michel C.
2001   El patrimonio es una responsibilidad de los ciudadanos. Los Tiempos (de Cochabamba), November 6.

Index

Paz, Octavio, 56
Peredo Antezana, Rafael, 32
Peredo Beltrán, Elizabeth, 97
performance: and role of patrimony in political discourse, 126; self-representation in political forms of, 186. *See also ch'alla*
personality (*personalidad*), and political speech in Quillacollo, 50, 160
Peru, and use of term *choledad*, 41
pinche (political client), and political corruption, 45–48
piqueros (agriculturalists), 6
política criolla (creole politics) 26–29, 42–43, 45, 46, 48. *See also* patronage
politics, in Quillacollo: *chola* cult and concept of cultural intimacy, 80–120; and fictive kinship, 58–79; introduction to and background information on, 1–29; negative solidarity and indigenous experience of, 187–200; and productive relationship of estrangement to patrimony, 121–51; and ritual libations or ch'allas as political performance, 152–86. *See also* Bolivia; Bolivian Communist Party; careers; CONDEPA; corruption; dictatorships; identity politics; life history; MAS; MNR; MRTK; neoliberalism; patronage; UCS; UDP
pollera, and image of chola, 80, 81, 82–83, 85, 86, 90, 95, 117
Polo Nájera, Teresa, 10
popular identity, and political careers in Quillacollo, 22–23
"popular leaders" (*dirigentes populares*), 22
Popular Participation Law (PPL), 36–37, 126, 206n5
population growth: in Cochabamba region, 202–203n17; in Quillacollo, 11
Postero, Nancy, 95, 119, 206n7
prebenda, and male political imagination in Quillacollo, 88–95
prebendalismo (exchange of material goods for votes), 20
problem-solving networks, and politics in Quillacollo, 17–21
propaganda: and elections in Quillacollo, 88–89; and image of *chola*, 118

qhanaymany (cajoling), 46
Quechua: and moral order of *ayni*, 76; and *Quechuañol*, 210n6; self-identity and local politics in Quillacollo, 60
Quillacollo, and politics: *chola* cult and cultural intimacy of, 80–120; and fictive kinship, 58–79; fieldwork in, 201n1, 201–202n4, 209n13; introduction to and background information on, 1–29; *llunk'u* and patronage

system in, 30–57; negative solidarity and indigenous experience of, 187–200; and productive relationship of estrangement to patrimony, 121–51; role of ritual libation or *ch'alla* as political spectacle, 152–86
Quispe, Felipe, 51

Ranger, Terence, 205n2
Rappaport, Joanne, 196, 211n11, 211n14
reciprocity: and Andean concept of ayni, 76–77, 79, 94, 205n5; and gifts by regional and local political parties, 90–95; and political *ch'alla* in Quillacollo, 164
Reinaga, Fausto, 42
Rejas, Damián Z., 14
religion. *See* Catholic Church
Remedios Loza Alvarado, Francisca, 80, 82
representation. *See* self-representation
Rivas, Sínforoso, 51, 171, 174, 184
Rivera, Silvia, 8, 40, 87, 97, 185, 206n10
Rocha, José Antonio, 106
Rocha Monroy, Ramón, 74–79, 114–15
Rodríguez, Casimira, 81
Rodríguez Ostria, Gustavo, 67, 124, 190, 212n2
Rojas, Gonzalo, 30
Rojas Rosales, Julián M., 9
Romanucci-Ross, Lola, 204n1

Saignes, Tierry, 200
saints, and religious dimension of *ch'alla*, 172, 173
Sánchez-Albornóz, Nicolás, 6
Sanchez de Lozada, Gonzalo, 181
Sandoval, Angel Herbas, 46
Sanjinés, Javier, 125
Santa Cruz (city), 195–96
Sapir, Edward, 65–66
self: anthropological approach to, 211n12; and political *ch'alla*, 185–86. *See also* self-representation
self-interest, and neoliberalism, 70–71
self-representation: centrality of self-narration to political, 209n16; *cholos* and "humble status" in politics of Quillacollo , 29; indigenous peoples and challenges of in contemporary Bolivia, 197, 199; and *llunk'erio* in patronage politics of Quillacollo, 47; nicknames and indigenous identity in Quillacollo, 61; and political performance, 186; and public implications of political careers in Quillacollo, 23
Seligmann, Linda, 83, 208n9
Simmons, R. A., 62
social club, as institution of elite control in Quillacollo, 65. *See also* Federation of Mothers' Clubs
social mobility: and *cholos* as clients in patronage

Robert Albro received his PhD in sociocultural anthropology from the University of Chicago in 1999. Since 1991, Dr. Albro has maintained long-term ethnographic research and published widely on popular and indigenous politics in Bolivia, with a particular focus on the changing terms of citizenship, democratic participation, and indigenous movements in this country. His current research is concerned with global cultural policy making, as it meaningfully shapes the ongoing terms of globalization, including the relevance of culture in contexts of security. Dr. Albro's research and writing have been supported over the years by the National Science Foundation, the Mellon Foundation, the Rockefeller Foundation, and the American Council for Learned Societies, among others. Dr. Albro has also been a Fulbright scholar and has held fellowships at the Carnegie Council for Ethics in International Affairs, the Kluge Center of the Library of Congress, and the Smithsonian Institution. Dr. Albro has held several leadership positions in the American Anthropological Association (AAA), including Chair of the Committee for Human Rights and Chair of the Ad Hoc Commission on Anthropology's Engagement with the Security and Intelligence Communities. He received the AAA President's Award in 2009 for outstanding contributions to the Association. Most recently he has taught at Wheaton College (Norton, MA) and at George Washington University. He currently teaches at the School of International Service at American University.